Cover: Oil Painting of Emmanuel Episcopal Church in
Killingworth, CT, by Sandra E. Smith

George Blodgett, "the hat uncle" *(p. 34)*   When I Was In Normal School
(Chapter III)

Father *(Chapter II)*

My Room at Berkeley *(Chapter V)*

Bishop Williams *(page 61)*

Our Wedding Picture *(page 78)*

Calling on an Immigrant Farmer's Family
in 1917 *(Chapter VIII)*

An Abandoned Country Church Reclaimed
(page 180)

Some Members of My First Parish *(Chapter VI)*

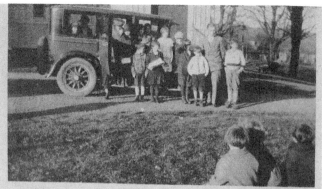

Bringing the Children to Church *(p. 152)*

"The more I worked
on my farm the better
I did my church
work." *(p. 137)*

—Courtesy *Hartford Times*

"I have given over
5,000 haircuts."
(p. 37)

THE PREACHER'S FAMILY, 1938
To my left Virginia; to my right Mrs. Gilbert, Charles, Closson,
Shelley and his bride. *Insert:* George, Jr.

The Preacher's Family, 1920

The Farm Home *(Chapter IX)*

"Gathered in that sheltered woodland spot." (*p. 298*)

"We eat at long tables." (*p. 116*)

The Farm Swimming Pool (*p. 146*)

The Killingworth Church *(Chapter VIII)*

Epiphany Church, Durham, July, 1939 *(Chapter X)*

"I'm very proud of that lily pond." (p. 143)

FORTY YEARS
A COUNTRY
PREACHER

By George B. Gilbert

. . . .

HARPER & BROTHERS PUBLISHERS

New York and London

FORTY YEARS A COUNTRY PREACHER

5-0

FIRST EDITION

D-P

To

My Beloved Wife

MARY JANE SHELLEY GILBERT

without whom there could have been

no occaision for writing

this book

Contents

. . . .

PREFACE

. . . .

YEARS ago, an Episcopal priest friend told me he had spent 30 years praying for God to speak to him, out loud and in English, and tell him "what to do." We were having lunch the week he was retiring and moving to an island off Maine and he told me his prayer had been answered.

After I picked my fork out of my salad and had a long drink of wine, I said, "What did God tell you to do?"

He shook his head and smiled. "God told me in an exasperated voice, "David, do whatever comes next!"

Forty Years a Country Preacher is the sometimes humorous, sometimes somber, but always insightful musings of George B. Gilbert, an Episcopal priest who spent his career in rural Connecticut parishes. Gilbert grew up in Vermont but came to New Haven to Berkeley Divinity and stayed on in the Diocese of Connecticut.

To call Gilbert "a parish priest" doesn't do him justice. During his time in the hills of southern Connecticut he was sometimes a farmer, sometimes a barber, often a cook, and always a community organizer — even before that term came into vogue. For the first four decades of the 20th century, he did whatever was needed by those he served and those in the community where he lived who had nothing to do with the Episcopal Church. He doesn't spend a lot of time in this book "doing theology," but he spent all of his ministry meeting the personal and spiritual and basic needs of those around him. His theology was just what God had told my friend David: George Gilbert did "whatever came next" for his 40 years as a country preacher.

He estimated he had given 5,000 haircuts to the rural poor he encountered. He rode his horse and later drove his oversized Nash over countless country miles to visit the many people he knew in his sprawling parishes. He helped cook and eat dinner (our "lunch," this is in the country, remember) almost every Sunday of his long pastorate. He cut wood for the stoves to cook the dinners and keep the churches warm. He repaired whatever was broken in his church buildings and whatever was broken in the people he served. He steadfastly believed that "feeding the body" of those he met needed to precede "feeding the soul." And for all that he was a passionate preacher, a devout keeper of the sacraments, a man of prayerfulness, if not prayer, and one who did all he did with a sense of calling and purpose.

I've been an Episcopal priest since 1976 — forty-one years and counting — and deeply admire Gilbert's attitude toward ministry. I think the "doing" of ministry comes out of the "being" of the minister, and George Gilbert fully embodied his priesthood. He was a "priest" incarnate — occasionally disappointed and frustrated that he couldn't do more for people, but through it all joyful and enlivened to be of service. His story reminds me of the response of Mother Teresa when asked by a cynical reporter how she thought she could save India. "One person at a time," she replied. Gilbert, in his time, lived out that commitment. His presence and energy seemed always totally focused on whoever was in front of him at the moment.

In my retirement, I have been serving, very part-time, three rural congregations in Connecticut, one of which is Emmanuel Church, Killingworth, where Gilbert became Rector in 1909 and served the rest of his ministry. So, I have some personal experience of the landscape where he rode his horse and drove his car and gave haircuts and cut wood and cooked and brought God to the rural folk. I also admire his attitude toward the institutional church. He was, in many ways, a rebel with a cause. He thought the church was out of touch with the needs of the people he served. And he, in many ways, set his sails against the wind of traditional Christianity.

Let me demonstrate that by quoting from Gilbert's own words: "It is not church form that makes good Christians. The essence of Christian ministry lies deeper than that and is rooted in human relationships. Too often the theologian doesn't know how to get along with people. The church cannot fail to be ineffective unless its clergy reach the poor and that can only be done by long and friendly acquaintance in their homes, ripening gradually into mutual affection — a link which brings them finally into the fold."

Those are the words of a person who truly understands the nature of priesthood. George Gilbert is that person.

May his words fill you with wisdom and give you some chuckles along the way!

—The Rev. Jim Bradley, February 14, 2019

FOREWORD

. . . .

WHEN Father heard that he was chosen "The Typical Country Minister of the United States" and was asked to write a book, he chuckled to himself, "Who would have thought I should come to this—I who have been called a fool for burying myself in the country? I can't write a book. Goodness, one hundred thousand words—never." But I knew he was pleased at having the opportunity to write.

We can't figure out where Father gets his energy. On Sunday he is up rushing around before seven o'clock. Before I have the breakfast ready, I hear the roar of the ten-year-old seven-passenger Nash. Like a locomotive it steams and sputters till it finally gives a last chug at the back door (far too often it has to be pushed around the block with the Ford before the faintest wheeze comes forth). Even the Nash isn't big enough—behind it is the two-wheeled trailer waiting to be filled.

Dad has jotted down, during the week, the various things he must take on Sunday, so it doesn't take him long to collect them. Sunday would not be Sunday to him if he did not eat at one of his churches. Into the trailer go three large pans of baked beans, specially done by Moms with a bit of pork and molasses. Six loaves of bread help to fill tremendous cavities. Twenty quarts of milk add needed nourishment. A box of cutlery and about forty white enamel cups supplement what the churches may have.

With what the parishioners bring, Dad thinks he has a foundation for a lunch. Magazines or books that may have come in during the week are carried along to be distributed where most needed. The barber's kit is always on the list—at least one way he can trim his congregation. On the way to church he picks up ten or a dozen men, women, and children. After holding four services, he wonders how he can fill the rest of the day.

Father is unusual—he is a minister who preaches only what he practices. He takes his sermons from people, from those for whom he has labored for forty long years. The simplicity and sincerity of each service make it the more sacred. All the children and adults take an active part, feeling it is their service and that their participation is needed. Father does not preach. He talks to his congregation in a language all can understand, illustrating his text, when he uses one, by homely anecdotes. There is something in his sermons for children, but more important is the stirring message for adults, bearing on everyday life and problems. No one sleeps in Father's churches.

Father is the happiest man I have ever known, due, I think, to his complete unselfishness. His deep compassion for the underprivileged never lessens, even though the slightest suggestion of appreciation on their part seems far remote. I sometimes wonder why he continues to clothe this one or feed that one, when neither seems to have any idea of helping himself. But Father has a reason for doing it — he knows there is some good in every person, and each has an important place to fill. Never a day passes without thought of Susie or Johnnie who hasn't very much. One day, as he started down country, I happened to look into the car. "Wait a minute," I yelled, for there beside him was my new spring coat he was planning to give away. It is only after persistent persuasion on the part of the family that we were able to convince him to buy himself a new suit or a new hat. There is always someone else who needs it more than he.

Let Father putter around in the kitchen and he has the time of his life. Everyone had better move out when he takes a notion to carve up his home-grown pork. On the wood stove (no electric one for him, although he bought one for Moms) he soon has some luscious tid-bits sizzling. He alone can make the sausage not too thick and not too sagey. If Mother and I happened to get home late for supper, we are pretty sure he'll have something ready—most likely chip beef gravy thickened to perfection. No matter how elaborate a meal—a Thanksgiving dinner, or Christmas feast—he must have a saucer of Vermont maple syrup with a cracker to dunk in it. Better put on some applesauce, too, for it always "goes perfect" with any meal. He dotes on eating outdoors. Summer suppers are usually by the lily pool.

Dad thoroughly enjoys going off for the day to make calls. With his mind on everything but driving, he crawls along at twenty miles an hour. Only by the grace of God does the car swerve to the right side of the road in the nick of time. Everyone knows when he comes to town – the muffler has a hole in it. The school children rush to the muffler has a hole in it. The school children rush to the windows when they hear him coming — no more work for them, "Mr. Gilbert has come with pictures." The day wouldn't be complete if he failed to stop at the neediest family for a cup of coffee. There's always some bread, corn beef, or eggs and bacon in the car, if a larder seems bare.

The bigger the job the better Dad likes it, and he always does it well. If the church needs wood, down he goes with one of two boys and the saw rig, to work till dark. He never has a sexton. He prefers having a group of young folks help him to clean the church, as it gives him a chance to talk with them about their school work and their future. Then too, he has a chance to cook his choice concoctions, and have the Sunday School children over from school during the noon hour for some crackers and cocoa. At Christmas time he loves to tramp in the woods with the boys, getting spruce and hemlock to trim the church. If the church needs painting, he gets a group of men together and tackles the job with them, mixing the paint himself. He may not be able to see out of his glasses at the end of the day, and the window panes may seem frosted, but nevertheless, the church is greatly improved.

We don't have to read the newspapers. Father reads them aloud to us. Whether we pay attention or not, he rolls back and forth giving out bits of news. A "listen to this" makes us come to. A new family has moved into his territory. He must look them up tomorrow. He likes to get the news broadcast while eating. No sooner does the first flash come than he drowns out the loudest reporter by his

[xxii]

own comments on why Russia won't be licked.

Just as Dad leaves the table, he shouts, "We're off!" even though we may not be leaving for two or three hours. Many a guest has appeared with hat and coat on, wondering why we were not ready.

To mention all Dad's accomplishments would be impossible. He can husk a bushel of field corn in five minutes. He prides himself on his skill at dissecting a pig, his speed in dressing a chicken, the amount of canned beef and chicken he has in the cellar, the quarts of applesauce canned in one day (maximum 138) and the way he cures hams and bacon.

Father has crammed a lot of hard work and horse sense into his forty years as a country preacher. He sees to it that life moves briskly at the Gilbert homestead, just as it does in his parishes.

MARY VIRGINIA GILBERT

Middletown
March, 1940

Forty Years

A Country Preacher

. . . .

Chapter I

THE CHURCH TAKES HOLD

. . . .

MY BROTHER Closson and I were cocking hay down in the witch grass lot south of the house on the old farm in Vermont when the minister came to call. We knew that it would be the usual parlor call and he wouldn't worry about us out in the fields. "It wouldn't hurt him to come down here and just say hello to us," I remember telling Closson. "I'd like to be a minister some time. I wouldn't hang around the house. I'd go out to the barn and down in the lot where the boys are, and I'd give 'em a lift."

I can still remember the preparations made for his coming. There never was any uncertainty about the visit, for he would announce on the previous Sunday what roads he might be expected to traverse that week, even to the very day. Then the whole household would turn handsprings getting ready for the visit. First, we boys would be sent around to see if the front door would open. As practically nothing else in our lives was important enough to warrant this desecration, there was ample ground for fearing that it might stick. Then the hall and stairway had to be scrubbed and cleaned, the parlor furniture rearranged, and the dining room slicked up. There was no need to touch any rooms but these. None other would be blessed with his august presence.

Although it was well understood that he would stay for supper and, therefore, wouldn't arrive before four o'clock, just to make sure of having a well-groomed welcoming committee on hand, Cousin Caroline would rush upstairs immediately after dinner to prepare for the minister's call. Even if she were sitting waiting in the parlor and saw him approaching far down the road, she would not stir toward the door until he had put both feet firmly on the big stone step, and with one hand flat against the side of the house, had given a terrific reef to a small knob connected by a system of pulleys and wires to a mighty gong up near the ceiling. With the reverberation that followed, the minister had arrived officially. Secretly we boys always hoped the rusty old wire would break as he gave it the pontifical yank.

Supper was the climax of the visitation. We boys never came near the house unless summoned to scour the barn for more eggs, or to get kindlings to make a roaring fire. This we gladly did, as we might get a whiff of the wonderful rolls Mother would be baking, or hear some tearful wailing over a fallen cake.

One of my clearest memories of the visiting minister was something he said that made me perfectly furious. We had an old cornstalk cutter on the farm. You turned a crank, and with its curved knives it drew in the stalks if you gave them a start. They would come off with a snap, flying right out on the barn floor. Father had told us we must never use it, for fear we should get cut. It was a terrible temptation, and one day I thought I would try my luck with a small stalk. Before I knew what was happening, one finger was drawn in and nearly cut off. A thrashing seemed inevitable, but Father prided himself on his first-aid ability so I think his joy in putting on the splints and tying them with a piece of sheeting made him forget to give me the punishment I had expected. I was always more or less prepared for the worst, like the boy who wired his mother that he had flunked all his exams and "please prepare Father." He got a wire right back, "Father is prepared. Prepare yourself."

The next Sunday, however, as I walked back from the family pew toward the stove where the minister stood, he spied the rag on finger. "Ah," he said, "I heard you cut your finger. Disobeyed your parent, I understand."

I can't describe how hurt, outraged and downright mad I was. Oddly enough, the more I saw in ministers that I didn't like, the more I wanted to become one. I don't recall that I disliked going to church. We all went as a matter of course. There was no debate about it, and we really had no place else to go. In the winter we often took the big two-horse sled. Closson and I cleaned it out, a much needed rite, as it was used for all purposes. We usually put wheat straw on the floor, placed the seats across, and added such horse blankets and robes as could be found. I was much mortified riding in this sled because of the length of loose chain that dangled from the traces, or "tugs," as we preferred to call them, and rattled as we went through the village. On Sundays especially I used to try to tie up these disorderly ends to the tugs with strings.

My ecclesiastical career really began in the little Episcopal church in Randolph Center where I was organ blower. My labors usually were rewarded with a jackknife at Christmas. Once, when I was sick, my substitute got one and declared in a loud voice that "it looked like one of

Fargo's ten-centers." Will Fargo ran the village store. There was much satisfaction, however, in performing this small function for the church. We could stay inside the organ all the time, sitting on the window sill in a narrow cubbyhole, or, when the weather was below zero, we could slip out and sit in an alcove by the door, ready to dash in at any moment. If we stayed in, we didn't have to look as though we enjoyed the sermon. Instead, we could scribble on the plastering. Once, with great boldness, I wrote on it, "I think I ought to have an ink pencil for this." I longed beyond words for one of these pencils. There was no ink in them, but you pressed one end and it opened its mouth at the other end and let out a large blue lead, upon which it clamped its teeth. I didn't dare mention the ink pencil as a hint for Christmas, for it cost twenty-five cents, but I needn't have trembled in my boots over my nerve in inscribing my heart's desire on the plaster. No one ever saw it, nor did I ever get an ink pencil. But the memory of this incident has kept alive in me the knowledge of how much a child can pine for something that other children have.

From organ blower I was promoted to bell ringer. Sometimes I filled both functions. I tolled the bell from the church gallery in the rear, then dashed downstairs and up the entire length of the church, finally reaching the organ hole, much as a rat might dash from the top of a corn crib to its burrow under the hen house.

Christmas was always a time of great ceremony in our church, and to this day my Christmas services are influenced by these early days. We go out and bring in our own cedars to trim my churches, just as we children used to bring in the Christmas trimmings from the woods in Vermont. One of us brought in spruce trees and hemlock for wreaths, while the other hunted rabbit tracks. In the evening we picked off the hemlock twigs and turned them over to the women to wind on long ropes. The Christmas Eve service was the event of the year to Closson and me. I seem to remember each one of them, but particularly the year when the big chandelier caught fire (the local paper said I coolly removed it from the building), and the time the ten-inch stovepipe near the chancel toppled down, filling the place with sooty smoke and disrupting the ritual.

From the beginning, therefore, I seemed to be closely linked to the church. I blew the organ, rang the bell, trimmed the chancel for Christmas. Even before I went to college, I began to read the service. It all fell in quite naturally. The church was a small one. There were few Episcopalians in that Congregational area—only twenty-five or thirty communicants. At first we had a settled minister, but soon the services became irregular, so sometimes Closson and I would officiate, because it meant so much to Mother. At last Closson decided to go into the ministry. He talked to me about it. Why didn't I go in for it too? Father would never have thought of such a thing for either of us, but he raised no objection. I don't recall that Mother said anything, although I'm sure she was pleased. Father was always interested in our marks. Scholarship was the big thing to him. But Mother would say, "Well, George, I wouldn't worry so much about the marks. Be a good boy."

As I recall it, we never had much of a Sunday school, if any, in this church. There weren't many children to begin with, and no one dreamed of any of the grownups being in a class. Not that they weren't just as good as the other churchgoers thereabouts, but they kept their religion more to themselves. Although I attended Sunday school for a while in a Congregational church and taught at one time in a Methodist church, I still think that one should attend church services from childhood up. This has always been the case with our children. The substitution of Sunday school for family church attendance seems to me to be helping to wreck our churches.

Although churchgoing was accepted as a family affair, Father would begin by the middle of the week to talk about the things we would have to do on Sunday. He would tell us that instead of going to church, we must stay at home and mend the bridle blinder or clip the horse's fetlocks. This would get Mother all stirred up, for to her Sunday meant a family churchgoing, and nothing else. Of course, Father fully intended us to go to church, but he had his own Vermont brand of subtle, unsmiling humor, and he liked to provoke Mother. When he got there, likely as not, he would clean his nails with a knife right through the prayers. Mother took her religion hard. She was a gentle soul and very pious. Some time ago I saw a poll of ministers in which they were asked where they got their religion. They all agreed that the first glimmerings came as they sat through the church services of their youth. This corresponds exactly with my own experience. I got mine sitting quietly in the pew and listening to the voice of my mother, which was packed with sincerity and devotion. It seems to me even now that I can hear her responding to the Litany. Children need that experience. I cannot emphasize too strongly my belief that children absorb religion in just this manner.

We didn't have family prayers in our home or even grace at our table, but we did have a genuine hatred of pretense and hypocrisy. A great deal of practical Christianity was practiced day in and day out. Before we were confirmed by the Bishop, we had to learn the catechism. I don't mean that we learned a part of it and just read over the rest. We mastered the whole business, word for word. In those days the Bishop lined up the candidates before him in the chancel and put the questions. He never used a book, thus leaving his keen eyes free to survey the row. We were instructed at home, and Father saw to it that no child said the responses any louder than his did. I don't think this catechism training ever did me much good, except perhaps one part of it. Of the two duties set forth—my duty towards God and my duty towards my neighbor—the first had little effect on me. No one gets to love God by being told that this is his duty, any more than one gets to love his country by being ordered to stand up and salute the flag. But "the duty towards my neighbor" had a profound effect on me. "To be true and just in all my dealings; to hurt nobody by word or deed; to keep my hands from picking and stealing"—these words sank right down into my life.

As our backs were turned to the congregation when we were catechized, I never could figure out how Father managed to catch every word we said. He seemed to single us out, even if there were a dozen in line, and he knew if we spoke up as loudly and clearly as he thought we should. As for the confirmation itself, it left a deep spiritual impression. It seemed to me that after it, I never could do wrong again. I am not much of a stickler for that mystic something that must have an unbroken succession through the laying on of hands, but I do know what that confirmation did for me.

Soon after it took place I entered the State Normal School, which was only a mile from our home. Nearly all my young companions went to this school whether they intended to teach or not. It cost practically nothing and they were all growing up virtually within sound of its bell. Randolph Center was a one-street village on the old stage route from Boston to Montreal. Like most of the original towns of New England, the people had all lived on the hills like the Indians until the railroads came. Then they had moved lower down until the floods came to bother them again.

The one street in Randolph Center was phenomenally wide and lined with fine trees. Perhaps a hundred people lived in the village proper and there were two or three shops, the most important of which was Will Fargo's grocery, where everyone gathered. There were always buggies hitched along the street, or sleighs in winter. We lived a mile out, in a simple frame house that was comfortable but far from bright. We were smack up against a hill and there was no view to speak of from any angle. A woodshed kept the south sun from the house, and the barn projecting to the southeast shut off the winter sun altogether. I can remember that the kitchen was always dark. We studied and lived mostly in the big dining room which opened off the sitting room or parlor. Plenty of studying was done by all of us in that house.

Father was long on education, having been a school teacher himself and having served on the local school board for years. We had a blackboard set up in the old dining room, and heaven help the youngster who disturbed Father in his reading of the New York *Sun* after he had been sent to that blackboard to do "figgers." The favorite problem was to divide one ten-thousandth (decimally) by one one-hundred-thousandth. Arithmetic came easy to me, and as he was rather upset one night by the ease with which I got the answers to the stiff problems he assigned me, he changed from arithmetic to reading. I read so dreadfully that he sprang from his chair and rushed into the kitchen to tell Mother that sad as it might seem, he had discovered an idiot in the family. Whereupon Cousin Caroline, who lived with us, took me over in the shadow of the big wood box and had me read to her. I got along much better with her than with Father, who had me scared to death.

Father was also great for having a town school-gathering at least once a year. In the winter he had all the elementary grades come together for a spelling bee. The children stood in two long lines around the walls and the teacher gave out the words, with Father striding along behind him as umpire. "Pursue," said the teacher to me. I hesitated a bit, and Father, anxious to see his son and heir do well, tried to help by explaining the word: "A father pursues his son." Heaven knows, I knew what he meant by that! "Persue," I spelled it, and took my seat in disgrace. Father glared at me, and I looked forward to some uncomfortable pursuing, after the bee was over. Once I did manage to spell down the school, but most of the scholars were absent that day, so I didn't get much credit for it.

But Father's love of education was not so profound that he wasn't ruthless about keeping us home from school to work on the farm. When I objected he went to Edward Conant, the principal, who played right into his hands. "Keep the boy home," he said. "He will pass all right." Well, I stayed out a fourth of the year and I passed all right. I could learn quickly because I was so healthy and exercised so much outdoors.

Mr. Conant, like Mother, greatly influenced my religious life. Every member of the school gathered in the assembly hall for prayers each day, and Mr. Conant's head always shook with earnestness as he prayed zealously for us. All my life I have had a most vivid picture of him as he started in on the Nineteenth Psalm, and I can hear the words today, as plainly as I did some fifty years ago—*"The heavens declare the glory of God; and the firmament showeth his handiwork—"*

All five of us went to normal school—my three sisters, Rebecca, Adelaide and Martha, as well as Closson and I. But we boys always had to hustle home, get into overalls, and do chores, no matter what the weather was like. We had debates every week for two years in this school, which gave us ease in speaking. All the time I was working toward the Episcopal church, sometimes reading the service and moving steadily in the direction of the ministry.

Along with my schooling I was getting an invaluable education from living on the farm. What a help that training has been to me in my work as a country preacher! While a man can function well enough in a country church without having lived on a farm, I think he is greatly handicapped without this experience. I loved it. I loved the farm animals, and Martha and I spent much of our spare time during the winter training calves to drag us around on our sleds. We had one black and white heifer we could drive anywhere. Years later Father took that grown-up heifer out with some of the herd, to lead them down a road to a distant pasture. He had a terrible time with the one we had trained. At last he gave up and rushed into the house dripping with perspiration and wildly excited. While he was being calmed down I sneaked to the barn. Imagine Father's chagrin when he saw me driving the recalcitrant cow down the road with a horse's bridle on her head and the reins through a saddle on her back!

About the time that I entered normal school I joined the Christian Endeavor at the Congregational Church, which most of the young people of the town attended. We boys filled the back seat every Sunday night, and took part rather mechanically in the service. I don't know that this did me much good, yet it did keep me up to certain standards. I became president of the local society and then of a large Christian Endeavor Union. It was most unusual, in those days, to have an Episcopalian even join such a society, much less lead it. Father was pretty proud of me when he saw me preside at a large meeting of that Christian Endeavor. He told a neighbor named Luther Harrington, "Some folks think Episcopalians have to read their prayers out of a book, but my boy George got right down on his knees and prayed like a cuss!"

Of course, we boys couldn't let the poor girls go out in the cold, dark world alone after Endeavor meeting. Sometimes I would have the buggy and the old horse, Bill, who got quite used to stopping at a certain house at the upper end of the town's main street, where my girl lived in a rented room. The house was owned by Miss Hayes, a queer old maid who was smothered in oddity and bore a rather laughable local reputation. Her clothes were all made out of bran sacks. She always planted her garden on the Fourth of July, when others did theirs in May. Strangely enough, it was a good garden too. A young boy named Joe lived with her.

One day Bill had been shod at the blacksmith's shop just beyond her house, and Father and I met at the shop to drive home. Father took the reins, but no sooner had we started than he placed them between his knees and proceeded to light his pipe, a favorite trick of his. Free, Bill just laid back his ears and headed for the old maid's. Before Father knew what was up, we had landed plump in the front yard. To make it worse, there were a lot of loafers on the store piazza across the street, and they roared. How mad Father was! "You old fool!" he shouted at Bill, as he whacked him with the butt of the reins. 'By thunder, George, that's the queerest thing that ever happened to me," he added. I, too, looked astonished at Bill's procedure, but I thought the less said the better.

There was an energetic Band of Hope at Randolph Center. Both boys and girls belonged to it and they used to go marching past our house at milking time on their way to meetings in the old Southey District schoolhouse. Usually they were yelling like a lot of maniacs. We boys knew the bunch. Had we not had many a bloody fight with them after school, because they made fun of our clothes and our bare feet? We would have none of them. The Band was broken up before the winter was over but not until the leader, a woman, had interrupted our peaceful milking operations one night. She was rather large; and her way of looking at things was as far from Father's as the east is from the west. Father would disagree with her, anyway, whether the issue was high tariff or hell's pavement of infant skulls. So, when she blew into the cow stable one night, the fuse was already laid to the gunpowder—and a mighty short fuse too.

If only there could have been a dictaphone in old Jim's horse stall that night and the conversation preserved for posterity! As a parting shot, she assured Father that both his sons would die drunkards. This impressed me very much, for it appeared to be a case of the Band of Hope or a drunkard's grave, and I felt exactly as the old darkey did, when assured that it was either heaven or hell, and he couldn't help himself. "In that case," he cried, "I'll take to the woods."

We were all brought up on the temperance basis, but not one of us signed the pledge. I take little stock in passing any laws about drinking. Man-made laws mean one thing today, and another tomorrow, but God's laws never change. Our job is to bring up boys and girls who don't want the stuff and who won't touch it, laws or no laws. The Episcopal church has always seemed to me to stand for temperance on good Biblical grounds but without fanaticism. It did not get greatly excited over the prohibition issue. But St. Paul's words in First Corinthians have always made an impression on me, and I have ever tried to keep them in mind: "Take heed lest by any means this liberty of yours become a stumbling block to them that are weak." I feel that all Christians, and especially Christian ministers, would do well to give up anything that might prove too much of a temptation to others. Sometimes I take a sip of homemade wine, when urged so strongly that I am in danger of hurting sensitive feelings if I refuse, but I do this very seldom. It's just as well to lean over backwards on such things.

As for smoking, Father smoked us out so thoroughly when we were young that neither Closson nor I ever felt any desire to take a puff. One of my Divinity School classmates used to urge me to smoke. He said it was restful, comforting, relaxing. But long ago he died from cancer of the tongue, caused by cigar irritation, so I think it is just as well I left it alone. I never have felt the need of it.

Chapter II

FATHER

. . . .

FATHER was a small man with a majestic beard and an excitable manner. He met large issues calmly but was in a continual ferment over trifles. His native Vermont reserve was shot all through with a strong dash of peppery temperament and sometimes I felt very sorry for Mother, who strove always to throw balm on his harshness. She was delicate, sweet and submissive, and when things got out of hand she meekly resorted to tears—like the day Father decided that her beautiful old syringa in the yard must come down. But her tears did not stay his ax. He dug around the tree and chopped it down without remorse. Some time later by a miracle of management she kept him from hacking up her favorite table. I can see him still, coming in and flourishing the ax over it, while Mother argued that it was a good table, a Blodgett table, and she liked it. Father thought the time had come to get some new-fangled furniture, like other folks thereabouts. I have the table in my own parlor today.

To understand Father, one would need to know something of his own bitter childhood. At the age of three he walked to school, a considerable distance, experiencing the rigors of a New England winter almost before he was free from his cradle. One day his father picked him up when he got home from school, kissed him and told him that his mother was dead. After that he had a stepmother who was so cruel to him that it shaped his attitude to women for the rest of his life. In his teens he ran away from home and by the time we got to know him, there was little softness left in Father. But life under his roof was never dull, for he had the knack of dramatizing every simple event around the farm—the result, no doubt, of his wandering days in the South when he played Shakespeare, taught school and wore the uniform of a Confederate soldier.

He had all the ingrained pessimism of the farmer and the beauties of nature left him cold. If he looked at the sky at all, it was merely to see whether it was going to rain, and usually he was sure that it was. The flowers and birds might have been so much cardboard, except that the birds would undoubtedly damage the corn and the flowers were traps for weeds. If a stretch of fine days came along, it was a "weather breeder" sure. We would have to get the corn in before it rained, or rescue the buckwheat from the deluge. A sunny stretch was bound to presage drought. Early in the fall he began to worry about frost. "Yes, the wind's swinging to the north, George, and the frost is on its way," Father would say. "And the corn not yet ripe," he would add mournfully.

I have actually prayed that there wouldn't be a frost to kill the corn, so seriously did I take Father's dire forebodings. One night he got us up at three o'clock to go down back of the barn and cut corn as, sure enough this time, the frost had come. We had no mittens, since it was too early for our woolens, so I remember Father holding the lantern while we boys, half asleep and shaking with cold, gripped the icy stalks with one hand and tried to wield the cutter with the numb fingers of the other.

But as I grew older, I noticed that the neighbors didn't seem to worry the way Father did, and still they got along all right. Father simply magnified everything to the proportions of calamity and kept us all on tenterhooks. That was one reason why the work on our farm was so hard. He was the same about politics and all the details, large and small, of everyday living. Mother was like a gentle breeze blown before a tornado. We all hopped to do his bidding. The house was full of women—my three sisters, our Cousin Caroline, and for several years Kate Robinson, who helped Mother when we were little.

The old north bedroom where Closson and I slept was terribly cold. Our covers were usually like ice. We slept on corn husk mattresses with socks on our feet and long woolen toques with tassels on our heads. When I wakened in the morning my head would be sweating, and I have always blamed my baldness on this. I started to lose my hair while I was still in college.

The winter cold of these days lives more strongly in my memory than the blossoming springs and fine autumns we had in Vermont. Father was more solicitous of his horses than his sons, so when Closson and I wanted to go somewhere, we generally had to walk, no matter what the weather was like. It was bad enough doing the mile and a quarter trek to school in the snow, trying to keep in the narrow ruts made by sled tracks, but getting back late at night in the dark from a church function was worse. Often there would be an icy crust on which I kept slipping, and the wind would cut right through me. I remember once getting so discouraged that I sat right down in the snow, despairing, and after a while crawled along on my hands and knees. It really seemed as though I never could get home that night. But I didn't get any sympathy from Father. "Nonsense!" he would say, dismissing the subject, when I dared to complain of the cold.

One night I was coming home from the grist mill in East Bethel after dark and heading all the way right into a north wind. My hands and feet seemed to be frozen right through the blankets. When I got home I went indoors and stood near the stove, whimpering with misery as my hands thawed out achingly. "Why didn't you get out and walk?" was the sympathy I got from Father.

Our sufferings were greatly aggravated by chilblains. Can I ever forget them? We wore hard, cold, cowhide boots made by our grandfather Blodgett, and sometimes rolled on the floor with pain, in spite of the woodchuck grease rubbed into the leather to soften it. There was one pair in particular from which we all suffered in turn, boys and girls. No one could tell on whose feet these awful shoes would land. They must have been a child's size twelve, and were made of heavy, unsplit cowhide just as stiff as a board. There were cut holes for the strings and no shaping in the back to fit the heel. Just low and painfully straight. How we hated them! They were summered in an old chest over the shed. Four of my generation had worn them and finally they fell to poor Martha. One thing I know, they never wore out. The one redeeming feature was that after going barefooted all summer, our feet would spread and the abominable shoes would not go on, no matter how much woodchuck grease, well colored with lamp black, Father might apply from his three-legged iron kettle with its rattail handle, all of which gave off a worse smell than the fried salt pork we had every morning. But when I was about twelve years old along came a new kind of shoe—a felt moccasin covered with rubber. I shall never forget the difference this made to me. My feet were warm at last. I was no longer driven half crazy with chilblains and blisters.

We had a big box stove in the dining room where we usually sat, and we boys kept it filled with wood. The whole top lifted up and the chances were that when we put in wood, the twelve-inch griddle that sat on it would go spinning to the floor. We boys had to jump and dodge when it did. Father had the idea that the more stovepipe you had draping the room the more heat you got—a notion that Mrs. Gilbert says has persisted with me. He had the stovepipe come up and out in the room, and across and back again with quite a fancy effect, before it finally disappeared in the chimney. It didn't improve the look of the room, but it did give out plenty of heat, and that was important with the temperature at 34 below zero.

But all that was forgotten when spring came and then the long busy summers. We had two fine maples and some big elms on the farm. There was a maple right in front of the house and a swing hung from one of its limbs. If a rope broke when the beds were being corded, we got the worn pieces to make swings for ourselves. I made up my mind quite early that when I grew up I would help children to have swings, for they meant so much to us. And I have carried out this intention in my various missions. I have furnished rope and chains in many places and have urged the use of automobile tires, which make excellent swings. I have one on my own farm. But in my boyhood no one would think of buying a new rope for a swing. That would be mad extravagance. We made up all our own games, of course. We hunted through the barn for odds and ends to help in making sleds and for pieces of straps to hold on old skates. When I was fifteen Father did interest himself enough to help me make a good traverse sled. I sold it to a neighbor when I was going off to college, and he still has it, half a century later. It was a stout piece of construction.

I can never forget the rattrap Father made. He got a big box, at least a yard square, made a sliding door for it, and put a hook over the door. This he put up in the cellar. A string ran up from the sliding door, through a knothole in the floor, and was tied to the bedstead right by Father's pillow. Some corn meal was put in the box as bait for the rats, and any old time that Father happened to wake up in the night, he pulled the string, just on general principles.

The morning after the box was first set up, there was a grand rush for the cellar. We hit the box and listened. Yes, it was occupied all right. We heaved it step by step up the cellar stairs and into the living room. Closson had been dispatched to the hay mow to hunt for the cats—Frolic, Spot and Beelzebub, the latter so-called as he was certainly the prince of all cat devils. They were to help conduct the massacre when the box was opened.

The women came downstairs from their bedrooms, and the men of the house armed themselves with clubs. The cats were all present or accounted for, and we opened the door of the box. Man alive, what a time we had for a few minutes! Men, boys, cats, rats, chairs, weeping and wailing and gnashing of teeth! We went through that performance a dozen times, whether there was one rat in the box or eleven, which was our score on one occasion. The women soon learned to absent themselves from those rat-killings, and to show up only after the carnage was over. Poor patient Mother never said anything, but my sisters made no pretense of liking it.

Another time Father and I went down to the cellar to open a barrel of cider. Cider, of course, begins to "work" about three or four days after it is made. Father had rolled a barrel of it to the foot of the cellar stairs and I noticed that there were decided signs of pressure and agitation within. But he said nothing until after supper that night. Then he exclaimed, "By thunder, George, I forgot about that barrel of cider. We've got to knock the bung out of it. Get a hammer and a lantern."

He took the light and I followed him down the cellar stairs with the hammer. We rolled the barrel over on its side and worked it around until the bung was on top. Father reached for the hammer. Now, you don't hit the bung itself in a cider-barrel. You strike the stave near it, with a downward blow. Father was never a man to do things by halves. When he hit a barrel, it stayed hit. And he hit this one. Bang! The thing blew out like the rear tire of a Model T. A two-inch stream of overworked cider hit the ceiling. Father, acting on impulse, pushed his hand down over the hole, to stop it. He might just as well have tried to stop the Mississippi, for he merely spread the shooting stream sideways. I ducked to the floor and Father got the full benefit of the flood. He was literally soaked with cider. His whiskers dripped streams of it—Aaron's beard and its oil had nothing on him. He was a sight to behold. The deluge put out the lanterns and we groped our way upstairs, in the dark.

Well, I never found that bung. Out of sheer curiosity I used to look for it, but it never did turn up. The force with which it hit the ceiling may have broken it to bits—who knows? Neither did I ever refer to this incident in Father's hearing. Whenever I thought of it, I had to get out of his sight, back of the kitchen stove, until I could quiet down. No one ever laughed at Father and survived.

The old gentleman fancied himself as an expert in many fields. He had a quart cup that he was quite proud of, black as the ace of spades from countless coffee brewings. He liked to tell how many minutes it took him to build a fire and cook the coffee. We did no canning, but we had a fine old New England cellar and I'll never forget the abundance of apples on our farm. I think the reason my right arm is longer than my left is the constant pulling and stretching I did after school hours all fall, groping for the high branches to pluck down apples.

Mother and Kate Robinson, who worked for us, were great cheese makers. This was always an elaborate ceremony. First, when a calf was killed, its stomach was stretched on a board, as one might stretch a woodchuck skin. There it dried and the pieces were then used to make cheese. One piece of rennet, an inch square, was put in four-and-a-half quarts of milk to curdle it for the making of a pound of cheese. When the milk was properly curdled, it was poured through a basket to remove the whey. Then the curd was seasoned with salt and sage, both well mixed together with the fingers. (The sage was raised in the garden, dried in the attic and crumpled up, ready to sift into the curd when needed.) The cheese was then put in a round wooden cylinder and thoroughly pressed down until hard, remaining in this state at least overnight. Finally, the cheese was removed and covered with a cloth, ready for use. It was cut with an army sword, a flourish favored by Father.

The churning was a great headache to Closson and me. We had the usual barrel churn that flopped over and over. If you didn't get the cover on just so, with all the "fingers" under the "hooks," then off it would come, as you turned the churn over, and the whole mess would go all over the floor. Besides the loss of the cream, there was the task of cleaning up, with the prospect of Father's fury hovering over us like a thunderbolt. "Has it come to butter yet?" was the cry that pursued us all over the farm for years, it seemed to me. Sometimes the wretched mixture would take a whole day and would even run over to the next— stubbornly frothing and foaming, everything but coming to butter, and in the end going to the pigs. Closson would get so bored that he would try to read and churn at the same time.

The washing was done in the hard old-fashioned way. No gadgetry lightened the task in our earlier years. Kate Robinson superintended this rite, relying solely on elbow grease. Kate looked after me from the time I was two until I was seven and I always remember her as most sympathetic and good-natured. I missed her terribly when she left and I would frequently waken up in the night and cry, "I hear her, Mama. She's coming, she's coming." She and her sister, Caroline, aged eighty-nine, are the oldest twins in Vermont today. There were ten brothers and sisters in their family.

Poor Mother! She always seemed so frail and delicate. I tried to help her around the house as much as I could. I put up clothes lines and fixed screen doors for her. She had pneumonia several times but she did not die until I was in Divinity School. Her work was never done and she had infinite patience with Father. She had fair hair and a sweet face, with a look of resignation. She was born Martha Pamelia Blodgett, daughter of the itinerant cobbler who made the terrible shoes from which we all suffered so shockingly. In those days cobblers went from house to house with sides of leather on their backs, making shoes for a whole family at a time. Mother had two brothers and five sisters, and the six Blodgett sisters all taught school. They were so adept at spelling that they prided themselves on carrying off the prizes at any spelling bee. So good were they that one night when they went to Tunbridge to a spell-down, they found a warning on the blackboard: "Anyone is entitled to enter this spelling contest except the Blodgett girls of Randolph."

My grandmother, Rebecca Blodgett, was descended from Benjamin Blodgett, a brilliant man who was born on an Irish ship coming to this country. Grandmother belonged to the Congregational Church until she became friendly with an Episcopalian family named Chase, who came from Cornish, New Hampshire, and were the first Episcopalians to settle in Randolph Center. It was through them and their friendship with a youth named W. H. A. Bissell (who later became Bishop Bissell) that the little

Episcopal Church was started there. A current joke in that region was that there were enough Chases thereabouts to blow the devil out of hell and enough Bellowses (in Bellows Falls) to blow him back again. The Episcopal community at Randolph Center was considered pretty gay. They drank cider, played cards and had dances. Today they would rank as great puritans.

Mother's family never even owned a horse but went to church with oxen, if they didn't walk. She and my aunts Hannah, Addie and Olivia all trudged two miles to the old Orange County Grammar School, which preceded the normal school in Randolph Center. They learned Latin and algebra and were fine scholars and a studious family of girls. Mother didn't have to travel far afield to meet her fate, for Father was soon to come home from the Civil War and make her his bride. They went for a local honeymoon after the fashion of the time, and it was seventeen years later that the horse and buggy which served as the wedding equipage was paid for with the first money I earned from teaching school. The original cost of the turnout was $40, but the interest mounted up over the years. I had $100 all told to meet the bill. "Well, let it go at that," said the patient creditor, pleased to have this forgotten account settled up. Father had not even paid a dollar down. Many a drive I had in that open buggy in my boyhood days and I was willing to pay for it. I can still picture Father sitting in it, the reins slack between his knees, while he lighted up his pipe.

Our home was not run on business principles by any means. Father was scrupulously honest but had all the genius of Mr. Micawber for letting matters rest, and Mother would give away the last thing she had in the house. Goodness knows, with five of us children, and poor as we were, things were pretty well worn out when we got through with them, but it was miraculous how Mother could always find something we didn't need to give to someone poorer than we were. No one can ever estimate the tremendous influence this giving propensity of hers had on my whole life. Of course, we had a good many things given to us, too. One aunt was quite well-to-do and her children never wore out their clothes. So, between the Blodgett shoes, the Blodgett hats (given us by Uncle George, a hatter), and the cousins' cast-offs, we sported fine feathers at times.

One of my great friends in town was Will Fargo, who ran the store. He was slack beyond belief about his accounts. He entered all purchases as they came along in a day book, but usually forgot to charge them up to the individual buyer. The result was a strangely muddled state of affairs. Gracious knows how far we Gilberts got behind, but as Closson and I grew older and began to worry about Father's debts, we kept at Will to see how much the family owed him. But could we find out? No. He would search through his day books for years back and get nowhere. Then he would give up. So Closson and I went in with $200 one time and insisted that he take it. We felt it our moral duty to pay for the groceries we had had as children. When he died, he willed his store and house to Closson, who had been very good to him in his last years. Will Fargo was a remarkable man, always doing the helpful thing, and he influenced my life very greatly.

Another interesting town character was the Washburn woman, whom everyone called Aunt Peaker, because her face was so peaked. She looked more like a turkey than one would believe possible. Every year her son, Julian, sent her a keg of red pepper from which she made red pepper tea— a keg of it to last the whole year. She lived to a ripe old age notwithstanding.

But we had one neighbor who never failed to get Father's goat. This was Colonel John Mead, a Civil War veteran who lived across the road from us, and put on the kind of dog that made Father froth at the mouth. He was a large and handsome fellow, tall and straight, weighing about 250 pounds. His black beard used to be rather intimidating to us boys, used as we were to hirsute adornment in our own home. He was a native Vermonter and very puritanical. He was a great temperance man and he wouldn't have a playing card in the house. It so happened that we were brought up on cards. Right after supper, Father would get us lined up for whist. He thought that a man who could play whist well could do virtually anything. By the time Closson and I came of age we were sick of the sight of cards, thanks to Father, and we never quite got over it.

The Colonel was very stern and I think it was from him I learned what not to be. He developed in me a terrible prejudice against a show of religion, so that we don't have household prayers even today, and grace only occasionally. The Colonel was strong on family prayers and he used to say he'd rather see his sons lying in the cemetery than have them touch a drop of liquor. He used to annoy Father no end as he swashbuckled around the countryside. His second wife had money and the Colonel was quite a swell, driving about on weekdays as well as

Sundays in a Prince Albert coat, his kid-gloved hands lightly holding the reins over the dasher, and two horses hitched to a shining buggy. It just didn't go down with the farmers, and it was a big joke at the Gilbert place. He had a double driveway and he used to make Father wild by swinging round a big tree in our yard to go up the other side. We children always scattered like hens before this equine onslaught.

The Colonel was on the State Board of Agriculture and passersby would always stop to admire his place in passing. This left the Gilbert farm unnoticed. "There is somebody down on this side of the road, too," Father would snort, as he watched the visitors, all agape over the Colonel's indifferently tended acres, knowing full well that his garden and crops were better weeded by far. But Father's sweet revenge came when three members of the board arrived to inspect the show farm. This day the Colonel was loading hay on top of a high hill. He was a good loader and his load was as square as a brick.

Henry Inman, who was working for him, looked up as the load went higher and higher and said humbly, "Colonel, haven't we got about enough on there now?"

"Put her up, put her up," roared the Colonel, "I know what we're doing."

So they put her up and up, until the eyes of the onlookers bulged like peeled onions. At last the Colonel called for the reins and swung the horses sharply, right on the brow of the hill. In a split second the front axle broke in two, and over they went down the hill—hay, horses, Colonel Mead and all. Father happened to be working in his garden and he had the laugh of a lifetime.

However, he was an erratic farmer himself. He had no luck with hens and he always hated the sight of a cow. He went in for old-style poultry and then wondered why they didn't lay. One trouble was that he was always full of great ideas and never confined his interests to the farm alone. He seethed with political feeling and at times felt that he was practically running the country from his quiet New England corner. He was the original isolationist—the lone Democrat in Vermont. Indeed, he was a man who would try anything, expecting nothing of it. After the Civil War, he bought the first mowing machine ever seen in Randolph Center. All the farmers came to see it work and he cannily tried it out on his father's best meadow lot right beside the road where all could see it. His father was furious over the new-fangled thing. "Cutting so close will kill every spear," he roared. As a matter of fact, there happened to be a bad drouth that year right after haying, and the whole lot turned berry-brown.

Father had firm notions of discipline and I shall never forget the look on his face as Uncle George told him about a ride he had with a friend of his who stood by helplessly while his grown daughter, indignant that he would not take the road she chose, ordered him to stop the horses, while she got out of the carriage, lay down at the roadside and went into a regular tantrum—yelling and kicking until she was tired out. With that whalebone whip right there in the socket, she would have got back into her seat in one shake of a lamb's tail if her father had only been my father. But I don't suppose it would have changed her character much at that age.

The spirit of adventure was strong in Father's family.

His grandfather, Nathaniel Gilbert, was visiting his uncle, Captain Gilbert, in Royalton, Vermont, at the time the Indians burned the town. On October 16, 1780, Nathaniel was sent off to warn a neighbor that the Indians were coming. When he returned, he found the house already occupied by the redskins. He started to run but soon stopped to look back. He saw that an Indian had him spotted. Knowing it would mean death if he went another step, he surrendered.

The Indians took him with them to Canada. One night all the captives were tied to trees, and the old Indian chief proceeded to go down the line, scalping each one. When he came to Nathaniel, then a boy of fifteen, the squaws made such an outcry to have his life spared because of his good looks that the chief passed him by. After that Nathaniel spent seven years with the Indians, his chief occupation being to help the women with the cooking. One day when the tribe went skating on the St. Lawrence River, Nathaniel pretended that he could not skate. Falling down frequently, he gradually separated himself from the others until the moment came for him to skate away at full speed. He came to a break in the ice and leaped over it successfully. The Indians followed him to that point, but were not so skilled on their skates as he, and didn't dare to bridge the gap.

After his escape Nathaniel joined the British army for a time, this being one way to keep from starving to death until he could manage to get home again. On his discharge from the army, he finally reached Connecticut and found his mother and sisters still alive. When he got to their door, his sisters begged their mother not to take him in, for they felt sure he could not be the brother who had been captured by the Indians. He had changed greatly because of all the experiences he had been through. At last he convinced some neighbors of his identity, and then his mother and sisters accepted him too. It has always been a tradition in our family that when Nathaniel finally was taken back into his own home, he remarked with some bitterness, "Always take people in. You never know who they may be." From that time on, no Gilbert has been known to turn away anyone without help.

So far as we know, Nathaniel married and lived in Connecticut, while the next generation moved to Vermont. Who can say what strain from this adventuring ancestor may not have run through Father's veins, for one day when Grandfather remarked, "Hen, you don't earn your salt," Hen laid down his hoe, retorted "Is that so?" and calmly left his home for good. He was just a boy at the time but was quite ready to see the world. He persuaded a brilliant youth named Levins, who had gone to the old Orange County Grammar School with him, to strike out for himself at the same time. Father always said in after years that Levins was smarter than he was, so he must have been good.

They decided to look up two school teachers named Moulton and Griswold who had written them from Mississippi that excellent teaching positions were available there. They got as far as Cleveland, Ohio, and there their money ran out, so they went to work in a boarding school. The principal was tight about food and fuel. He used to buy a firkin of cheap butter at a time, and when the young blades realized that thirty pounds of frowy butter lay ahead of them, they couldn't stand the prospect, so they got up during the night and daubed butter over every doorknob in the school. There was good butter after that. This was only one of many similar tricks played by the traveling duo. Levins had a strong sense of humor and one of his fancies on their travels was to pretend that he was crazy and that Father was his keeper. Father would tell by the hour of the escapades that this entailed. It was while they were in Ohio that they both managed to get on the stage, acting in *Macbeth* and *Uncle Tom's Cabin*. Levins got so intense playing in *Macbeth* that after the performance was over he used to rip up chairs in his absorption, repeating the dagger scene.

The pair finally got to Mississippi and there taught school. The man on whose plantation Father boarded paid him out of his own pocket to teach the slaves and he came back North with a different idea from anything he had picked up in *Uncle Tom's Cabin*. When the Civil War broke out he joined the army of the North, although he drilled with the Confederate soldiers. He was at the Battle of Gettysburg but did not figure in the fighting. He gave up his watch and money and was all ready for action but at the last minute he and his tent pal, Bill Perham, were sent back to help guard a pack train. Bill was a great character, who used to go foraging around in the night and come back with plunder, much to Father's distress. "These cookies seemed to be lying around loose down at the Commissioner's tent." Bill would apologize, depositing a huge bag of them in the tent. Father would plead with Bill to return the loot, but Bill could see no valid reason for undoing his sleight of hand, so in the end they would eat them, and share them with any soldier discreet enough to keep them out of sight.

Father was born in 1842 and he lived to be exactly eighty-three. He was full of ginger and opposition right up to the end. Shortly before Mrs. Gilbert and I bought our farm in Connecticut he came to see us. It was during the Christmas season, when we seldom had much snow, and we thought it would be nice for him to come down to our place, where it would be warmer than in Vermont. It was a hard trip for him—two hundred miles on the train, with several changes. As usual, ill luck and calamity pursued Father. He had no sooner started than it began to snow, and by the time he crossed the Connecticut line the snow lay two feet deep, with a bitter wind to freeze it.

He weathered the trip all right but was tired out when he arrived, and we put him to bed immediately, in a room facing on the street. But that didn't end his woes. The streetcars that passed our house had great trouble with a sharp curve just outside. A snow plow was summoned and soon it began bucking a big drift right under Father's window. It would back up and come crashing, ca-*bang*, into the drift. Behind it came the trolley—snapping, popping, flashing. The wheels ground and slipped, sand was spilled over the tracks, sparks flew. Every flash struck Father's room like midnight lightning. On top of all this was the highly appropriate language of six trolley men.

Next morning Father came down to breakfast with an ultimatum: "Thunderation, George, this may be a warm climate, but I wouldn't live in such a confounded place if you gave it to me. Why, the Civil War was a sleepy hollow compared to this house. I'm going home."

And home he went, the first day the roads were opened. That was Father all over.

Chapter III

SCHOOL DAYS

. . . .

THE annual hat agony took place in the fall. From the breakfast table on the first day of the school term, Father used to march us up to a cupboard in which rested a collection of Dunlap derbies worthy of the Mad Hatter himself. He would twirl one on his hand. He would pinch in the top with his fingers and show how it would snap right back. "Any boy should be proud to wear a hat like that," he would announce. "Why, it's a five-dollar Dunlap." But we did not share his conviction.

The hats came from Uncle George Blodgett, who kept a clothing store in Amherst. His trade was mostly with the boys of Amherst College—luxurious young men who were able to buy new hats every season, blithely tossing the old ones on Uncle George's counter. Uncle obligingly waited until he had a huge box full of the cast-off derbies. Then he sent the whole batch to us, express prepaid. We looked them over without enthusiasm. Such a collection of styles, shapes and sizes! There were flat low hats with narrow brims fit only for pigmies, and others with crowns nearly as high as the lordly plugs. Starting on the lower shelf, Father would bang down first one hat and then another over our ears, admonishing us all the time, "Yes, you ought to be proud to wear a hat like that. A hat like that will never wear out."

That was just the trouble. The college boys were a lot older than we were, so the hats as a rule were miles too big, and we had to stuff out the hat bands with yards of newspaper. Remember, we were mere boys going to school in derbies. Probably not a man in Randolph Center wore one, to say nothing of the boys. Catch Father showing his face under one himself! Poor Closson acquired a nickname that stuck because of one of these detestable hats. He was attending Bethel High School at the time, and it was his sad lot to go forth every day in a tall, jet-black derby. He walked to school, and as he came over the brow of the hill, the boys playing out in front could see that hat long before they could see anything under it. "Here comes the hat," they'd shout. And "Hat" was Closson's name until he graduated.

If Father kept us all on the run, Mother's family certainly gave us a lot of anguish, between the Blodgett hats and the Blodgett shoes. I prefer to remember the good times we had sugaring. During my normal school days, I used to work at it all night, leaving home in the morning just in time to get to class. I love sugaring, as I suppose all boys do who have tried it. There would be a fine crust of snow at that time of year, and we would slide over it through the bare maples. Afterwards would come the big roaring fire, the steam, and plenty of syrup around for us to spread on our slices of bread.

On Saturdays Mother sent us our dinners from the house. There would be a six-quart pan with mashed potatoes and now and then a fried egg, depending on how Father's hens were doing. Sometimes we cooked our own dinner. We liked to boil eggs in the sugar sap, and we made a weird concoction which we called "coffee." It was brewed by toasting slices of bread until they were black, and then boiling them in maple sap. We kept the milk cold by burying it in snow, and we washed our hands in a snowdrift. It was hard work. I can remember seeing Closson come in at night, so exhausted that he would collapse in a chair and Mother would bring wash rag, towel and water to wash his hands and face for him. A grown man, too tired to wash!

During a great "run" one of us would stay and boil all night, getting catnaps on a board bunk. There were many loose boards on the old sugarhouse, and sometimes we would just be dozing off at the break of dawn, when a big wood pecker would start in pecking on one of them, about a foot away from our heads. Mother Nature's alarm clock!

In those days there was no such thing as an evaporator with a regulated flow of sap. If the sap got scorched, that meant a lot of trouble. Once I poured a big mess of scorched sap down a woodchuck's hole. I thought this would be a good way of getting rid of it. If any woodchucks were down there, they must have had a sticky time getting out. But the great thrill came at "sugaring off," when the sheet-iron pan was pulled off the fireplace and the syrup dipped out. Father would stand by the pan with a long-handled dipper, stirring the boiling mess to and fro, holding it up every minute or two to watch the syrup drip off the edge. If two or three drops ran together and made a big flat drop, it was called an "apron." This meant that the sap was boiled down enough for syrup, but if the drip came off the dipper and made a long "hair," it was done well enough for granulated sugar. Father would get excited when it aproned. "She's down," he would yell, and we would run around to the other side of the fireplace to lift up each end of the pan, so that he could push a board through. Down would come bricks, ashes and all sorts of debris, right into the tops of our boots. A delay of half a minute meant that the mixture would be scorched and spoiled so we had to work fast, no matter what the consequences to ourselves. The last run of sap, when the leaves had started, made a ropey syrup that turned into vinegar. We were sorry when sugaring time was ended. It was hard work but great fun.

During this period I did my first barbering, a hobby which has followed me right through my ministry. I figure that I have given about 5,000 haircuts in the intervening years—to men, women and children—and I would no sooner start for church without my barber's kit than without my prayer book. I carry it in a tin box—apron, scissors, comb and clippers. Whenever I see the need for it, out comes my kit and a head of hair is shorn. When I was in Bethel High School I got all my spending money this way—cutting hair at ten cents a head. Had it not been for Father, I might never have set up as an amateur barber. He said to me one Sunday forenoon, "George, cut my hair."

I was dumbfounded and frightened. Cut Father's hair? What a responsibility! But before I could say a word, he reached for a towel and put it around his neck. "Just cut right across the comb," he shouted. "That's all there is to it."

I went at it in fear and trembling, and I must have taken about seven snips when Father jumped up to look at himself in the mirror. I can't recall just what he said, but I know the remarks were appropriate. When he had recovered from the shock of seeing the jagged stairway running up the back of his head, he ordered me to hitch up Bill in the buggy as fast as I could. There was no barber shop in Randolph Center, but there was a man named Fred Eaton, commonly called Crocket, who cut hair. What Father said to him has been lost to the world, but Crocket got busy and repaired the damage as well as he could. Father proceeded to church, which in those days was held in the afternoon. After that I practiced on a little dog a cousin had given me and I kept at him until I could do a fairly good job.

Father preached education to us all the time. Both he and Mother had high respect for academic attainment, so it was not strange that Closson and I should turn our attention to teaching before we eventually found our way into the ministry. My first school was at Brookfield. Martha and I set out on the ten-mile trip there with the same old Bill that landed Father in front of Miss Hayes'. We had a dog cart by then, a two-wheeled affair that Aunt Olivia had gladly given us, as her husband had been killed in it. I was sixteen and Martha was twelve, and we were so childish that when we came to a flat ledge beside the road we drove Bill out on the rock, turned him clear round on it and then went on our way. That was our idea of fun. I got along better at Brookfield than anyone my age might have been expected to fare.

They "bid off" the board of the teacher in those days, and a man by the name of Richards got the privilege of boarding me for one dollar and ninety-nine cents a week.

It was a winter term. I had twenty-four scholars representing eight or nine grades. Children weren't graded in those days like milk—A, B, C, D. Now they are run through the school mill like cornstalks through an ensilage cutter. I had one big boy from up Northfield way who would rather be cutting up any time than studying. He had long hair, and the minute I saw it I remembered hearing Father tell of how in his teaching days he used to run his fingers through a boy's long hair, pull his head back and tell him a thing or two. That kept two of the lad's senses occupied at the same time. I tried it on this boy but only once. Next day he came to school with his head shaved smooth as a doorknob. For the rest of the winter I managed to warm some other parts of his anatomy, although the hair-pulling was at an end.

I had been in this town only a few weeks when I was invited to a party over on East Bear Hill. I had made friends with a younger crowd who were considered pretty free and easy by the older, puritan set. The Episcopalians in Randolph would have had some card playing, dancing and cider, but the puritanical spirit prevailed in Brookfield all right and there was none of this unseemly gaiety thereabouts. I asked a Congregational deacon's daughter to go to the party with me, and I skidded logs all one Saturday so that I could have the horse and buggy for the evening. We got there and soon found there would be no card games, no dancing, and not a drop of sweet cider. But they *did* play kissing games. I never had played kissing games, but they said I learned the quickest of any man that ever came into that town. By ten o'clock we were playing "Post Office" at a great pace. At eleven we paused a few minutes for refreshments. We needed refreshments. By twelve-thirty I realized clearly that I had joined the wrong church!

I didn't know the roads home, so my girl took it upon herself to guide me. She knew them all too well. She'd say, "This way" or "Take that road now," and we drove around in a circle most of the night. It was all over town next morning that the teacher got home at six a.m. This was my first and last party in that town, but the school committee, at the end of the term, reported that "although the teacher is young, he immediately put the school in running order and carried it through with profit to the scholars and with credit to himself."

Just after I had finished at Brookfield, a school committee man wrote to Father asking if I would go over to Chelsea and teach. "It doesn't take much brains to teach in Chelsea," he wrote, "but one has got to have a lot of sand to get along there." Most of the pupils were hired men and kind of rough. This letter was later reprinted and laid on the desks of every legislator in Vermont. The consequence was that instead of the old district committee having power to select the teachers (usually favoring their kin), a town school board was created by law—the system which still prevails.

I didn't go to Chelsea because Closson, who had been engaged to teach in Rochester, wanted to go on to a better position in Massachusetts, and he urged me to take over the post he was leaving. I taught there for two terms. It was a graded two-room school and I never liked it. My experience there was most unhappy. The meanest boy I ever taught was in that school—a Methodist minister's son.

Half of the students were as big as I was and many of them were older. In those days it was considered quite the thing to throw out the teacher and lock the door. Father, who had had just such an experience in his younger days, wrote to me, "If they put you out, take an ax, smash the door in, and lay the ax on top of your desk." But they didn't go that far with me.

Greenleaf's old arithmetic was in use in that school, and it was the bane of my life with its impossible and improbable examples. Soon I noticed that some of the class could do examples in ten minutes that kept me up most of the night. I did the janitor work of the school myself and one night I found a book with practically every difficult problem from cover to cover worked out in the margin. For the rest of the winter I got along quite well. In summer I worked on farms for a dollar a day. One season I loaded and pitched off 119 big loads, earning enough to pay for a two-horse spring-tooth harrow for Father's farm. It was a grand affair that ran on four wheels and had a seat. After studying it carefully, Father put the seat down cellar and stowed it well out of sight over a beam. Nothing as lazy as this could get a footing on his farm. He stormed when wheel rakes came around, and clung for years to the old flop-over, man-killer type. Father was ever a critic of the soft and effete.

Even in those days I used to pick up yarns here and there that greatly pleased him, like the one about the old fellow who was always doing odd things, and who, when he went up a steep hill in front of the house every evening to get his cows, used to grab a tree stump, swing right around it and then go on up the hill. Some boys went up one day when he was away and sawed the stump almost off on the upper side, close to the ground. Then they hid and watched. He came up as usual that night and swung around the stump. Off it broke, and down the two rolled, over and over. This was the same old chap who always carried his own chair around with him, wherever he went. He would go to a party with the chair on his back, and never stir out of it until the party ended. Then he'd put it over his shoulder and go home.

He had never seen a railroad train. So when a line was put through near his home, he took up his old chair and went out and sat on a hill, waiting for the iron monsters to roar by. It was a double-track line and within a few minutes he saw a train go east. Two minutes later he saw another one on the other track, going in the opposite direction. "Good heavens," he cried, "how did that train get turned around so quick?"

When I had had enough of Rochester I went back to Bethel High School for further study. I hadn't had Latin or Greek in normal school and now I wanted to catch up in the classics. I stayed with my aunt, Mrs. Adelaide Stearns, in a house full of roomers. They all took down food from their farms and stayed through the week, then went home for week ends. The principal of the school taught too, so I got my tuition free by looking after his pupils while he was busy in other rooms. This, with the proceeds from my hair-cutting, helped considerably.

I had been studying at Bethel for a year when I saw in the local paper that a teacher had given up his job in a village six miles away. I decided I could teach and study at the same time, so I rose before daylight next day, stuffed doughnuts in my pockets and headed for Gaysville to see the school committee chairman. He happened to be the town doctor too. When I rang his bell, he shouted from an upstairs window, "Well, well, what is it? Do you want to see me officially or professionally?"

"Officially," I replied.

"Sit down in one of those chairs on the hotel porch across the road. I'll be down as soon as I get dressed."

He came down and we sat and talked for a few minutes. I got the job and agreed to start the following Monday.

I set out for Bethel again, walking five miles of the way and being picked up by a farmer for the last mile. I had gone eleven miles since daybreak, obtained a job and still was only ten minutes late for school. In my youth and enthusiasm I fairly loped along that country road but I was somewhat dashed to find that the family were opposed to my taking this job. They wanted me to stick to my studies and they didn't think that I could do both. Father and Mother both thought I was crazy, and I'll never forget the amount of work I did when I went home at the week ends, in order to smooth Father down. The first Saturday I went back I found him groaning about things not being done around the farm. So I drew out and spread twenty-six loads of manure, which was a job almost beyond human strength.

But this was a fine period of my life. My oldest sister taught at Gaysville for a year and I stayed there for two years. We played tennis and thoroughly enjoyed ourselves. We had fewer hardships and more variety in our lives than ever before. I used to get a team and drive fourteen miles to Randolph Center to read the Episcopal service on

Sunday. I put money into the farm for painting, and paid outstanding bills of all kinds. Then I bought a piece of land with my new riches. It cost $1000, and I paid $300 down and borrowed the rest. It had wonderful first growth hemlock and I felt it would give us some return.

By this time both Closson and I were figuring out ways and means to go to college. Closson had already put in three years at the University of Vermont and now we both planned to go to Trinity in Hartford. We didn't want to give Father any excuse to cite us the case of the proud parent who exclaimed, "My son went to college and got a B.A. and finally an M.A., but I notice it's the good, old P.A. who is supporting him all the time." So during the next summer we worked like mad in our newly acquired forest. We cut timber and peeled bark. When we counted up the money we earned we found that we had $99.40 between us. This was for the bark; we sold the timber later. The year was 1892, the world was comparatively peaceful, and life looked good ahead of us.

Chapter IV

COLLEGE

. . . .

OUR departure for college was more or less of a foretaste of much that was to follow. We planned to take our food and to board ourselves. Besides our trunks and bags, we fixed up a box shaped like an egg crate, with rope handles at either end. This we packed with food. I can see that box as if it were before me now. The baggage man at Bethel picked it up and threw it on the baggage truck with a vengeance, in his amazement at finding it so heavy. It split right across, spilling potatoes and beans all over the place.

We were embarrassed almost to the point of flight, for the train was due any minute. Luckily there was a piece of old clothes' line round the box and with this we were able to pull the split pieces together. We learned afterwards that baggage was supposed to hold wearing apparel only and not groceries or cooked food. But the baggage man, seeing our confusion, had pity on us and let us go through. We cluttered up the coach with so many bags and bundles, however, that the conductor reminded us there was an express car on the train.

During that freshman year Closson and I kept our potatoes in the janitor's cellar, getting out a few as we needed them. We had a two-burner gas plate and an oven. If we put the potatoes on when we went to recitation at eleven o'clock, they were done by twelve. We ate quite a bit of meat, for meat was cheap—ten cents a pound for pork chops. In the fall we ate sausage, day in and day out. Indeed, we bought so regularly that one day when I was telephoning the clerk at the old Hartford market, I hesitated a minute in giving my order, and in a second she shouted, "Sausage!"

One day I left a little too much fire under the potatoes. As I came down the walk at noon, one of two brothers named Gage who roomed over us had his head out of the window, gasping for breath. "For heaven's sake, Gilbert," he moaned, "there's a terrible smell coming up from your room. What is it?" The potatoes had been burned to cinders and he was getting the carbon dioxide.

I entered college with a barrelful of conditions, for I had never been graduated from high school, staying out too much of the time to teach. I found out right off, however, that I was to study Latin, Latin prose, Greek and Greek prose—the very subjects I was conditioned in. This way I killed two birds with one stone, and passed off my last condition by the end of my freshman year. My teaching experience stood me in good stead. I got 100 in my first algebra exam, which nearly floored the professor. I liked mathematics, and in my junior year made a key to the calculus, which I sold to a sophomore for two dollars when I was through with it. He used it the next year, and flunked.

Although things went well so far as my studies were concerned, I look back on my college days as probably the most wretched of my life. We were poor. We were farm boys. We were classed as grinds and the tendency was to jeer at the studious. Although we never had to worry about our exams, we were out of key with the general atmosphere. These were very wet days in college. We neither smoked nor drank. The place was snobbish, and one of the small things I remember was that one youth got $1000 as a birthday present to spend as he pleased. That, of course, would have been a fortune to us. Our eating habits, our clothes, our high marks, the fact that we never went in for athletics, all were matters of comment. Of course, the professors were all right, and would do anything for a man who showed some interest in his work and had high marks. But although I have lived for more than forty years near Trinity, I have never gone back to a commencement and never expect to. Perhaps I should, but I just can't make myself do it, for I have never quite forgotten those bitter days. I must have shown my sheepskin to the folks at home, but I cannot remember having done so, nor have I any idea what became of it.

Closson advised me strongly to have nothing to do with non-scholastic activities—athletics or anything else. This was a mistake. As I look back on those days I feel that if I had gone into baseball and football I would have got along better and it would have been more help to me afterwards. I was twenty years old. I was strong. I had chopped wood all summer. I was fleet-footed as a deer. I could have been a tremendous football player, I am sure. That would seem like nothing compared with rolling logs in the wood. But we kept out of it entirely, and suffered accordingly. I have often wished I had piled up more athletic knowledge in place of such high marks—an average of 92 for four years and finishing up as salutatorian of the class. I always remember one of my classmates saying to me: "Gilbert, you think you're smart but I'm a good deal smarter. A man who can be at the foot of his class for four years and not get dropped out, is the smartest man in it."

The city fellows seemed to think that to be hazed and made a fool of was a joke. To me it was just impossible. I had some bad boils one fall, so I had a bowl of soaked bread in water on the mantel that I used for a poultice. A hazing gang broke in one night, and I kept them at bay with a ball club. Not daring to attack and trying to hide their faces, they discovered this mess in the bowl. What a time they made over that! They stared at it, smelt it and passed it all around among themselves. Then, still wondering, they piled out, promising that they would come again.

Many of the freshmen were mere boys and terribly homesick. To meet them with nothing but abuse seemed to me to be criminal. As soon as they got there, they were warned about what they might expect on "Bloody Monday." I don't believe there is anything of this at Trinity now, but I can testify that I was anything but happy there. The one bright spot in college was my roommate, George N. Holcomb, a Connecticut lad who shared quarters with me after my freshman year. I bought the food and cooked it, and George did the dishes. We had cocoa and crackers for supper because they were cheap and easy to prepare.

George claimed that we had them every night for three years, and he was probably right. He had stomach trouble before coming to room with me, but it cleared up quickly after I got him on my crackers and cocoa diet. When I reminded him one day that his stomach was in very good shape, he remarked, "No wonder. It's had a long, long rest."

George was good at languages and I was good at maths, so together we made an unbeatable team. At commencement he delivered the valedictory address and I the salutatory. Unlike me, he did no work outside college, so he had plenty of time for study. He was one of the most spiritually consecrated fellows I have ever known. Now I suppose spirituality is a prime requisite for the ministry, yet I feel there are other things the preacher needs just as much. One must know boys, for instance, as well as books. One must know men as well as manners. One can't be wholly academic and still be an effective shepherd of the Lord in an unacademic atmosphere.

A candidate for the ministry lives in a college atmosphere for four years, and that is certainly the atmosphere of the well-to-do. Then he goes to a seminary and spends another three years in the same rarefied air. When he comes out and takes his first parish he finds himself in such a different world that often he is helpless. This is one of the major tragedies of the ministry. It was then and it is today. The pursuit of learning is apt to make a one-sided character. Several of the instructors at Trinity made me dislike the subjects they taught. I had been to a normal school. I had taught school myself. I had studied teaching and my father and mother both taught school, so I had been brought up with certain ideas on pedagogy, and it seemed to me that the methods of my instructors in college were just about as bad as they could be. They didn't have the power to make their subjects attractive, for it is all too true that a professor is often maintained not for what he can impart but for his own abundance of knowledge. Some of the professors seemed almost inhuman with youths who were having difficulty in their particular subjects. Either you had it or you hadn't. You did it or you didn't. They would flunk boys without a scrap of sympathy. They never thought to ask, "Can I help you with this?" No, it was take it or leave it, know it or flunk. George and I didn't suffer particularly from this sort of thing, as our marks were so high, but we could see it operating cruelly around us.

I got on particularly well with Professor Flavel S. Luther, who was a farm boy himself, and who seemed to feel that he and I had much in common. He was my type and he was very nice to me. His subject was maths and that, of course, was my particular forte. I always found him sensible, kind and just. He was smart, witty and his discipline was good, but he was not by any means the sporty type. He was very careless about his clothes and his pants were a sight—usually three or four inches too short for him. The students made much fun of him but when he liked he could cut them all to pieces with his sarcasm. Somebody asked him one day why a divinity student should spend time learning mathematics.

"Perhaps if more of them studied maths their sermons would come out with an answer at the end," he retorted.

He was always quick on the trigger. I remember meeting him on the walk one beautiful spring day and saying, "Fine morning, Professor. Good time to sow oats."

"Yes," he said instantly. "Wild oats."

I first won his respect with a difficult question that he had put to seven men in a row. Every one got a zero and flunked it. I didn't know an awful lot about it, but I had given it some study, so I had a shot at it, and got nine or ten. Fortunately, I could always learn quickly. I can remember getting up at two-thirty a.m. to study for an examination on a subject in the Divinity School that I knew nothing about—one that required a fifteen-weeks course. I went in at ten that morning and passed. I had a system which enabled me to offer something on every question. I would run through a book pretty fast and get the gist of things, absorbing something from each chapter. This was useful, when it came to exams.

But on one occasion Professor Luther left George and me high and dry after we had worked for six hours on a tough problem in advanced algebra. I had a little edge on George on stating a proposition, but he excelled me in working out a difficult equation. We sat on the lawn and went at it for hours and hours. Finally we solved it and went into class feeling quite well pleased with ourselves. But before we had a chance to show what we could do, Professor Luther got up, and taking it for granted that no one in the class could possibly have solved this poser, he went to the blackboard and did it before our eyes. We sat speechless and he never knew that we had mastered it ourselves.

Professor John J. McCook, a relative of Justice Philip J. McCook, was our German professor. For some reason or other I never enjoyed his classes. He was a wise man, with a wonderful reputation, and no one in Hartford would dare to whisper that he didn't worship a McCook (some members of his family are among my best friends), but I never was happy with him, although I passed in German with a good mark. Although he was both learned and just, to my mind he lacked the tenderness, sympathy and consideration that go with what I call a Christian gentleman. He made me thoroughly dislike the subject he taught.

Professor "Boo-hoo" Johnson, as we called him, was good to work with because of his enthusiasm for his subject and for anyone who showed any interest in it. His English class was always entertaining. He had an odd way of marking, but he generally got things right. One day a student went up to get his month's marks, thinking he had it on the professor, as he had not been called on to recite for the whole month.

"Your mark, your mark?" echoed Professor Johnson. "Oh, yes, it is two point five." The highest mark was ten.

The student was astonished. "Why, professor, you never called on me the whole time," he protested.

"I know, I know, but I looked down at you every day, and if you looked as though you knew anything about the lesson, I gave you a five and if you didn't, I gave you a naught."

The boy raised a hullabaloo over his mark, but the professor never changed it.

Another day he announced that there would be a written recitation. The boys hated these exams, as it was hard to bluff on paper and it also took a little energy to do the writing. The professor slapped a whole ream of faculty paper on the edge of his desk. The pile must have been two inches thick and it suggested a long and difficult exam. Instantly one of the students stepped up and engaged him in conversation. Now, the slightest sign of interest in any literary subject was so beguiling to him that he gave the fullest possible response. While they were thus engaged, another of the students slipped the paper off the desk and under his coat, walking casually out of the room with it.

When the professor finally looked around and saw that the paper was gone, he was furious. He gave the class three minutes in which to produce it, or they would all get three marks and a zero for the day. The students started an industrious search, looking under and over everything, even shaking a great globe on the table in the corner to see if the paper was inside. One got down on his knees and crawled under the desks, holding aloft sundry scraps of paper. Soon the three minutes were up and we all had our three marks and a zero—all but the chap who took and kept the paper. Incidentally he was studying for the ministry— a meek and kindly fellow.

Plenty of pranks were played on "Boo-hoo." Another time the boys concealed six alarm clocks, set ten minutes apart, in different parts of his classroom. When the first went off, he stopped and gave us a good lecture. Just as we were ready to settle down to work again, off went another. Then another. The third or fourth time the class broke up in turmoil.

Dr. Thomas Ruggles Pynchon was another interesting figure at Trinity. He had odd traits. He never smiled or laughed and he was very careful of his speech. He was devoted to church ways and particularly the sacrament of the Lord's Supper. His course was Christian Ethics. Holcomb and I elected this course, in spite of the fact that around college it was considered a snap course. For instance, it was so easy that one morning when we went in, Dr. Pynchon started the recitation and turning to George, said: "Mr. Holcomb, what is the opposite of right?"

"Wrong."

"And what is the opposite of wrong?"

"Right."

"That is so," conceded the professor and gave him a ten spot.

A rich young blade who went about looking like a rag bag and wore long "football hair," popular at that time, decided to profit by the easiness of Dr. Pynchon's course. He was a great burly fellow, uncouth and sporty, who could get along only by being coached. He was a distasteful object to the good doctor, who was astounded to see him walk into his class. He simply couldn't face the prospect of having him in the course for twenty weeks. So looking at him over his glasses, he demanded: "Is that you, Mr. H--?"

"Yes."

"May I ask what you have in mind here this morning?"

"Yes, sir. I have elected to take your course."

"Is that so? Well, I must tell you right now that the course in Christian Ethics presupposes some moral nature in the student, and, sir, as you have no moral nature whatever, I shall have to forbid your taking this course. You may leave the room."

I agree with what William Lyon Phelps says in his autobiography about my old friend "Shorty" Martin—that he was more devoted to pure learning than any man he ever met in his life. Nothing under heaven took the place with him of just knowing facts. He was a great French and Hebrew scholar and a kindly man, but like many another professor, he had so much knowledge that he was out of sympathy with the students. It was hard for him to be patient and sympathetic, or to understand a man who was not gifted in his subjects.

Professor Martin was a Presbyterian and one day he nearly threw me out of class for levity. He was quoting the collect for Good Friday, pointing out that prayers were read for Jews, Turks and infidels. But he omitted the final category.

"And heretics," I added pointedly.

Now, in the eyes of many in the Episcopal church, the Presbyterian is a heretic. Professor Martin got what I meant and came near to expelling me.

He was quite an impressive figure—a really huge man with commanding whiskers. He was straight as an arrow and was always turned out rather formally in a Prince Albert coat. His recitations were conducted in the old gym, which looked like a Vermont schoolhouse. I used to think how unsuitable the building seemed for his dignified and scholarly bearing. Three wooden steps led up to the entrance and his long legs took them in a single stride. One year, on the eve of St. Patrick's Day, the students carried off these steps. It was easy enough to get in without them but out of thirty students, only six or seven elected to go in. George and I were among them. The others assembled outside and said they couldn't attend the class because the steps were missing.

Soon "Shorty" appeared. He didn't smile, but just rolled his eyes when he took in the situation. "Well," he said, covering the gap with one long step, "a kind Providence has enabled me to enter the building." Then he began to call the roll and the students answered through the window. "Shorty" stopped at once and debated with himself as to whether a man who answered "present" through a window was present or not. His decision was that unquestionably he was absent. The men outside argued that they willed to be present but were debarred by the absence of the steps. By and by they began to boost one another head first through the window, with terrible wheezing and groaning. Shorty stood there like an indignant giant, without a smile on his face, watching them come in.

My three years of Hebrew seem so much waste of time to me now. I would rather have learned how to umpire a ball game. It was the same with Greek. Infinitely better would it have been for me to have spent my time studying the English Bible and learning long portions of it by heart. Often during the years of my ministry I have had this thought. And French and German would have been of much more use to me than Greek and Hebrew. I must confess that I look back on these hours as time and effort utterly wasted. We had compulsory chapel, but I don't believe that this did me any particular good either. It was perfunctory, and the boys read Sunday papers under the pews. They were a wild crew. A college official spoke later of these days as the "wet era" and the wet era it certainly was. The whole tone of the place was such that I was terribly unhappy.

Uncle George, who sent us the derby hats, wanted me to attend Amherst College and help him in his store. He had done so much for us that I felt it my duty to go, and go I did. I would stay in the store while he went home for lunch. One day a farmer came in with a big hulking boy, for whom he wanted a suit of clothes. I sold him one for

$13.00. It was marked "Cost M.R." which meant $9.50, and "Sell C.G." which meant $13.00. The man counted out the bills, and I felt deeply guilty over what seemed too big a profit.

Really, with what it cost to do business there, I suppose it was not. But this was the only thing I ever sold in that store. I never liked it, and I never liked Amherst College. After three days of it I went back to Trinity.

The morning after my arrival I met Professor Luther on the campus.

"Well, Professor," I smiled, "I'm back again."

He had a quick answer. "So I see. Well, many men make mistakes, but few have sense enough to correct them."

He thought there was no college on earth like Trinity.

It was lucky for me that I went back there, for I was stopped one morning soon afterwards by old Professor Pynchon, who said, "Let me congratulate you, Mr. Gilbert. "On what?" I asked.

"On your award of the Toucey scholarship."

"What's that?" I demanded, never having heard of it.

It was a scholarship worth $250 a year paid in cash, and I held it every year until I was graduated from the seminary five years later.

I had a fair amount of social life while in college through the church work I did outside. This gave me great satisfaction, for although I was not homesick, I missed the companionship of women. I was used to Mother, sisters, aunts and cousins coming and going at home, and I found a world where there wasn't a woman in sight, where even the waiters were men, a distressing change from the lively family life I led in Vermont.

In my first year at college I assisted the rector of St. Thomas's, Hartford, and got many a thick beef steak to eke out the crackers and cocoa diet, even though my earnings were nil. For the next three years I assisted the Rev. Dr. James W. Bradin, of St. John's Church, Hartford, getting $100 a year for this, a $20 bill each Easter from two sisters in the church, and many a free meal—which was a great consideration in those days. I had charge of the boys' club, and we played Crokinole and Barnyard, a game that was hard on the chairs. I often wonder whatever became of the splintered remains of all these church chairs that I tucked away in a dark corner of the attic, out of sight of keen-eyed Sam, the Negro janitor.

Dr. Bradin was a fine Christian gentleman and I enjoyed working with him. I remember one morning as he began to read the second lesson he announced "Here beginneth the Epistle of Jude." Then I saw that he was looking for Jude. After much fumbling of the pages, he started to read, but I knew the passages were not from Jude. When he came back to the prayer desk he whispered to me, "For heaven's sake, where is Jude?" I reminded him that as Jude had only one chapter, it *was* rather hard to find.

For two years I had breakfast every Sunday morning at the home of a Hartford bank president whose son was in my boys' club and Bible class. This gave me some insight into a way of living I had not seen on the farm, but it failed to arouse in me any longing for this type of social existence. Things in that house were most unhappy. The home life of the boy really was distressing. His mother was a society woman and his father was the most miserable man I have ever known. Brought up poor, I was fool enough to believe that the rich must be happy. But I soon came to the conclusion that poverty on the old farm might be better far than a bank presidency. The son, a happy-go-lucky fellow, came up and boarded with us for several summers after that.

But I got the other side of the picture in downtown Hartford where my church work opened my eyes to some of the problems of actual human existence. I had to do everything from running boys' clubs and attending old ladies' teas to sitting up all night in tenement houses with the penniless sick. There was no organized charity at that time, hygiene was a little known word, and housing conditions were wretched. The church was the one agency that got close to the misery of the people. I learned a lot about social conditions from "Nosey" Brown, a policeman who used to drop in to get warm at the mission where I worked. He and I would have great talks about life in general. It was around this time that I saw the old wooden bridge from Hartford to East Hartford burning up. I also remember seeing the first trolley car ever run in that city. It went down Broad Street and the motorman failed to take a sharp curve. The trolley jumped the track right in view of all the people who had come to observe civic progress.

While I was assistant at St. John's, something happened that made a deep impression on my mind and heart and ministry. One of my club boys came to tell me that his sister was "bad sick" and he wanted me to visit her. It was my first contact with a real slum. The tenement in which the family lived was owned by the local gas company, and the minute I saw it I felt sure that the girl was sick because of the filthy sanitary conditions in her home. Why the whole family didn't die is still a mystery to me.

I sat up all night with the unfortunate girl. Her pitiful, wasted face haunted me and cockroaches ran all over my feet when I fell asleep in my chair. (I had never seen a cockroach until then.) She died just before morning. On my way back to college, in the early dawn, I passed the great mansion where the president of the gas company lived, and my heart boiled within me. I could have told him a thing or two that morning, for I was aflame with indignation.

As I sat in the chancel of the church the following Sunday morning and watched the finely dressed parishioners coming in, I kept thinking of the girl's pale, wasted face on the pillow. That incident haunted me and had a profound effect on my future. Probably more than any other single factor, it made me resolve to give my ministry not to rich people in fine clothes, but to those who needed me more—the humble ones whom God must love, as Lincoln had it, because He made so many of them.

Chapter V

SEMINARY

. . . .

It WAS late in the fall of 1896 that I gave all my everyday clothes to a man who happened to be working for Father, and headed for Berkeley Divinity School in Middletown. The hired man was dumbfounded to find himself with such a wardrobe all at once, and Father was surprised at my recklessness, but on the whole it was a good exchange. The man needed the clothes and I needed the education.

Bishop John Williams was in charge of Berkeley. As a matter of fact, he was the whole school. He was old and quite sick and he spent most of his time in bed, but even there his sense of humor never deserted him. He may have seemed gruff at first contact but when we boys in the school got to know him, we loved him.

Everyone rode on bicycles in those days. As Hartford was only eighteen miles away, I used to slip back to call on my old friends and flames. One night when I returned to my room I found a message from one of the boys: "You left the faucet running on the top floor, and the water has seeped clear through to the Bishop's bed. He is terribly angry and wants you to come to his room at once—no matter how late you get in."

I was paralyzed with fright as I tiptoed towards his room. I looked in and there he was, fast asleep in his bed.

Who was I to waken a weak old man who needed his rest? I promptly tiptoed back upstairs, where the boys were waiting for the explosion.

"What did he do to you?" they asked.

"Nothing. He's asleep."

"Asleep your eye!" they answered. "We were just down there."

That was typical of him. He probably saw the funny side of it by the time I got back, and, besides, it is doubtful if he wanted to pounce on me at all. He seldom went after any of us, except in a kindly way. When he did, we needed it. He had a lot of good old Yankee horse sense in dealing with the problems of the school. He arranged, for instance, for devotional periods that were just about right—neither too long nor too short. I wish more schoolmasters would do the same thing. It has always seemed to me that an overdose of any kind of medicine is bad.

In every way Bishop Williams was an attractive figure to me. I liked his humor as well as his common sense. His whole life was run on a sound and unostentatious basis. He was far removed from the bishops who like to surround themselves with pomp and flunkeys. Making his diocesan visitations he often stayed overnight in the parish, and on one occasion he noticed that the woman of the house where he was billeted was not preparing to go to church.

"Aren't you going to church today?" he asked her.

She hesitated. "Well, I'm not planning to," she acknowledged.

"I'm afraid it's because I'm here for dinner," said the Bishop, "and you're staying at home to prepare it."

She didn't deny it.

"What does the dinner consist of?" he pursued.

"Well, I haven't got the pies made."

In those days a dinner without pies would be a mortal offense to most bishops, but not to Bishop Williams.

"What kind of pie is it?" he asked. "Apple."

"Well, why can't we do something together about it? Where are the apples? Where is the paring knife?

Let me help you."

The woman hurried to the cellar, came up with the apples, and produced paring knives. Bishop Williams betook himself to the kitchen and pared and cored the apples while she made the crust. She went upstairs and dressed for church while the pies were in the oven cooking, and she got to the service after all, with the aid of this kindly bishop.

Usually a student accompanied him on his sojournings, to drive the horses. On one occasion they put up overnight at an old country house where the windows were glued down fast. They were ushered into an unaired room. The Bishop couldn't sleep that night. He turned and tossed and finally wakened his companion.

"John," he said, "this is awful. I can't get a wink of sleep in this stuffy room. It's terrible. We've got to have some air."

John tried to open a window, but it was stuck fast with paint.

The Bishop relapsed into his feather bed and made another effort to sleep, but without success. He roused John again. He had reached a decision. "We'll break a pane of glass and I'll pay for it in the morning," he announced.

The windows had small panes in the fashion of the

period. John reached under the bed, got one of the Bishop's size eleven shoes, aimed at the glass and let fly. There was a resounding crash and Bishop Williams drew a deep breath. "Ah," he said. "Fine!" In no time at all he was fast asleep.

Morning dawned and the Bishop wakened from a sound and restful sleep. He stared at the window, astonished to find it closed and the panes intact. He nudged John, who sat up, but promptly collapsed again when he saw that he had heaved the Bishop's ancient shoe through the glass front of a bookcase, the most highly prized piece of furniture in the house.

Bishop Williams was thoroughly indifferent to appearances and, indeed, to worldly possessions of all kinds. He cared so little for money that after his death a forgotten bank account of $6000 was found in his name. He was careless about his clothes and his shoes were so worn that the people of the diocese felt mortified to have their Bishop traipsing around in such shoe leather. Finally they assembled a committee to suggest to him as tactfully as possible that they were quite prepared to buy him a new pair of shoes if only he would wear them. They hemmed and hawed and finally blurted out their proposal: "In all kindness, Bishop, we feel that we must give you a new pair of shoes."

The Bishop listened attentively, then turned to them with a glint in his eye and remarked, "Perhaps that is so, but I want to tell you one thing—there are plenty of men in this diocese just waiting to get into my shoes, old as they are."

Bishop Williams overshadowed with his personality

everyone at the seminary but I have vivid memories also of good old Dr. John Binney, who taught Hebrew and Old Testament. Everybody liked him and everybody dreaded his courses. We took reams of notes while he rambled around, but I never got a thing out of them and the hours I spent in his classes now seem to me a colossal waste of time. What I know of the Old Testament I learned after my Berkeley days were over—certainly not while I was in the seminary. Had Dr. Binney only taught us with the idea in mind that we had to take what he gave and weave it into intelligible sermons, it might have been a help.

But he was a great fellow to take a ride on a bicycle. He didn't like to wheel through the fine countryside around Middletown alone, however, so one student after another would hear the refrain, "Well, after lunch supposing we take a little bicycle spin." Those were the days when the highways were dotted with frantic cyclists, male and female, pedaling along as if their lives depended on it. Of course, we showed the greatest enthusiasm, even though tennis or swimming seemed a more exciting pastime than pedaling along behind the Hebrew professor. Dr. Binney was a tall, powerful man who took no exercise except this, so he made it a rite.

One hot day he invited me to join him on one of these expeditions. I said I would be delighted. We started off, heading for New Haven. He had had a good meal but I was not eating enough to hurt me, especially at lunch time. It had rained and the road was rough, with sandy spots and water bars. Bikes were not made then to run as smoothly as they do today. I found it hard work. Well, we took our little spin to New Haven—a mere twenty-five miles. There

Dr. Biriney refreshed himself with a glass of beer. "Well," he remarked optimistically, "we don't want to go home the way we came. Supposing we go to Meriden."

That made forty-three miles altogether. When we reached Meriden he thought it would then be all right to head for home, which meant fifty-three miles after two o'clock on a half-empty stomach, and we were supposed to get back for chapel at five! Good Dr. Binney seemed to have no idea how far to go when he got on a bicycle.

But the bicycle was very useful to me then and throughout the early days of my ministry. During my college and seminary days I used it to go up to Randolph Center to visit my family, for it saved railroad fare. I remember late one fall running into freezing weather just south of Springfield and cycling until my clothes were sheeted with ice. I took shelter in a freight shed and as I thawed out, the water ran from the bottom of my trousers. Another time I bicycled to Putney, Vermont, a distance of a hundred miles and thought nothing of it.

The divinity course at Berkeley was by no means stiff in those days. I did the three years' course without any difficulty in two and I earned $5 a week by tutoring. We had some very hard-working youths in the seminary. I remember one—William Jepson, who before embarking on his divinity course, worked in a factory for ten years soldering spouts on tea kettles. He had never been anywhere near a prep school or a college, and he had to slave to keep up with the rest of us. "Little Jep," as we called him, was married, had one child and lived in a flat. His wife took in students as boarders. One Monday, when she was ill, I went over to help wash the week's clothes. It made me his friend for life. I needed a friend like this. His knowledge of human nature, gained in that factory, must have been of more use to him than all the book learning of the seminary was to any of us. Preachers need contacts like that, to hold their feet on the ground and to keep themselves human.

Another of my classmates, William Woodford, had peddled pies from door to door in New Haven for nine years. He knew something about human nature too—about woman nature, anyway. And he made one of the best ministers I have ever known. Neither of these men went to college. I doubt if they even went to high school. They illustrate a favorite theory of mine that a lot of our ministers have too much education and not enough practical experience among men. I believe in an educated ministry but a preacher must also know how to get along with people. Otherwise, instead of drawing members into the church, he will drive them away—like the parson who was asked how he was getting along with his congregation, and replied: "Oh, splendidly. I'm weeding them out."

The late Bishop Robert Paddock was in Divinity School with me, one of the finest fellows that ever lived. He was impulsive and highly emotional and a pep talk of any sort always got him. In those days we were exposed to a great many talks by missionaries who came around recruiting men for the foreign field. One of them got Paddock. He was all set to leave—until vacation time came and he went home to say good-by to his family. A few days later I had a letter from him saying he couldn't go to China just then, as he had to take care of his two sisters.

He hadn't thought of them when he volunteered for

the foreign field. "I want your prayers, Gilbert," he wrote at the end of his letter, "that the obstacles to my going to China may speedily be removed." It wasn't long before one of the sisters died, but I hope my prayers had nothing to do with it.

We students used to go out to the missions as lay readers. This was good. It is something all divinity students should be made to do, but with intelligent supervision by someone who knows what it's all about. Not by some high-hat Bishop whose days have been spent in a rich city parish or as a seminary professor—God forbid! I knew one minister who worked like a Trojan building up a mission and got along in fine style until he asked a seminary president to come and preach for him. That killed it. He never could bring that mission back and he went on to another job within a year.

Almost as bad as the visiting preachers were the gushing mothers we used to meet in those parishes, with their marriageable daughters. What a menace! They would sit enraptured during those student sermons, secondhand theological compositions horrible to contemplate, worse to listen to. We could have preached almost anything to them, and got away with it. Too often we heard "Oh, Doctor, what a lovely sermon!" We know now in our hearts that it was awful. I remember preaching my first Christmas Eve service at Randolph Center. For a wonder, I didn't go into a long discussion of the Virgin Birth, as most students do. But I settled the whole question of the Incarnation that night in less than fifteen minutes!

The fact is that about ninety per cent of our sermon and preaching instruction was utter waste. Luckily, I had sense enough not to pay much attention to it, anyway. Berkeley, and I suppose most of the other seminaries, taught the young preacher to write out his sermons in full, from the announcement of the text to the closing words. At least, we were supposed to keep writing them out until we had crystallized the academic style that is impossible for the man in the pew to follow. The best criticism I've heard of this type of preaching came from a minister's son. When his father asked him if he thought the congregation had approved of the sermon that morning, the youngster replied, "They sure did, Dad. They were nodding all the time you were preaching."

I remember the tomfool hours I spent in a rocking chair at Berkeley, writing these learned sermons and preaching them to myself over and over again, making sure of the points. My rocking chair used to creep around the room with the fervor I put into it. Finally I got a big staple and hammered it into the floor, then fixed an eyebolt in the rocker and roped it to the staple. The time wasted in writing out long dry sermons is argument enough against them, but the effect of them on the average small congregation is one of the great tragedies of Christendom. It may be that some preachers read their sermons because they lack the courage to face their congregations. The old idea that you should write out your sermon word for word, and then "rub out with your nose what you've written with your pen" when you get up to preach, has driven more people away from church than ten thousand Bob Ingersolls. It may be all right in a big city church, although I doubt it, but it is pure poison in a small church where people come to hear real preaching. They'll soon let you know they don't like it by getting restless, or drawing pictures in the hymnbooks, or winding their watches. I like the story of the parson who said to one of his watch winders, "I don't mind your looking at your watch, but when you hold it up to your ear to see if it's still going—well, that gets on my nerves."

During my last year in seminary, I worked as assistant in Christ Church on the outskirts of Middletown, which was later to become my first parish. I was lay reader, then deacon, before becoming rector. There was a large factory nearby, and many of the workers came to church. A big farming and rural section was within reach and, of course, being the product of the farm, I went after the farmers and their families with holy zeal. I loved to get out among them and into their homes. There was one grand old farmer named Elijah Roberts with whom I used to spend the night. He provided the best meals and the finest beds in the county, and he made a point of shaking my hand as I mounted my bicycle. There was always a dollar bill in that handshake. When I told my fellow divinity students about it, they almost mobbed me, shouting, "Lead us to it. Give us a chance at him." They had never found a hotel where the host paid the departing guest instead of expecting to be paid!

I didn't think, during my Berkeley days, that my own ministry would lie so near at hand in the years to come, or that I would live to see a gas station on the site where I studied theology. At the turn of the century the chapel bell could be heard along Main Street in the heart of the town. Now on the site of the chapel is a large international chain store. Where the dormitory stood, Montgomery Ward and

J. C. Penney cater to the public. One reason for the Divinity School being moved to New Haven was the noisy trolley track that ran past it. But by the time the change was made, the tracks had been pulled up and busses were running by, much more quietly. It is all more or less symbolic of the times.

I have Bishop Williams to thank for the fact that I settled in the Diocese of Connecticut. I did not wish to share the fate of my brother in Vermont. Closson, a graduate of Cambridge Divinity School, went up to take his candidates' orders examination before Bishop Arthur C. A. Hall of Vermont. The Bishop was very High Church and set the most rigid examinations for my brother, coming from Cambridge. Closson didn't pass. One question put to him was:

"Supposing that the spiritual condition of the recipient is in each case just the same, what would you say as to the efficacy of the holy communion of the Congregational church, compared with that of the Episcopal Church?"

"Just the same," said Closson.

"And where do you find the authority in the New Testament for infant baptism?"

"Well, I don't know that it is especially emphasized anywhere in the New Testament that infants should be baptized."

"Don't you know that in certain cases the whole family was baptized, and in an Eastern household it would be most likely that there would be infants in the family?"

"If that's all the authority they have for it, they should give it up," Closson retorted.

After his experience I could see what lay ahead of me,

so I decided to get outside the diocese of Vermont. This was not so easy, for Bishop Hall was in straits for ministers, and the only way to get clear of him was to have another Bishop ask for me. I thought at once of Bishop Williams, who was in bed and very ill. Closson urged me to hurry before he died. So I asked Bishop Hall if he would transfer me.

"Only if the Bishop of Connecticut requests you," he told me.

So I went to Bishop Williams in fear and trembling and told him what I wanted.

"I'll do that all right," he assured me.

There was quite a form to fill in, and the Bishop was so ill and weak that the whole process was slow and difficult. I fussed plenty until that form was filled in and mailed, for I felt that things would be made difficult for me in Vermont. Yet I have often thought how much I could have done in my native state that I have always loved, with all my knowledge of the people, their ways and their needs.

Chapter VI

MY MINISTRY BEGINS

. . . .

F RESH from the seminary and aglow with zeal I took over my first parish in 1899. I had no premonition then of the difficulties I would encounter, the ancient prejudices I would stir up, the petty fires that would flare in my church. I had been in and out of churches, done mission and parish work, and read the services. But this was different. It was my domain. I have often thought since how hard a young man works in his first parish, and how the results either make or break him.

What a thrill I felt that first day when I started my ministry at Christ Church! It was with sheer joy that I mounted my bicycle and rode around the parish. The terrain was familiar enough. I had been up and down the winding roads of the Connecticut River valley all through my seminary days, and the slopes and vistas, the creeks and hamlets, the distant view of the Meriden Mountains, were as familiar to me as my native Vermont.

At the beginning of the century it was by no means the Middletown of today, with its population of 24,554, its large modern bridge, its college, up-to-date shops and its paved Main Street seventy feet wide—one of the broadest thoroughfares in all New England. When I began my ministry, Main Street was wide all right, but it was still reminiscent of the days when lawns fronted the houses and people beat paths to the front doors of the shops, until finally the lawns were abandoned altogether in favor of the wide streets characteristic of this region today. Main Street in those days was not paved and wagon teams frequently stuck in the mud. We all used kerosene lamps and life moved at a leisurely tempo. Old plugs of horses pulled the streetcars. The platform in which the driver rode had no side or front protection whatever. There was a little roof over his head, but he got the full benefit of storm, wind and cold. What with guiding the horses, plying the whip and winding up the brakes (quite likely all three covered with ice), he had plenty to do. There were coal stoves in the cars for heat, with funny little stovepipe chimneys sticking out of the top. The wheels were under the middle of the car, and on the uneven rails the whole thing went up and down like a teeter. Not only did the driver have all he could do to stay on his feet, but as likely as not the passengers in each end of the car had difficulty staying in their seats. I doubt if there were any timetable arrangements. The old saying, "Never run after a streetcar or a woman—there'll be another along soon," didn't apply in those days. But the chances were you could walk along and overtake one.

Then, as now, there was close contact between the farming community and the town. My church was on the outskirts, in the region known as South Farms, and I had both urban and rural parishioners. My bicycle was the handiest thing in the world for getting around. It was easier than the automobile is today. I used to carry all sorts of things on it and my little dog always trotted behind me. When the weather got too icy for cycling, I took a horse and wagon but I enjoyed my bicycle more than anything.

I went fishing with the farmers, pitched hay in their fields and on Sunday afternoons led religious services for them in a local hall. Every Wednesday evening we had a prayer meeting. One afternoon I stayed out too late fishing. I was always spearing suckers—in fact, this is what I was up to the night I was elected rector of Christ Church—but this time I caught a big trout. I stuffed my pocket with grass and shoved the fish in on top. I hurried to the meeting, knowing full well I would be late. Although the proceedings were under way, the chairman insisted on my taking the chair. After the meeting I showed them my fish. If those farmers had seen it sooner they wouldn't have paid so much attention to what I had to say.

Right from the start I went exploring around the country sections, calling at homes, especially where there seemed to be need. I met a lot of people during this period who left their imprint on my life, just as every young preacher does. One was an old lady well over eighty, with whom I used to have regular prayers and Bible readings. She was terribly sick, yet I never once heard her complain. When I left the parish she insisted on giving me a small milk pitcher that belonged to her wedding set. I've kept it all these years. It is more than a hundred years old now, and every time I look at it I remember her great patience in her suffering.

We had one old farmer in that congregation with a particularly long-legged horse named Tyball. What an animal he was! When he got tired of pulling his wagon, he'd lie right down in the shafts, and I don't believe the angels in heaven could have moved him. I helped pull turnips in his owner's field, and for pay accepted a loan of old Tyball to take a wagonload of my Sunday-school youngsters on a nutting party. Tyball soon got tired and gave up, but the children kept at him. He never had such stimulus as that. We'd all pile out and walk ahead of him. He would watch us with his rheumy eye, and then, rather than be left alone, he would rise slowly to his feet and amble after us. We'd all pile in again and encourage Tyball to keep at it.

I gave my best energies to the young people, organizing ball clubs, hunting expeditions, game suppers, picnics and nutting parties. We had a Sunday school that averaged one hundred and fifty, but I had to work seven days and seven nights a week to keep it up, and stimulate the interest of the young folk. It was hard, continuous work, but it paid off in results. Preachers seem to be afraid to work like that nowadays. Too often they think that Sunday is their day of labor, and Sunday alone—like the case of the preacher who fell down a manhole. Someone saw him and rushed pell-mell to the home of one of the men in his parish, crying, "Hurry, hurry. The preacher's fell down a manhole."

"What's your hurry?" asked the layman. "We don't need him till Sunday!"

Christ Church was dominated by the family who owned and ran the near-by factory. The church was endowed by this family and at the end of the year the unfailing deficiency was made up by them. This gave them a stranglehold on the parish, and my first experience of church politics centered around this Lady Bountiful, as we called the rich widow to whom we were beholden. When she decided to build a rectory she didn't consult a soul as to where to put it, how large to make it, or how it should be arranged. Nor was it ever deeded to the church. Her dominant thought was to model it after her summer home in Bar Harbor. It was nowhere near the parish house or the church, an obvious disadvantage. Close to the parish house was a building that would have been simply perfect—just the right size, easy to heat and with a good garden plot. But I, the rector, was not consulted about a single thing, nor even shown the plans.

In due time Martha, who was then keeping house for me, and I moved in. The new rectory was both beautiful and expensive, but it proved to be a great, headache. It was much more pretentious than my salary warranted. We didn't need a butler's pantry, with our simple way of living. Situated on a corner lot, there was a terribly long stretch of sidewalk to shovel and sweep. The lawn was an enormous piece to mow, and the house was difficult to heat. Moreover, we were under constant strain. Any day our patron was apt to arrive with wealthy guests, to show off her handiwork and her benefactions. I had never had any experience in toadying to the rich or kowtowing to a Lady Bountiful. I expect I wasn't very good at it.

It was during this period that the course of my own life changed considerably. I was holding a mission down Maromas way when a girl came up to me and offered to play the organ and lead the singing during the services. A colony of summer boarders swarmed over this picturesque spot on the Connecticut River from June to September, and she happened to be one of them. I had a boys' camp near the house where she was staying, and what an excuse that turned out to be for seeing her all summer! It seemed to me I spent a lot of time following the winding River Road that leads from Middletown to Maromas.

This light-haired, blue-eyed girl with the lovely voice was sent from heaven and no mistake. She was soprano soloist in the Vermont Avenue Christian Church in Washington and a teacher in the Sunday school. She pitched in and helped to take care of those Sunday-school children of mine, and the more I watched her, the more I knew I wanted her to help me all my life. So Mary Jane Shelley and I were married one February day in 1903 in her own church in Washington, without benefit of Episcopal ministration. Nobody can ever say that I rushed her out of her own church and into mine. She was confirmed in the same class as our oldest boy—fourteen years later.

We went to Vermont on our wedding trip. It was February in Vermont and Father was our host. My fair bride came down with the mumps. Her in-laws gasped at the first sight of her, but Father measured up to it pretty well. He had a pet hen that was tuneful, and every morning he brought in the hen to cheer up the bride with song. Eventually the mumps succumbed to this barnyard euphony.

We went back to our magnificent rectory but did not live in it long. If I had had troubles before, they were intensified when I dared to bring a bride into the church, and a bride who was neither an Episcopalian nor a New Englander. Her family came from Virginia and her soft southern ways were under suspicion in this more frigid atmosphere. When she dared to wear a black lace dress and the best jewelry she had to do honor to her hostess at a party, she was accused of putting on airs in the parish. Moreover, I brought a heap of trouble on myself with one thing and another. I worked very hard to get the parish to pay its bills and become independent, so that the annual genuflection would not be necessary. It was quite a struggle, and perhaps it was not worthwhile, for it took so much time each year trying to raise the money.

We had more than seventy boys in our clubs and we kept two baseball teams going most of the time. Every fall we took a roomy express wagon with an old horse and went on hunting trips. When we returned, we gave a game supper for the club members. The die-hard members of the church who had run it for years didn't take to all these new-fangled ways. One of the things that irritated them was the imitation college yell the boys gave in front of the parish house before their meetings broke up. The parish treasurer, who seldom came to church, said that every time this happened, the boys drove another nail in my coffin. The greatest shock I have had in my whole ministry was the discovery in this, my first parish, that the old church members actually did not want these young men to belong to the church or sit in its pews. In the old country church in Vermont there would have been joy over one new member entering the fold. As I look back upon this period now, with the knowledge gained about church life over the years, I think I may have carried the club business too far. We had something going on in the parish house every single night of the week, and even on Sundays. As assistant at St. John's Church, Hartford, my chief business had been to run boys' clubs. It is so easy for us all to do what we think we know best how to do.

I hope divinity students now get better training in what might be called parish work than I had. I knew nothing about hospital work or calling on the sick, so I neglected this side of church life. Whatever else a man may fall down on in the ministry, he must not be amiss in caring for the sick. And I realize now that even though old and gospel hardened, the established church members are a great asset in any parish. It is comforting for a preacher to look out over his congregation during the first hymn and see those familiar faces before him, even though their glances may not always be wholly approving.

All the time the storm clouds kept gathering around me, but they really closed in with a Labor Day sermon I preached. It must be remembered that my church was closely welded to the life of the adjoining factory. When things got slack, the factory just shut down and the owners took their families and went off to Europe, leaving their employees to shift for themselves. This irked me, so I gave vent to my feelings in a Labor Day sermon. The Lady Bountiful didn't hear it preached, for she came to church only once a year, but she soon heard plenty about it and so did the rest of us.

I doubt now if that sermon was wise. Nothing was gained by it for anyone. Having grown up on a farm and never having stepped inside a factory, my knowledge of it was based on hearsay and that was one-sided. The factory bosses asked, not without reason, what I knew about it anyway? They said I might get a different slant if I had to handle the bunch I had rushed to defend. As time went on, I found that there was a lot in what they said. I don't suppose conditions are the same now, but during that period the superintendents and employers had plenty of trouble on their hands. The girls got into terrible fights among themselves and had to be separated by force. They stole anything they could lay hands on, concealing needles, thread and yarn in their clothing. In their mad rush to make a cent more, they would spoil material and damage machinery. This was a side of which I knew nothing. In matters of strict right and wrong, the pulpit stands adamant, but on controversial issues both sides should be presented, and if possible, at the same time. This cannot very well be done at a church service. It needs the forum type of gathering where people can answer back. Any young preacher who tries it from the pulpit is heading into trouble. The Labor Day pronouncements of the Federation of Churches are good, and in presenting these, which arc probably just about what the average minister would want to say anyway, one has tremendous backing.

But the Labor Day furor was mild compared with the choir rumpus that followed. I realize now that if there is one hot potato for a minister to handle, it's the church choir, which is more or less of a sacrosanct institution. With so many young people flocking around our church, and a minstrel show being staged every year, we were often asked by casual members of the congregation why we didn't have sweet young voices in the choir. There was no denying that the voices we had were neither young nor sweet. About half a dozen of the faithful who had sung for so long that they felt as if they owned the church, raised cracked voices in faulty unison Sunday after Sunday.

In my youth and inexperience I was persuaded that fine music and a vested choir would pack the church. Now

I know that it won't, for although good music is a help, it isn't the making of a church or even a small part of it. For a few Sundays proud parents will drop in to see Johnny wearing his big white collar and Susy her black bow tie, but that is just about all a new choir will mean in the way of attendance. The best soul-saving work I have ever done was in a mission which has never had a choir.

It was obviously impossible to combine the old and young voices in the same choir and still have good music, so I went ahead with my plans and assembled a youthful choir to sing on Sunday evenings and at special services. The members of the old choir were consulted first, and they said they would welcome this innovation, but when comparisons began to fly through the church, they piped another tune. Mrs. Gilbert trained the youthful choir. She was a newcomer to the place and of course she was not an Episcopalian. Soon the church seethed. On the one side stood an embattled church choir of long standing, supported by the conservative members of the parish. On the other side were the younger and more liberal members. It was a battle royal, brought to a head when the regular choir resigned in a body two days before the Sunday service, believing that Mrs. Gilbert would be unable to carry her youthful choir through the morning ritual, and particularly the chants. But she fooled them. What they didn't know was that she had sung for five years in an Episcopal church in Richmond, Virginia, and was thoroughly competent to train a choir in any part of the Episcopal service.

The morning service went off remarkably well, although the whole congregation was agape for developments. The members of the old choir came to scoff, but they never showed their faces inside the church again. The organist, wife of the church treasurer, played that day, although she was one of our meanest critics and had tried for weeks to embarrass us, bringing her small son to church with her, and whispering and giggling right through the service. Before the second Sunday she had followed the example of the choir, thinking that we certainly would be blocked by this double defection. But Mrs. Gilbert pitched in and played the organ herself until we were able to train a young organist to take over. Eventually one of my club boys transferred his interest from the piano to the organ and continued as organist at Christ Church for more than thirty-five years.

We had won, but the victory was empty. I realize now that the church could ill afford to lose these faithful members who had been in the choir for so many years, and I doubt if it was worth all the ill-feeling that was stirred up. We might just as well have used our energy in other directions.

Before long a letter arrived from a lawyer asking me to call at his office. There he informed me that the rich widow wanted the rectory she had shown off with such gusto and piety. Our eviction came because of all the complaints that had reached her about hurt feelings and woeful treatment of old members. I believed that the growth of the church, and the large number of baptisms and confirmations we had had, would offset almost anything, but I was wrong. Our record in this direction didn't count an iota. Her action was a great blow to us. No one thought we could stay on in the parish after this, but we did for seven years, and by the time we left, the choir feud was almost forgotten and a well-trained vested choir was in full operation.

But at the time we were wretched. It was difficult to find a place to live, for no one thought we had money enough to pay rent. Mrs. Gilbert went to Washington on a visit with Shelley, our son, who was only a year and a half old and very frail. But a good part of the congregation was behind us, and all the young people helped us to move when finally we found a place to live—the first floor of a modest frame house, a great comedown from the rectory. I liked it well enough, for here we had a fine garden plot, a hen house and a tool shed. After factory hours, some of the young people came with a borrowed horse and wagon and helped me move to the new home. Here three more children were born to us as the years went on—two boys and our only girl. These were hard days for Mrs. Gilbert, with no conveniences and a delicate child to care for. She was outwardly cheerful when I was around but I felt sure— and she acknowledged it later—that she was crying most of the time when I was out. We had no bathroom, no hot water, no furnace, and no electricity. The house was lit by gas and we had a gas stove beside the coal stove, which was a help.

I never told her what happened on our last night in the rectory. I heard a noise at the back door, opened it, and a huge railroad tie fell toward me. Just in time I managed to push it away with my hands. It seemed the darkest night of my life, as I lay awake planning to get up before daylight to carry off that dirty tie so that she would never know it had been there. It seemed to me to be a symbol of the dirt that was continually being thrown at us by our enemies. It was another drop in the bucket that was to drown us out, and eventually drive us from that parish. A few persistent faultfinders and scandalmongers can wear down the strongest resistance and at last I resigned.

At the last business meeting I attended in that parish, we needed one more voter to make a quorum. I went down the street and asked a man to come into the parish house for two minutes. Heaven knows, I had done plenty for him and for his family. But he refused. It cut me to the quick. Later, when I resigned, he told me how sorry he was and how badly the children felt to think I was going. I reminded him of that night. "If you had just stepped over to the parish house," I told him, "I would undoubtedly have been in this parish today, and quite likely, for the rest of my life."

He seemed to be stunned. He stood speechless and motionless. It is wonderful how God can turn the cussedness of one into the cure of many, for it was lucky for me, in the long after years, that he didn't show his face at that meeting. But it didn't seem so at the time. Our worst financial difficulties came after we left Christ Church. Things got really desperate. I picked up a little supply work here and there and did the best I could for my wife and small children. Butter was missing from our table, but fortunately we had some hens and our garden. I took long trips with my bicycle, picking great quantities of blackberries for canning, and wild grapes for grape juice. The woman next door had some fine pears which she let me pick at the halves.

The year 1909 was perhaps our lowest ebb. One of the really bitter moments of my life came when I started out by bicycle for a schoolhouse in Maromas on the chance of collecting a few children and holding Sunday school. I had no church, no salary, my family was virtually in want. As I passed my old church the choir, on which I had worked so hard, stood out in front ready to march indoors—a choir of twenty-seven young people, vested and trained, which we had built up from nothing. Well, I held Sunday school for three children under a tree in the yard, as we had no key to the schoolhouse. I had some popcorn in one pocket, Sunday-school papers in the other and some good stories in my head. We had a fine time, and I walked home with the children, pushing my bicycle. They had scattered my mortification.

There were many poor children in this region, so my mission grew tremendously. Often they came barefooted. There was always something to eat and we played games and stayed around with them for four or five hours. We sang out of the Mission Hymnal published by the Episcopal church. The children's favorite hymns were "What a Friend we have in Jesus," "I will sing the Wondrous Story" and "Yield not to Temptation."

In 1910 I took the census of the town of Haddam, eager to pick up money wherever possible. I had thirty days in which to do it, and I can remember those fresh budding April days when I rode around on my bicycle, checking up on the 2000 inhabitants of the town and the farmers in the outlying districts. We needed the money badly and my check for $119 was a godsend when it came. It was good experience too. Part of this area was in my territory and it gave me fresh insight into the lives of the farmers and the various encumbrances and mortgages that held them down.

I had always liked Sunday-school work from the angle of laboring with large poor families, so I decided to fit myself for this branch of the ministry by taking a course at the Hartford School of Pedagogy. My first class was with Dr. Edward Porter St. John, and he began it by telling us a story entitled "How the Half Chick Came to Be on the Weather Vane." I was startled by his procedure, until I realized that he was impressing on us the tremendous possibilities of good storytelling. I worked feverishly over his book on storytelling, and Sarah Cone Bryant's *Stories and How to Tell Them.* The field opened wider as I learned to tell stories to anyone who would listen.

I remember coming home one night, taking Shelley on my knee, and starting in on a story. Moms, as she had now become, was frying cakes at the stove but she listened. Pretty soon she turned, shook the cake-turner in my direction and remarked, "I hope to goodness you never tell a story where anyone can hear it. I'd hate to have to count the thousands I have sprinkled around since then!

While I was taking this course and doing some supply work on the side, Dr. St. John said to me one day: "If you don't do better in your history of education, you won't graduate."

"Is that so?" I retorted. "For that matter I don't want to graduate." "What do you mean?" he asked, plainly quite knocked out by my answer.

"I've graduated from enough schools already. I came here to get certain things. This study is of no interest to me and I care nothing about it. That's why I'm neglecting it." "Oh, oh, but we want you for an alumnus!" he cried, terribly upset.

He seemed to feel so badly about it that I braced up and was graduated. Ever since, I have been chased up for contributions to that school and every other school from which I was ever graduated. But I found the storytelling course most valuable to my ministry. I can't sufficiently emphasize the pleasure and profit this sort of thing is to children and even to grownups. When you go into a country school the teacher is only too glad to let you tell stories to the children. Every seminary should have a thorough course of this sort, making clear how a story is built up, and showing the difference between a joke or an after-dinner story, and a story with a moral to it. When a parson tells a story and sees how interested both the adults and children are, and then preaches a sermon and sees the children fidgeting and the grownups napping, he begins to do a bit of thinking. Whether he changes his technique or not is another question.

Something happened to me in the School of Pedagogy that changed my whole life and outlook. I was never the same man or the same kind of minister again. It was almost like St. Paul's vision. Dr. Kenyon S. Butterfield came to the school to give a series of talks on the rural church. He said the supreme emphasis should be on people—their needs, their desires, their happiness, their decent living, their social life, and their good health.

I was troubled enough by the fact that when I went out in the country for a social time with games, stories, a Virginia Reel, and a cup of coffee, the place was invariably packed with everyone from babies to grandmothers, but when I appeared for a straight, orthodox service, I would find only a handful of timetable saints. Since many a neighborhood feud has been wiped away at the sociable, why couldn't there be a combination of the two? If eating together provoked Christian feeling, visiting together yielded good fellowship, and children playing together taught unselfishness, then why, in heaven's name, shouldn't they do those things on Sunday? It seemed to me that if you had twenty people doing a good thing on Sunday, and sixty people doing good things on weekdays, you might get fifty or sixty doing all these good things at the same time—and what better time than on a Sunday, when they might drink of that spirit that furnishes a right basis for all their actions?

This new outlook changed my work, myself and my people. "How does your church go?" a city minister was asked. "Why, it goes when I kick it," came the answer. But I didn't kick the missions any more. My work just became natural, instead of artificial. It was fitted to the people instead of to customs and traditions. Children weren't Sunday-school fodder. People weren't pew fodder. The church was made for them instead of their being made for the church, as most church members seem to suppose.

After being graduated from the School of Pedagogy, I was in the field for any Sunday-school work that might come along. Soon I was asked to do some work for the State Sunday School Association. I went around speaking, mostly on boys' work. For this I got three hundred dollars *a* year, which was a great help to us. I was also on the Sunday School Commission of the Diocese of Connecticut, which at that time was contemplating hiring a state-wide worker. Of course, my qualifications came up for consideration. The Sunday school of Christ Church had grown from a mere handful to a roll of 149, and I had worked out an opening-and-closing service that was considered good enough to be put on exhibition at the office of the New York Sunday School Commission in New York. But my Sunday-school work had merely increased suspicion of the soundness of my churchmanship. At our county Episcopal gatherings in those days the Archdeacon always went out of his way to speak about this minister or that minister as being a "good churchman." Then the so-called sound churchmen would glance at one another knowingly.

This attitude was to pursue me for some years, but I did not lose any sleep over it.

On this occasion, at a meeting held for discussion of the candidates, I was asked to leave the room. As it didn't seem altogether right to send me out alone, Dr. John L. Lewis, of Waterbury, went out with me. It must have been a hot discussion for we had a long wait. When we went in again, we found that I had been ruled out.

Chapter VII

HORSE AND BUGGY DAYS

. . . .

WITH the new idea given me by Dr. Butterfield burning within me, I went at my mission work from a different angle. I took my prayer books and hymnals, to be sure, but I added a great deal more. I got hold of an express wagon, which would carry more than my trusty buggy, and it was invariably full. I paid forty dollars for a portable Graphophone to take around for combination services and sociables. When we had something to eat, people would stay for games and talk. Magazines and papers were added to my collection, and the libraries furnished me with books.

I usually took my stereopticon lantern and slides, which have been a tremendous help to me all these years. I began assembling a library of slides, buying a few at a time and in my collection are some of Joseph Boggs Beale's highly treasured drawings. I soon had sets on all the parables, and many on the life of Christ. Now I have a good representation of the whole Bible. We also have hymns, passages of scripture, the whole catechism and psalms that we can throw on the screen. With movies so popular one might think that my slides would no longer make a hit, but they do. "Got your movies with you?" the children cry when I show up. It did trouble my conscience a bit to answer "yes" to the movie idea, but then the slides do move back and forth. Anyway, they still seem to enjoy the old-fashioned slide and they laugh uproariously at the funny ones, like Beale's. We also have nearly a hundred slides on our own work over the years.

I used to have a terrible double one-can arrangement to generate gas by the drip system. Why that contraption didn't blow up and send the whole shooting match skyrocketing with it, I don't know. As time went on I got a compressed gas tank, such as was used on automobiles, especially trucks. This was a godsend, and I still use one where there is no electricity. We took long strips of draperies or old curtains to hang over the windows to darken the room. The children loved to have me come with my pictures and my barrel of stories. Bible pictures, Bible stories and good, old gospel hymns would all be used before we were through. Why shouldn't the church do that oftener than it does? Why shouldn't it put on a happy program? Why should it move forever on the assumption that the folks in the congregation are just naturally wicked?

Old Bill Perham, Father's tentmate in the Civil War, said they used to sing this doleful hymn over and over in the Baptist church he attended in Vermont:

How vain are all things here below,
How false, and yet how fair,
Each pleasure hath its poison, too
And every sweet its snare.

The brightest things below the skies,

Give but a flattering light,
We should suspect some danger nigh,
Where we possess delight.

This terrible theology must have been depressing to a happy, jocular soul like Bill. I found a good illustration of the pernicious effect of this sort of thing in the man who insisted that I baptize his children at home and not in church. When I pressed him for the reason, he said that he never entered the doors of a church, because his father had let one thumb nail grow long so that he could stick it in his children's legs when they got restless during the sermon. I couldn't blame the man much for feeling the way he did, any more than one could blame the woman who had been listening to an hour's praise of the Pilgrim Fathers and finally interrupted to say, "What about the Pilgrim Mothers?" "Well, what about them?" the speaker inquired.

"What about them? Why, they endured all the Pilgrim Fathers endured, and they endured the Pilgrim Fathers besides."

In Connecticut the Episcopalians talk a good deal about "Connecticut churchmanship." Not that anyone knows what it is, but it gives them something to feel good about. I told a diocesan convention once that the matter could be summed up in the words of an old fellow who took his oxen, his worldly goods and his family from an old farm down below Moodus, and went up into Massachusetts, where he was supposedly settled for the rest of his life.

It so happened that he got into a nest of godawful New Englanders. The old fellow couldn't stand them, so the next spring he returned to Connecticut in time for the plowing. His friends tried to get out of him why he came back. At last he cried, "Thank God, I'm back in Connecticut, where I can chew tobacco and enjoy religion." Now, isn't there a lot to that? I often say that we don't pretend to have so much religion down in the country places, but we enjoy what little we do have.

Soon my mission work spread out in all directions. We had baptisms, confirmations, and sociables without end. I don't much believe in elaborate preparation for confirmation. In fact the catechism did more to keep me out of church than in it, with Father glaring at us and knowing we'd get thunder if we didn't know our answers. But we had many large and interesting confirmation classes in schoolhouses in the back country, and I can even remember the Bishop officiating in the parlor of an abandoned farmhouse. When I celebrated communion in schoolhouses I passed up and down the aisle, so that the people could put out their hands for the reception instead of kneeling by a communion rail. Our baptisms were just as informal.

One day I stopped in to visit one of my families near Maromas. They had a fine crop of potatoes, cultivated after they had nearly ruined my brand-new cultivator on their rocks, but that was a small matter. In my church work I have always tried to get people to help themselves by giving them a start, especially with their gardens. When we bought our own farm later on, I let my parishioners take horse, wagon, fertilizer, plow, harrow and anything else they needed—even seeds—if they couldn't get them elsewhere. For many years I got small seed potatoes from Closson in Vermont and little pay he asked or got. From the ministry he had turned to the land, a pursuit which he followed until his death in 1934.

Well, the potato grower was in the kitchen with various members of his family when I arrived. I saw a big kettle of these beautiful Green Mountain potatoes on the stove. It seemed a fitting time to suggest baptism.

"Have your children been baptized?" I asked.

"Why, yes, all but six."

"Well," said I, "that might be enough to start making plans for, anyway."

Later, many of these same children were confirmed by Bishop Brewster at a service held in the schoolhouse. He arrived on a very hot day. "Are you going to wear vestments?" he asked. "Well," I said, "I'm not very heavy on vestments at these mission services." "Let's neither of us wear them then," said the Bishop.

So the class that had grown from the three children under the playground tree, until it reached clear across the schoolhouse, was confirmed by a Bishop in a business suit, a novel state of affairs in the Episcopal church but one that was all right with me. This way the congregation could think about the service instead of reflecting on how hot the Bishop must be in all his togs. Afterwards we had lunch in the school yard, and it was the first time the good Bishop had ever eaten a hot dog or an ice cream cone.

At this school we always had lunch after "meeting." I usually took along a can of coffee or cocoa, a good supply of enamel cups, and some frankfurter sandwiches. The country women came in with cakes and things they had baked. While we ate we had time for discussions on farming and politics, town affairs and the extension of electricity through the rural areas. When the voting machines were first put in, I had a model brought to the schoolhouse for them to practice on.

For a time we could not use the schoolhouse in this locality, so we looked up empty farmhouses and assembled some strange congregations in them. We had one old fellow who refused to take off his hat. He never did at home, so why should he here? In time he got a little self-conscious about it, and went so far as to pull the old hat well down over his ears, and finally off altogether. He never came except in summertime. As there was no spittoon, I always put him near the window.

It was while we were worshiping in farmhouses that our wooden cross and organ were stolen. They were carted away in a truck, for we later found the organ beside the road where the truck got stuck in the mud. The rain had ruined it. But these unused houses were really ideal for mission work. We sat around big fireplaces, roasting hot dogs and popcorn, and brewing cocoa or coffee. We also told stories and had games. The old Graphophone rattled out its tunes most of the time. It was a good way of getting close to one's congregation. I had one practical joker in this group—George Whitmore. One night when we were having frankfurters he cut the end off one, dug out some of the meat and carefully refilled the skin with a long piece of coiled string. Then he handed the frankfurter to Albert Scovill, one of our more serious local characters, who took an eager, lengthy and inclusive mouthful. After chewing for all he was worth, Albert reached in for a piece of the meat to find out what made it such tough going. He got hold of the string and pulled out yard after yard of it. I thought his eyes were going to pop out of his head.

We had one family in this section who would have nothing to do with ministers. One day I gave the children some pictures. They took them into the house, then returned immediately and handed them back to me. When I urged them to keep the pictures, they threw them in the road. The woman of the house stood in the doorway and practically dared me to go in. I didn't. Several weeks later I passed that way and the children came out to tell me that their mother was sick in bed. Knowing no minister had ever entered these portals, I didn't venture in even then, but I asked the children to bring me a dish. It was an awfully hot day. I filled the quart-bowl with luscious smooth ice cream which was left over from a party at the school- house, and I told them to take it upstairs to their mother. The victory was easy after that. It wasn't long before those children were climbing into my old express wagon and heading regularly for church. Long afterwards, when I was under fire in the press, a big brother of this same family, unable to compose a letter on his own, paid a lawyer $2 to write one answering my critics and praising me. I was greatly touched.

One family in this region gave me a good chance for work. Eleven children all at home, and the man was a shiftless no-good who came home only on weekends and sometimes not then. How many times I went down to that house! They were quite impoverished, and the little boys worked so hard cutting wood and tending the garden that I decided to help them. One of the most strenuous trips I ever had was when I went down there with a horse, lumber wagon, and cultivator. I cultivated their garden and crops, for I couldn't bear to have the little fellows trying to hoe the hard, weedy ground. Hoeing is hard enough even when land is well cultivated.

Now and again I read this poem about hoeing to my country congregations:

Said Farmer Jones in a whining tone to his good old neighbor Grey,
"I've worn my knees through to the bones, but it ain't no use to pray.
Your corn looks twice as good as mine, tho' you don't pretend to be.
A shining light in the church to shine, and tell salvation's free.
I've prayed to the Lord a thousand times to make this here corn grow,
And why yourn beats so and climbs, I'd give a world to know."
Said Farmer Grey to Farmer Jones in his easy, quiet way,
"When prayers get mixed with lazy bones, they don't make farmin' pay.
Your weeds, I notice, are good and tall, in spite of all your prayers.
You may pray for corn till the heavens fall, if you don't dig up the tares.
I mix my prayers with a little toil along in every row,
And I work this mixture into the soil, quite vigorous with a hoe,
An' I've discovered, tho' still in sin, as sure as you are born,

This kind of compost, well worked in, makes pretty
  decent corn.
"So while I'm prayin' I use my hoe and do my level
  best
To keep down the weeds along each row, an'
the Lord, he does the rest.
It's well for you to pray both night an' morn,
as every farmer knows,
But the place to pray for thrifty corn is right
between the rows.
You must use your hands while prayin' tho',
if an answer you would get,
For prayer worn knees and a rusty hoe never
raised a big crop ye
And so I believe, my good, old friend, if you want to
  win the day,
From plowing, clean to the harvest's end, you must
hoe as well as pray."
                                        —Anonymous

One night when I stopped at this house I found things in pretty bad shape. The oldest girl, about fourteen, had had a terrible row with her mother. Although it was nearly dark, she was down in the valley below the house, wandering around in the woods. A boy named Johnnie was sick and running a high temperature. A doctor had been there, had left some medicine, and said that he could do nothing more. I really didn't think the boy would live till morning. The father was not at home either.

As soon as I arrived, some of the boys rushed to the back of the house and shouted to the girl in the woods,

"Mr. Gilbert has come. Mr. Gilbert has come."

Soon the girl appeared. Then we all had supper together. I told stories to the little ones, while the others were doing the dishes. We sang hymns and when the tots had gone to bed, I talked to the older ones. We gathered round Johnnie's bed to pray that he might get well, and that there might be peace rather than quarreling in that home. And there did seem to be some sort of peace before I left, with the baby asleep in a carriage I had brought down, and with Johnnie breathing quietly. With the recuperative powers of his age, he was better the next morning, and was up and around in a few days.

I really think I have never had a family that needed more help or in a greater variety of ways than this one. Things reached a crisis when the twelfth baby was due and the mother was in a deplorable condition. I had a telephone installed so as to keep in touch with the family at this juncture. Someday I must reckon up how many telephones we have had put in around the countryside.

When the baby arrived a few days later, the woman was worse, and the situation seemed desperate. Mother and baby were rushed to the hospital in an ambulance. Three weeks later the woman was much improved and could leave. But how could she return to that home, with eleven children and no conveniences? We decided to bring her into our own house for three weeks. From there she was able to talk to her children by telephone every day, and she helped the older girls in their planning. I went frequently to their place to see that things were going along all right.

At last the time came to take her home. Never shall I forget that day! It was winter, and I had a long-bodied express sleigh, for the snow was deep. I loaded it up with provisions—beef of our own killing, potatoes, bread, butter, milk and more of the necessities of life. We drove across the white fields, and the cold air whipped her cheeks and brought a transient gleam of health to her face. As we drove up to the house, there were eight staring faces at the window, watching their mother come home. And happy I was that it was not in a coffin! It might easily have been a funeral sleigh coming across the snow toward that house. I looked up into the sparkling winter sky and thanked God that that mother was riding home alive.

In time the family moved away, and all the children grew up and scattered, but every now and then one of them turns up at my door, or at one of my meetings. The look on their faces repays me a thousand-fold for anything we were able to do for them long ago. There are many people, of course, who think a minister has the most thankless job on earth. A man said to me once, "Do you really believe there's one minister in this state who actually enjoys his work, and is happy in it?" And I replied, "Well, I can't speak for all of them, but there is one at least who is not merely happy, but who has the time of his life every day."

What if it does seem hard at times? If it is good work, why should we think of it as being hard? I don't believe God Almighty ever intended us to think of it in that way. He expected our work to be joy, not hardship. The very hardship of it should be joy. We are told that Christ even endured the cross for the joy that was set before. If the first fruit of the spirit mentioned was love, then the second was joy. Bishop Irving P. Johnson of Colorado says that "a preacher ought to be a lovable person, and no person is lovable who is too solemn over his status in life." Good for the Bishop! What we need is more preachers who can laugh, more ministers who can see the funny side of the toughest situations.

I have found a sense of humor one of the greatest assets in the ministry, particularly in the country, where any conceivable sort of situation is apt to arise. For instance, one fall a neighbor of ours who had a great many pullets had neglected to have his fences fixed, so two or three hundred of them spent most of their time on our farm. What a chance for a row! But I looked at them and said, "Boys, they'll begin laying soon. Let's treat them kindly." I was right. One day my sons went hunting and found 134 small pullet eggs. We sent a basket of them to the owner, who promptly sent them back, saying that he had more than he knew what to do with, and we had a fine time frying them around at missions and large-family homes.

But a flock of misguided hens brought nothing but discord into the lives of two families of the same nationality whose houses faced each other down in the woods. There were no other farms within sight or hearing, so helpful and friendly relations seemed to be called for, but one of the men, mowing beside the road, uncovered a nest of fourteen hens' eggs, worth at that time about fourteen cents. These eggs were laid by the neighbor's hens. Now whose eggs were they? The question never was settled, for the two families had a violent row about it and didn't talk to each other for fourteen years—just a year for each egg. All efforts on my part to get them together failed lamentably.

One day I was cutting a girl's hair in the Maromas

schoolhouse when she became very chatty and told me about her playhouse at home. She said she was Burt Bailey's daughter and that they had two cows and a horse.

"Two cows and a horse?" I echoed, having heard of their extreme poverty.

"Yes, the two front tires of an old truck are the cows, and the one big rear tire is the horse. Every night my brother rolls them down to the brook for a drink, and then puts them back in the barn."

Later I saw the little play barn made of white oil cloth and the playhouse made from the cab of an old Ford truck. But things were not so good on the small farm where they lived. I found that Burt's barn had no shingles, and soon would be rotting down. He had some good level land, but he never could improve his living status without a barn, and the moral effect of seeing it rot would be terrible. So we got busy. I managed to find Burt a job as a laborer, taking him to work and bringing him home. Then we got shingles of various kinds, and in a few days the barn was watertight. Now he could mow his hay and keep it under cover until he sold it to pay the taxes. He got a horse for its keep, too, and that was a help.

Soon they had a garden with a good crop of potatoes. I bought young chicks for them, and let them raise them at halves, furnishing the feed for them myself. I took the roosters and they kept the pullets. I helped them get some cement and we built a much needed chimney. Then I got a good stove so that they could bake their own bread; also a hanging lamp to brighten up the living room, a big table for the kitchen, a Graphophone, a cutaway harrow and even a barrel in which to salt down shad from the

Connecticut River. I gave the children various articles for their playhouse, and there we roasted hot dogs, fried salt pork, and had many a good time together.

Burt hadn't been to church for twenty-four years and he had no suitable clothes to wear. Although he was a big man, I was fortunate in getting him a complete outfit from shoes to collar buttons. (The wife of a friend, who had died, sent us all her husband's clothes. I was sorry he died but then—!) When Burt appeared at a local gathering in his tailored and imported trappings, his own neighbors scarcely knew him.

My mission work has taken me from place to place— Tylerville, Maromas, Chester, Ivoryton, Killingworth, Durham and Ponset—all within an area of a hundred square miles or so. When my job seems done at one mission I am always ready to move on and breathe life into another. As archdeacon for three years in charge of the mission work in Middlesex County I then supervised them all. There are few byways around Middletown that I haven't traversed with my horse and buggy. While of course these days are gone forever, I can't help thinking that traveling in a buggy had its advantages over the automobile for the country minister. Someone has said that civilization takes as much as it gives. Sometimes I am inclined to think that it takes more.

If, when going along with a horse, you met a team, the custom was to pull up for a little chat. The main idea, of course, was to run your eye over the other fellow's horse. What couldn't one tell about a man by the look of his horse! A great deal more than by looking at his car today, for the horse wasn't bought on the instalment plan, nor obtained by turning in the old one. It was only a horse, but it belonged to its owner and not to a finance company. How many ribs could one count? Had the horse been curried that day? Was the harness tied up with strings? No one was so poor that he couldn't mend the harness with rivets and oil it once a year. "Nice limber harness," a little Italian boy said to me on one occasion, as he was helping me put the horse up. That boy sized up his minister then and there.

"That minister is no good," said my sister one day up in Vermont, as the new preacher drove around the corner on his way from Randolph. "Why, he hasn't washed the old spring mud off his buggy yet."

I used to dread the long trips home at night, although any horse would make better time going toward his "master stall" than away from it. Whenever I think of a horse stall, I recall the story of the boy who said to his father: "What do they do when they install a minister, Dad? Do they put him in a stall and feed him?'

"Oh, no, my boy, far from it. They hitch him to a church and expect him to pull it."

Traveling with a horse frequently made it necessary to stay all night with some family and I delighted in this. If I got away from home and the farm work on Saturday afternoon, my custom was to work up my remarks or "sermon" on the way. I read as we climbed the hills, the reins over the dashboard, the horse taking his time. In summer I usually took ice cream for the Saturday night party. After working all day on the farm, I had to hustle to get the chores done and make that night's milk into ice cream, then drive eighteen miles to the party, but I have done it often enough.

In winter it was apt to be hard traveling. One night I was following the "over the hill" route which took me on a lonely stretch through the deep woods. It was just getting dark, when, quick as a flash, the horse jumped to the right of the road, throwing me into the bushes and overturning the whole wagonload of papers, magazines, grip, Graphophone, records, and whatnot. Father had often told us, "If your horse ever tries to run away, hang onto the reins." So I hung onto the reins, and was dragged fifty yards before I could stop that frightened horse. I have always thought that some animal, either a deer or a wild cat perhaps, jumped out of the bushes at the side of the road, and frightened him. The lantern was smashed, of course, and I had no light. The horse was astride one shaft but fortunately the shaft wasn't broken. I got the wagon righted, picked up everything I could find in the dark, and went on. When I arrived at the home in which I was to stay all night and rapped on the door, a woman came with a lamp in her hand. She took one look at me, gave a scream, and started to slam the door in my face. I must have been something to look at, my face all smeared with blood.

Although I never traded a horse on a Sunday, many a time I felt like saying with David Harum, "Now, if 'twan't Sunday, what would you take for that hoss?" Some mighty funny situations developed in the horse and buggy days, like the time two young men from our town went to a social and dance without changing their work clothes and ended up by scrambling half the horses in the parish. They had no idea of causing trouble when they arrived, but they looked pretty tough and when they handed in their money at the ticket window, the cashier pushed it back. They weren't wanted. They were out in the cold and they were mad. They vowed they would get even with that crowd if it was the last thing they ever did. A little way beyond the dance hall were the horse sheds, where the crowd had parked their horses and buggies. It didn't take these two lads long to put the horses into the wrong buggies. They mixed up eighteen of them and then stood around in the shadows till the party broke up. What a time those people had that night! To drive a horse that had come from Candlewood Hill in the opposite direction, towards Turkey Hill, was something of a proposition. If a man turned back to get his own horse, there was no telling when it would be found. As for the next day, what could one do? There were no telephones at that time.

Just as you could judge a man by his horse, harness and buggy, you could size up the female side of the home by glancing at the family wash, as old Dobbin jogged along.

By the degree of whiteness, you could appraise the thoroughness of the woman. The shapes and sizes of the various garments told the passerby the size and approximate ages of the children. It was easy to tell if there was a baby. And the sheets frequently disclosed where the family bought its grain, for it takes much washing and bleaching to get the lettering out of grain bags. Some of the sheets would have made a good billboard—*Worthmore Feed, The Coles Company, Purina Chow,* or *Meech and Stoddard.*

I have always liked this slow ambling around the countryside, noticing the state of the crops and the ways of the people. One Sunday afternoon twenty-seven years ago we were coming home from church and were deep in the backwoods when we overtook a gay procession. It proved to be a wedding party on its way to a Bohemian hall. When we reached the hall I pulled up and we went in. The celebration was in full fig. It didn't look much like Sunday afternoon in New England. One accordion player had imbibed too freely and had passed out. The second was rapidly following suit. Obviously the bridegroom was in distress so I went to him and said, "It looks as if you're going to be short of music before the feast is over. I have a fiddler here who can help you out." So in place of hymns, my fiddler played dance music for the Bohemians that afternoon, and when the people asked, "Where did the fiddler come from?" they were told, "The minister brought him."

The bridegroom was so pleased that he urged me to rest under a pine tree and partake of food and drink. But I told him I had ice cream in my wagon and would be pleased to treat the whole crowd, so we brought in the freezer and packed cones as fast as the wedding guests came up for them. The afternoon was waning before I took my fiddler and we went on our way. We still had twelve miles to go through the woods and we had to get home in time to do the farm chores. The wedding party danced until six next morning.

When you're on a long cold trip with a horse, you can get out and walk or run, and whip your arms to keep warm, but in a car that is not so easy. My son, Shelley, had to give a music lesson down country one night, so, as we had a gift piano to deliver to one of our parish families, I suggested taking the big trailer. It was late when we got started and very cold. My second son, Closson, went with us to help with the piano. He seems able to lift as much as two ordinary men. We arrived all right, but the family seemed rather puzzled that we should have chosen that time of night to bring a piano, and in such weather. The radiator seemed doomed to freeze, even though we had alcohol in it and kept covering it with coats and blankets. When we were eight miles from home, we ran out of gas. The boys thought there was plenty when we started. They had forgotten to figure on the extra load, which necessitated more. Of all times and all places to have such a thing happen! Luckily we found a house with a light in it. A woman came to the door. "Oh, Mr. Gilbert, is that you?"

"Then you know me?" I queried.

"Why, certainly," she said. "You used to show pictures and tell stories in the old Turkey Hill schoolhouse where I went to school."

So she heated a tea kettle of water for us, and we found a garage man who brought us some gas. After a while we were off again, but not until the garage man himself had got stuck and had to be pulled out by us. Twice more we had to stop for water. About three miles from home a farmer named Eugene Spencer got out of bed to give us our last pail of water. Where he raised it I don't know, for everything in sight seemed to be frozen, but I'll never forget how he appeared that night with a milk pail full of water in all that bitter cold. Some years afterwards his daughter came to me to be married. I told her what her father had done for me, and I made her a wedding present on the spot.

When we got home, we found it was 18 degrees below

zero, and the next morning the temperature had dropped to 21 below. Once I saw the thermometer standing at 32 degrees below in Middletown. I have considerable competition with a neighbor of mine as to which has the colder farm. Often when I am having breakfast on a winter morning, Myron Harris, commonly known as "Buster," will call up to ask what the thermometer reads at the Gilbert place. Usually we go him one better. Then the local paper calls up, and spreads the news that it's really a cold day. But it no longer matters as it did in the horse and buggy era. We can jump into a car and drive through the snow in comfort. In some ways life is easier for the country parson today.

Chapter VIII

CHURCH IN THE WILDERNESS

. . . .

IT WAS on a hot July day in 1909 that I first saw the church in the wilderness which has been the heart of my ministry ever since. I came tearing along a rough road on my bicycle, knowing I was late, and suddenly Emmanuel Church emerged from its frame of trees—a building that had been standing there for more than a hundred years. It was twenty miles from my farm. I had lost my way going over and it was not until I heard the peal of a church bell across the valley that I headed in the right direction. This must be my church. I rode like a madman, and got there twenty minutes late. Good start for the new rector!

The church had been closed for some time, and no one thought that it would be opened again. The population of the surrounding country had been thinning out for years. Most of the natives either had moved away or were about to do so. The building was large enough to hold a Park Avenue congregation, but it needed painting and was in a state of general disrepair. What a call! Terrible roads, rocky little farms, the old natives gone and no one taking their places.

When my good relatives in Vermont heard all this, there was weeping and wailing and gnashing of teeth. To think that George should have come to this! But come to this I had. I had no idea then that this little country church would become so important a part of my lifework, or that one day it would emerge from its obscurity and be heard of far and wide throughout the country. Strange things have happened in this church. Here we have fed the hungry and had cabbages in the baptismal font. We have baptized an old lady of eighty-eight in a rocking chair and cooked stew within sight and smell of the chancel. We still have the old communion table, the prayer desk with sockets for candles, the original Eucharistic vessels and the preacher's gown with great ballooning sleeves that must be at least 125 years old and was worn by the father of Professor Simon Greenleaf Fuller of Berkeley Divinity School. The old and new are happily combined in our little church in the wilderness but alas! so scattered are the parish families now that only when the wind blows can the bell be heard at one distant farmhouse. All around is the deep quiet of the forest. A brook runs like a silver thread through an avenue of white birch, maples, hemlock, wild cherries, oaks and pines.

My predecessor at Killingworth was a remarkable man, a type of fine old country preacher that one doesn't often come across today. His name was William C. Knowles, and his theology was the simple kind of knowing what to do for the sick and the troubled, and how to give practical aid to his parishioners. He was full of native lore. Once, when his own son John was terribly sick with fever, Mr. Knowles went out into the woods and plucked armfuls of brakes. He covered the boy's bed with these damp rich ferns and half buried him in them, until they literally drew out the fever.

He was never trained for the ministry, but worked as a deacon at a stipend so modest that when a fellow clergyman offered to sell him a horse and buggy for $150, he said, "I thank you gratefully, but you see, that is a large part of my yearly salary." He was not ordained until the summer of 1884. At that time Bishop Williams stopped him on the street one day and told him he was going to ordain him to the ministry.

"What!" gasped Mr. Knowles. "That can't be. Don't you know I have never even attended high school, much less college or seminary?"

"Aren't you doing the work?" said the Bishop. "And so I am going to ordain you to the priesthood."

At that time there were nine houses in the vicinity of the church, all of which have since disappeared, leaving it in solitary stillness among the trees. Much of Mr. Knowles' early work was done with the old native stock, but toward the end of his ministry the immigrants were beginning to swarm over the countryside, attracted by the prospect of farm life instead of city slums. He had the real spirit for country work. I was fascinated by what I heard him tell about his rural activities in Emmanuel Church. Soon I was encountering the same sort of thing myself.

Once he and his son John were riding along a country road when they saw smoke pouring from an attic window. Taking it for granted that the house was on fire, they rushed up and pounded on the door. An immigrant woman opened it and they shouted at her, "Fire, Fire! Your house is on fire. The smoke is pouring from your attic window."

"Oh, yah. That's all right," answered the woman. "We're smoking hams."

"You're what?"

"We're smoking hams. We made a big hole in the chimney in the attic, put a flat stone over the top of the chimney, and hung the meat on the rafters."

They drove on, wondering what the local insurance man would think of this method of curing meat. Nor was that the end of it. One cold morning Mr. Knowles remarked to a neighbor, "Cold morning, isn't it?"

"That's right," replied the neighbor. "It sure was cold, when I took the stone off the chimney."

"What do you mean?"

"Why," said the astonished neighbor, "don't you cover your chimney with a stone every night? You see, the heat from the house will go up the chimney unless you cover it."

I can just imagine taking a great flat stone to the roof last thing at night, then going up to get it down again first thing in the morning!

Another time Mr. Knowles called at a house where he wasn't sure who the occupants were. He rapped on the door and a woman opened it.

"Is this Mr. Smith's house?" he asked.

"That," replied the woman, "is a question that has never been settled." She slammed the door and left him there.

Knowing the intimate type of work Mr. Knowles had done, and liking it, I was glad to take on his parish, although the church had closed up after his retirement and things did not look very promising. But my ministry here proved to be abundant after all, and I often look back on the day of my arrival at Killingworth as one of the fortunate landmarks of my life.

I was invited out to dinner that July day, and what a meal it was! I wish I had a record of all the roosters that have entered the ministry. Of course the minister is supposed to go to the house of the biggest shot in the parish, where he is duly treated to the good things of the flesh—roast beef, chicken, ice cream, coffee, cigars and a nap. But I cared for none of these things. There were several small boys at the church, some of them living two miles away, and I longed to see more of them. I kept thinking of how far they had to walk and how hungry they must be before they got home. I remembered how ravenous I used to be as a boy before Sunday dinner. So after a few Sundays, I declined these invitations to sumptuous parish feasts, and arrived with cocoa, bread, bacon and a frying pan, all piled up on my bicycle. And under the horse sheds, the boys and I, watched by my little dog Maida, who always trotted behind the wheel on my forty-mile Sunday trip, would cook dinner before I started for home. I couldn't stay too long, for I was now preaching at two schoolhouses as well, and was not getting home until about eleven o'clock at night.

Before long the girls took to lingering around the campfire and some of the menfolk who had come quite a distance smelled the bacon and hamburger and joined us too. Right away they started bringing bread, eggs and milk. But cold weather came on, so we put the cocoa and stew-pan on the big box stove in the church. This was indeed a questionable innovation, and the old church members eyed it with misgiving and alarm. But it looked all right to the Rullman boys, the Nigrella boys, the Bristols, the Blatchleys and to me.

Things came to a head before long. The stove was then near the front of the church, and on it that morning we had a six-quart stewpan filled with cocoa. The fire was good evidently, for right in the middle of my sermon the pan boiled over. Up rushed one of the men to take it off. As he lifted it, the handle buckled, and the contents spilled all over the seething hot stove. A cloud obscured the Master from the apostles' sight, but it must have been as nothing compared to the cloud that cut off chancel and preacher from the sight of the congregation that morning.

A conference was held after the service. I refused to back down on the dinner-in-church idea. For eighty years dinner had been eaten after the morning service in that church, although the custom had been dropped twenty-five years before my ministry began. Moreover, my idea of making a church into a true community center had been fostered by my observation of what went on in the old Congregational Church at Randolph Center. My normal school principal, Deacon Edward Conant, and a committee of church members, had taken some unused space in the church and put it to community use. They had their "eating floor" upstairs. Well, we kept ours downstairs after a battle royal. I met the criticism of my parishioners at Killingworth by proposing that we fix over the building and have regular parish rooms, like those in city churches. So we sold a useless piece of property that had been left to the church, and this more than paid for the alterations. Our own parishioners did most of the work. Upstairs we now have a social room with easy chairs and a piano, plenty of space for Sunday school, and even beds. When we go down to paint or to chop wood, we stay all night and many a good sleep I have had looking down on the pews of my church. Windows from this upper room open out onto the main auditorium of the church. This extra space is used by the congregation on special occasions, such as Old Home Day. And by opening the windows in winter, one gets heat from the church. So that instead of the gallery, empty in so many churches, we have a glassed-in parish hall where we can sleep, have music, attend Sunday school or worship, as we see fit.

Our kitchen and dining room are downstairs, right where we enter the church. The kitchen is curtained off with burlap—and is equipped with a stove, a cupboard for dishes and a sink. Here the pots may boil and bubble while the service goes on. We all take turns cooking, serving and washing the dishes. We eat at long tables, with only a hinged partition separating us from the pews, and at times we open this up, particularly in cold weather, when we need the warmth from the big stove in the church. The kitchen stove does not throw enough heat to keep our church dining room as warm as it ought to be. I am a crank on having churches warm. I know that country churches are apt to be painfully cold in winter, a state of affairs well illustrated by the city girl who was asked what the text was, after she had paid a visit to a country church.

"I'm not quite sure," she said, "but as near as I can make out, 'many were cold, but few were frozen.

I honestly believe that hundreds of country churches could have been saved, and many more might still be saved, by rearranging things along community lines. One room can always be partitioned off with a curtain at trifling expense, and it is easy to arrange a social program suited to the community. I told the clergy gathered in diocesan convention one time, "You have had parlor religion. What you need now is kitchen religion." And this I firmly believe.

Of course, the city preacher is apt to be at a disadvantage in an environment of this kind. One of the problems with our mission churches is to keep the fires going and plenty of preachers would have no earthly idea how to chop wood, handle a fire or warm up a church in an hour. This is where my hardy Vermont childhood comes in handy. I would no more go down to one of my country churches without an ax than without my prayer book or barber's kit. I'm janitor, sexton, bell ringer and sweeper all in one. I'm a bit like the preacher who started out on a circuit of three churches and ended by being jack-of-all-trades. He found the first one to be quite High Church, with candles, incense and the perpetual light in evidence, so he put on a very High-Church service. A warden at the second church called up the first to find out if the minister were High or Low, so that things could be arranged properly for him. This church happened to be extremely Low, so it had none of the High-Church paraphernalia. When the minister arrived he took one look around and put on a very Low service. Wardens of the third church he was due to visit made inquiries of the other two.

"How is this new fellow?" they asked at the first church he had visited.

"He's High Church," came the answer.

Then they called the second church.

"He's Low Church," was the response this time.

Puzzled, they put the question to the minister direct, saying, "We want to arrange things here to your liking and we are trying to find out what your inclinations are. What are you, anyway? High or Low?" "I'm high, low, jack and the game," said the new minister affably.

Well, that's me. There aren't any chores around a church, or a farm either, that I haven't done at one time or another.

In the spring of 1921 we nearly lost our beloved church by fire. When we went down there on a May day for the Sunday morning service we found a forest fire raging in the region around the frame building. I was considering whether we should go and fight the fire instead of starting the service when I noticed that the grass was burning close to the church. I wondered how this could be until I glanced up at the roof and saw it was burning near the edge, and that the hot cinders had dropped to the grass below. A car drove up most opportunely with three men in it, and one of them, an athletic youth, volunteered to climb to the roof if we would pass up water from the near-by brook. He went up through the belfry, and then jumped down more than ten feet to the roof. He was wearing tennis shoes, which helped, but he was agile as a cat in any event. We all went to the brook with teakettles, pots, dishpans, pitchers and every utensil we could lay hands on. Our kitchenware came in handy that day. We formed a line and relayed the water to the young man on the roof, who kept slopping it on until the fire was out. In the meantime the members of the congregation who had assembled pitched in and helped. The communion table, prayer desk and silver vessels were carried to the grass plot in front of the church. The local fire company was notified by one parishioner, but the firemen lost their way getting out to the church in the wilderness, and by the time they arrived, the fire was out. What a look of disappointment came over them! It made me think of the story of the country fire company that was rushing through the town to a fire. "Stop!" yelled a man in the road. "There's another fire down at the south end." "Good," answered one of the firemen. "You go down and keep it going till we get there."

One of the happiest moments I have to look back upon came at the old Killingworth Church on a hot summer morning. I was alone, and hustling like all get-out to have things ready for the service, when I saw a ragged youngster peering at me around a corner of the building. He ran when he saw me looking at him and I had to yell pretty loud to stop him. He seemed scared, but he stopped. I had some ice cream with me, and I rushed over to the car, tore open the freezer and filled three whopping cones for him. He looked at them suspiciously. He didn't know what ice cream was. "Take it," I urged him. "It's good. Eat it before it melts." He took a bite, his face lighted up and he went off down the road.

I never saw that boy again. Later I learned that he and his father and mother lived in a hut in the swamp near Tittering Brook, where his father burned charcoal. The father had gone off on a drunk and the mother had sent this boy, nine years old, to go out into the great world to find him and bring him back. Probably he never found him. I often wondered whether the mother was left alone in the woods to burn the charcoal, tending it night and day.

One of the first Sundays I was in the parish, out in front of the church was a man with a group of boys, and he hollered at me: "What do you think? These boys want to go to a ball game. On Sunday too." He thought I would be shocked beyond anything.

"Where is it?" I asked at once. "Let's go over. I'd like to go there myself."

I took my horse, they took theirs, and we all went over to the ball game. I knew they were planning a beer party afterwards for I spied a buggy with a beer keg in it back of the barn. When I arrived there was quite a crowd, and there was much comment on the fact that the minister had come to a ball game on Sunday. I hitched my horse. "Let's have a good game," I said. "I'm not a good player, so I'll umpire." We organized two teams. I umpired and we had a great ball game. They never opened that keg of beer.

Some time after this I was driving through the woods one day when I saw George Shoens sawing logs alone with a one-man crosscut saw. I could see at once that he wasn't used to that kind of work. So I talked to him a little, sounding him out to see if it would hurt his feelings if I offered help. He had an ax with a terribly long helve. Being a city man, some shopkeeper had foisted this off on him. Within a few days I took some young lads around there with axes, saws, wedges and sledges. We all went to work and cut enough wood to last him a long time. Shortly after this we got some neighbors to draw the wood into the man's yard.

Then I noticed that the neighbors, who had not been long in this country, both needed haircuts badly and I told them so. I got my barber's kit from the car and went to work on them. This was the first time these men had heard about the parson cutting hair and they were dumbfounded! They knew I cut wood but they didn't know

I doubled as a barber.

Between one thing and another I soon found in how many different ways the church could help to build up community social life. Remembering church life in Vermont and adding a few touches of my own, I launched gatherings which we called "parties." If we labeled them dances, only the young folks would come, while the older people stayed at home, disapproving. Not being sure of always having some one on hand to call off the old-fashioned square dances, I went at it and learned to do it myself. It was not an easy thing to do, as I had never danced and was not supposed to have any music in me. Indeed, I never could carry a tune further than the first line of a hymn. I am like the chap who said, "I am no musician, but there are two tunes I am sure of—'God Save the Weasel,' and 'Pop Goes the Queen.'" In time I got so that I could call "Pop Goes the Weasel," "The Girl I Left Behind Me," "Virginia Reel" and a great many others. As I could not be sure of having a fiddler either, I used a graphophone, which can always be adapted to a small place. People came from miles around to these parties. Many a dance I have conducted in a barn since then. As time went on my sons made up a proficient orchestra for me.

Aside from our barn dances we always had plenty of games for the children and short talks on co-operation and unselfishness, for I maintain that a social gathering is the best training ground for the helpful spirit. Indeed, one of the first gatherings we had in the Killingworth Church was a poultry meeting. We had an expert poultry man, editor of a farm paper, come down and look over three crates of hens brought in by the local people. On the way to church I stopped at various farms and had him inspect the hen houses, and examine the roosts for the red lice that stay on them during the day and feed on the hens at night. We found them the worst enemies of egg production. There was so much interest in this subject that we had an evening session, followed by games and dancing. It was two o'clock in the morning when I arrived home by horse and buggy.

Another time, after we got the farm bureau organized, the country agent came down to give practical advice. When some parishioners who we thought needed help did not show up at the meeting we went around and visited their farms in the senior warden's ox cart. No one had cars in those days, so we did many errands for people that we would not have to do now. One family wanted a couple of young pigs and did not know where or how to get them. Living near the city, I could watch the paper until I saw that some were for sale. Finally I got a pair of nice Chester County Whites and took them down to church in an express wagon the next morning. I put the horse and wagon in the horse shed farthest from the church, knowing that the pigs would do some squealing during the service. (It was said later that there was no need to ring the bell that day.) That same fall we had a good roast pork dinner one Sunday at the church.

Another pig incident involved Bill Mildrum, who lived in Tylerville. He and his wife were getting along in years and Bill was not at all well. He had been unable to work for some time. His wife told me that he was very worried about not having a pig that spring. They had never failed to have one and they didn't see how they could get through the following winter without their accustomed pork.

I told them nothing of what was in my mind, but two weeks later my Sunday route took me around their way. I had had my third and last service for the day, and was headed for home, when I pulled up at their house about ten o'clock at night. Bill was in bed but his wife came to the door.

"Where shall I put the pig?" I asked.   v

"Pig? What pig?"

"Why, the pig I brought for Bill, and it's all paid for, too. Ask no questions and I'll tell you no lies."

The woman was too overcome even to talk about it for a while. Then she began to think of another difficulty. "But the pen," she said. "It's in bad shape. It has to be fixed up a lot. If I had only known, I would have hired a man to fix it."

"That's all right," said I. "It won't hurt my best clothe to fix it right now. We've got to put this pig in."

She brought me hammer, nails and a saw, and I went at it. It really was more of a job than I had figured on, but I got it in shape, put the pig in and rode off. It was late enough that night when I got home, but sometimes I have wondered if I ever did a better deed in my life. It was the last pig the old man ever had.

By another spring a pig was out of the question, for Bill was dead.

While fixing the pig pen I had learned that he didn't have a comfortable chair to sit in, so I took him down a Morris chair. He was deeply grateful to me and when he knew his end was near, he insisted that his wife show me where his tools were, as he wished me to have them after his death.

We raised pigs on our own farm for a few years. They happened to be Duroc Jerseys—red pigs. When a litter of them were running around the barn one day, a car from New York pulled up in front of the house and a good-sized boy came to the door. "Papa wants to know if he can buy one of your puppies," he said.

"Puppies?" exclaimed Mrs. Gilbert. "Why, we haven't a puppy on the place."

"Yes, you have," the boy insisted. "We saw a lot of them running around the barn."

I got into one bad mix-up over pigs in those early days and for a time lost one of my best families because of it. A reporter from a Hartford paper arrived one Saturday, stayed overnight and attended church next day. He was going to write up our work. I took him to see one of my parishioners, a woman who happened to have a fine litter of pigs. While there, I took her picture standing beside them. By ill chance I happened to make this the occasion for telling the reporter what I thought was an amusing pig story—about the shoat I bought from another woman in another town. The facts were that I bought this particular pig one afternoon and paid for it, telling the woman I would call for it on my way back. I arrived about seven o'clock. Out came the woman from whom I had bought it. "You'll have to pay a quarter more," she said. "I had to give it supper."

With grain about a cent a pound, this was a steep price, but I paid it, took the shoat home and put it in the pen. I wouldn't have believed it possible, but that pig got out. Next morning he was gone. We hunted everywhere and at last advertised for the vagrant pig. About a week later he was reported in captivity fully three miles from home. He had gone through a regular wilderness to get there. At last we got him back and put him in a pen from which he couldn't escape. But in the meantime our lost pig had caused a lot of commotion.

The reporter to whom I told this story inadvertently used it with the picture of my parishioner taken beside her pigs. Underneath was printed "The Source of All the Trouble." Someone promptly sent her the clipping. Next time I stopped in at that house, I was met by a perfect cloudburst. "So I'm the source of all the trouble around here, am I?" she demanded. "You needn't worry. I certainly won't be the source of any more trouble *at your* church."

My explanation seemed to make matters worse. Next trip down I took the reporter with me and let him face the music, which increased mightily in volume as he was sighted coming up the walk. No appeasement on his part had any effect whatever. A long time after this episode, she came to church, but things were never the same again.

When one stayed overnight in these old farmhouses in the winter, some forethought had to be given to the trifling matter of keeping from freezing. It takes skill to keep warm on a bitter cold night with one feather bed under you and another one over you. Feathers are apt to run around in a bed tick like juice in a cherry pie. You put one over yourself and begin to doze off. Then you dream you are putting ice in the ice house, your feet are soaked in ice water, and you have a belt of icicles around your waist. All the feathers have run off either side of the bed, and you have just a rope of ticking across you. You pull it up on the bed again, and it makes a haycock pile of feathers over, your stomach, but it has rippled down the sides once more by the time you start a second catnap.

When your hostess suggests that you hang your overcoat in the hallway, it is wise to tell her that you will take it upstairs to your room where "it will be in no one's way" and where—you do *not* tell her—it will keep the shivers out of your bones. If you are fortunate enough to stay in a room on the first floor, you can usually open a door leading toward a stove and thus keep warm.

The talk of quiet restful nights in the country can be overdone. I remember a spring night after one of our parties when I got settled down in bed by one o'clock, and almost at once a whippoorwill decided to perch in a tree right by my window, and go through his throat exercises. I began to count and, honest to goodness, he shouted "whippoorwill" 756 times. Now I like to hear the whippoorwill within reason, but that next day I would not have paused beneath an orchard bough to listen to one, if the branch were breaking under its weight of ripe Macintoshes.

In my early days at Killingworth I often stayed with Harry Blatchley, a warden of the church. His hospitality was as expansive as his family—a wife and nine children. The rooms were cheery and homelike, and no bed here ever needed an overcoat blanket. These comforts for me, and a warm barn for the horse, made it a really good place to stay overnight.

Mr. Blatchley and I got talking about fishing one morning at the breakfast table. I told him that I hadn't been fishing that year, so he urged me to go to Bristol's meadow, right in front of the church, where I might catch a few trout. We got some worms, went down to the church, opened up the building, and then went over the fence to fish. We failed to get a single fish of any kind, although I believe I did get one slight nibble. Of course, we left the brook in plenty of time to get ready for the services, to ring the bell, and have things in shape generally. But as chance would have it, a reporter got wind of the fact that I had gone fishing on a Sunday. He wrote up the incident for a Hartford paper, saying that I had gone fishing on the way to church, and had become so interested in the trout that I had forgotten all about the service, finally rushing in half an hour late, to throw my fish pole into the back pew, put my fish basket beside it, mount the pulpit and preach a wonderful sermon. When the wardens took a peak inside the basket and saw it filled with speckled beauties, they forgave the minister for being tardy.

This was taken up by papers all over the country. One minister wrote from West Virginia, and enclosed a clipping. "I know this cannot be true said he, "but, to assure my people, will you not write me a letter to that effect? If they really thought it were true, I fear a large part of my congregation would quit."

I wrote to this man that I certainly did go fishing on Sunday, and that if the attachment of these members to his church was so weak as to be affected by my actions, then he had better let them go, as they were not worth keeping anyway. But from Ohio came a pastoral call on the strength of the fishing episode. The men of this particular parish thought I was just the minister they wanted. They would guarantee me good fishing, for there were plenty of brooks around there, and all well stocked.

About the same time the papers got hold of another incident and soon Killingworth was labeled the "Rocking Chair Church," because of old Mrs. Emily Pervis Nettleton who lived in a little farmhouse four miles from the church but had refused to attend a service for thirty years. The woman who took care of her belonged to our church, so one day I went over with the car and persuaded Mrs. Nettleton to leave her fireside and join us. She was badly crippled with rheumatism and I could see she was uncomfortable in the old-fashioned church pew. So it occurred to me to bring down a comfortable old-fashioned rocking chair for her use. You should have seen how the old lady enjoyed the service after that! She had never been baptized, so I baptized her at the age of eighty-eight, and then she went back to rocking herself in comfort by the stove. She had her dinners in church from then on and got great pleasure out of this weekly expedition.

Later, in another church, I noticed a woman swaying back and forth, trying to put her fretting baby to sleep. So I got a rocking chair for her, too. The papers took notice of all this and said that I had substituted rocking chairs for pews in my missions, that I urged the women to bring their fancywork and knitting, and that croquet sets adorned the lawns of my churches. When people read this, it created quite a stir. A few of the very orthodox wrote to the Bishop saying that they would give no more funds for local missionary work if this sort of thing were to go on in mission churches. A good share of my salary came from the Diocesan Missionary Society. But I was merely trying to humanize the church—to make it fit the people instead of having the people fit the church.

Bishop Brewster sent me some of their letters and suggested, as I recall it, "that I leave one or two pews in sight, just for old custom's sake." Although I do not pretend to say that I have always been at peace with my bishops, I must say that Bishop Brewster and I got along well. When things were dark and I was encountering much opposition, he came to my support, attended one of our unorthodox services and had dinner with us in the church.

I have worked under three bishops in Connecticut—Chauncey B. Brewster, E. Campion Acheson and Frederick G. Budlong—and because I am on the missionary basis and am paid by the diocese, my relationship is slightly different from that of the rector in his own parish. Bishop Acheson also paid a visit to Killingworth when my methods were under fire, and it was obvious that they made him uncomfortable. But after the service I said to him:

"Did you see that family of eight with their mother and father in the front seat?" The Bishop had observed them.

"Well, they walked three miles to get here, and they must walk three miles to get home, the youngest being drawn in a hand cart. They have little enough to eat when they get there. Would you give them a bite in the church, or would you send them over the hill afoot with empty stomachs?"

"It would be a shame," the Bishop conceded. "By all means give them something to eat."

But Bishop Acheson was used to wealthy city churches and it was hard for him to comprehend the meaning and purpose of many of the things I did in the country. On the whole, we got along fairly well, but now and again there were ructions. His whole training and upbringing were so different from mine that it was difficult for us to find mutual understanding. One time things came to a head when he made some disparaging remark about me and my work at a church luncheon. Two of my good friends in the ministry happened to be present—Dr. Lewis, of Waterbury, and William B. Lusk, of Ridgefield. They went to bat for me there and then, and ever after that the Bishop had a different attitude toward me and my work. He let me alone. That was fine. That was all I wanted.

When Bishop Budlong came along as coadjutor, Bishop Acheson, in discussing the various clergy in the diocese with him, finally reached me. "The only thing to do with that fellow," he said, "is to let him alone. You can't do anything with him. You can't change him. I tried it and got nowhere. Just let him alone."

Bishop Budlong has never found fault with any of my strange ideas, although he didn't like my going into politics and indeed asked me not to. In any event, as soon as I had done what I thought I could do in that field, I stepped out, for I wasn't a politician at heart. I was essentially a preacher. I feel the same way about my parishes. When I have built one up and have done all I can in it, then I am ready to go on somewhere else. I like to see things moving.

I got into plenty of hot water in and out of the diocese about the time of the Russian Revolution, when Berkeley Divinity School invited a lecturer to give a talk on the new Bolshevik government. A reporter from *The Middletown Press* went to see the Dean about it. He was treated rather curtly and next day his paper blazoned headlines reading

"Berkeley Divinity School a Spawning Place for Bolshevism" The whole town was stirred up, and the excitement was intense. I took the stand that all this fuss was a lot of tomfool nonsense. A hearing was staged in the town hall, with a judge sitting unofficially as arbiter. I considered it a silly proceeding. The paper reported that I attended the hearing "with a copy of *The Nation* sticking out of my overcoat pocket." This made it perfectly evident in those excitable days that I was not only a liberal in religion, but a radical politically—a dangerous combination.

When a new minister was called to the Episcopal Church in Middletown, he was duly warned by the Suffragan Bishop of the diocese to have nothing to do with me. With the exception of a few ministers I was thumbs down in the whole diocese. But Lusk, Lewis and Ernest DeF. Miel, of Hartford, all prominent clergymen, stood by me from the beginning. They invited me to speak before their men's clubs, and to preach to their congregations. They fought for my cause with all comers—bishops, priests or deacons.

The east could be no farther from the west than the archdeacon of Middlesex County and I were on our methods of running a mission. He was my immediate superior in the diocese and this was awkward, for the sparks flew every time we got together. One day he sent for me to come to his study, and there he hauled me over the coals. It wasn't a pleasant interview. He went into the question of vestments—I didn't wear them often enough. I didn't use my prayer book enough. My stereopticon lantern was a "flash in the pan." I didn't leave it at home enough. And the crazy coffee pot idea—I didn't let that cool off enough.

He never mentioned what I might be doing with boys and girls, with the young and old, with the poor and the sick. Instead, he ran on and on, ignoring these more important aspects of my work. It all struck me as being something worse than tragic. It was comic. When he stopped, I just laughed right out loud. That was too much for him.

"Get out of here," he cried, "and never come into this place again while I am here."

Of course you can argue with an archdeacon. You can tell him that what he says isn't true. You can even use that short and ugly word to him, but if you laugh at him, look out. That is the limit of insult.

I kept pegging away at my job, however, regardless of the kicking around that I got. The clergy listened to me at the diocesan conventions and laughed at my stories. I could see that many of them were gradually swinging around to approval of my way of doing things. More and more I was asked to preach around the diocese and for several years I preached in the Cathedral of Hartford. However much trouble I had inside the church, I always felt that I had the laity with me. There was never any doubt of that. They have an eye for results, and little patience with haggling over methods.

A few years after my set-to with the archdeacon, I was elected to the executive council of the Diocese of Connecticut by a majority of one vote. Since then just about everything that I can handle has come my way. Where once I stood trembling on the carpet, I now lounge in the seats of the mighty. No longer do wrathful archdeacons banish me from their presence, for I have even been my own archdeacon, working for myself, reporting to myself, bossing myself—how handy! I have also been with the Department of Missions, deputy to the New England Synod, and the requests I get to speak are more than I can accommodate.

Chapter IX

THE FARM

. . . .

FARM life gets into your bones once you've lived on the land, for it's a way of life and not just an occupation. When one has been at it for twenty years there's no escape from it, and my own life has always been close to the land. Even in my college days there never was a time when I wouldn't lend a hand in the hay field, and preaching has never kept me from being in close touch with the farmer.

Sometimes the question comes up of how much farming a country minister should do. In the little parishes in the old days most of the local resident ministers had small farms which they ran in conjunction with their parsonages. They worked with the farmers round about, driving teams of oxen, getting up wood piles with them, and bringing in the harvest together. There isn't so much of this sort of thing now and, of course, if the parish is large, it can be argued that the minister should not spend his time this way. But it's a great link between church and rural parishioner.

We had rented a house in Middletown for seven years, after the rich millowner turned us out of the rectory of Christ Church. During this time we had a fine garden and kept a few hens, which laid very well. Our church work did not take much time during the week, for by staying at a place for four or five hours on Sunday, the equivalent of the pastoral call was made in reverse order—the parishioners called on me. (At Killingworth I never found out for seven years where the senior warden lived.)

Right through this period Moms and I both yearned for the land, so at last we began to look for a place. We had considered one or two when we read of the death of the owner of a farm not far from where we lived. I had often had mission services in that section and knew the people well, so I went to see the widow. She thought she would sell the farm—$3,500 for twenty-three acres of land, a good house and excellent outbuildings. As I approached the place on foot, I kept my eyes open. Father had told us many times: "If ever you buy a house, boys, look well to the cellar and the underpinning. And if ever you buy a farm, look well to the water supply—a farm with stock takes an awful lot of water."

I saw at once that there was a brook right back of the barn, and I knew it would never run dry, for it started from the foot of a big reservoir not half a mile away. That brook caught my eye at once. We had one on the old farm at Randolph Center, and many a dam we built there in our boyhood days. There was a good well on our prospective farm and the cellar seemed to be fair—rather damp but it had a drain. No place has everything, even if you spend a lifetime looking for it. We knew it was low ground, but then you can't expect a brook to run on top of a mountain. It always amuses me to see city folks come out to the country insisting on "a farm with a view, and a brook right near the house that will never run dry." It takes the patience of Job to persuade them that brooks don't run up one side of a mountain and down the other.

Before I bought the farm I asked the owner's son how wide the farm was, for I knew its depth. "Why," said he, "if you start hoeing a row of potatoes on a blazing hot day, you'll think it long enough." And he was right. It was forty rods across. Anyway, it suited us. Although Mrs. Gilbert came from Washington, her home was on the outskirts of the city. Fourteenth Street then was not so urban as it is today. Her family had a pig, cows and chickens, as she called them—we called them hens in Vermont. So she was not only willing but glad to get out in the open country. Our children were growing older. We needed space and outdoor interests for them, so Moms packed up joyfully and at last we were ready to move. I drew three hundred dollars from the bank to make a down payment. It was about all we had laid aside, and Moms' bad knee in a way had got that for us. Soon after our wedding she stepped on a rotten plank at the railroad station and twisted her knee. She collected $350 for this injury. Later she received a legacy, and I had some life insurance fall due, with which we made payments amounting to about $2,500. The first year the taxes were $35. Now we pay more than $135, but we have better roads and better schools, and we have things pretty much as we like them around the place. By an eight-hour system—eight hours of work in the morning, eight hours from noon on—and much scrimping, we worked off the rest.

The day of moving was one to remember. I went ahead to receive the family. We had borrowed a lumber wagon and hitched our horse to it, making three trips altogether. I can still see the last load coming up the hill to the farmhouse. On the driver's seat sat Moms with two of the boys—young George and Closson. Back of them rode Shelley, hanging on to the baby carriage that held Sit, the family name for Mary Virginia, our only daughter. That carriage, by the way, is in our attic now, after being used for the transportation of five little Gilberts, and it's just as good as new. That's the way Moms is with the family possessions.

Speaking of carriages reminds me of the time I advertised for a few to give to needy mothers. Moms didn't know I had put that ad in the paper, and one day she came home and found four baby carriages lined up on her front porch. She said she simply wouldn't have this array on the front porch, so I trundled them around to the woodshed. Next day I drove nineteen miles into the country to give one to a mother, and ten days later I baptized her baby in my church. Even a baby carriage may become the chariot of the Lord.

Well, when our equipage drew up at the door of the farmhouse which was to become our permanent home, we somehow knew that we had a lot of work ahead of us. And how we slaved on that farm during the next few years! It didn't have a single fence, and the land was run down. At the start we sold butter and buttermilk, cream, eggs and lambs. Moms made from ten to twelve pounds of butter a week and disposed of it all. The blankets we have on our beds were made from the wool of our own sheep. One year we had cloth made from our sheep's wool and we all had suits of it.

Mentioning buttermilk reminds me of the time I decided to take a can of buttermilk to a sick friend in

Hartford. When I went to get off the trolley, right across from the old state house, I had so many things to carry that I asked a man to help me. "Will you carry the can (a six-quart one) and hand it to me at the door? I asked.

He willingly complied. But instead of grasping the bale of the can, he took hold of the cover. Holding it aloft, he came down to the platform where the conductor was standing. Just then the cover came off the can with a kerplunk. The can hit the floor right side up and a stream of buttermilk shot up and took that conductor right under the chin. Then the can tipped over, its contents running along the platform, down the steps and into the car rail groove for nearly a block.

I found that the more I worked on my farm the better I got along with my church work. Putting in less time on sermons and more on hoeing helped rather than hindered my chosen work. The farmers and I had everything in common. We sang hymns, prayed, went to Holy Communion together, observed the Old Testament *Agape* in unison and then farmed together in spirit during the week. It was glorious. It still is. I wouldn't swap it for all the city churches in the universe.

As we had a brook and a good deal of water, we went in for geese. We bought a gander from a family that had moved up from New Jersey. His name was Jerry and no one knew whence he came, except that he had been raffled off in a saloon. Whether he learned his evil tricks in that environment or elsewhere I don't know, but he had plenty of them. Yet one couldn't help liking him—he was so plaguy smart. We wondered who kept leaving the gate open and letting all the animals into the pasture. One day we set a watch over it. A latch opened on one side by pulling a string. Old Jerry, the villain, led his flock right up to the gate, calmly took hold of the string and raised the latch.

Could the Faith be defended as well as he defended his two wives, there never would be a heresy trial. One day a city chap came out to buy a goose. Jerry's favorite spouse was then setting on a nest full of eggs, with Jerry standing guard night and day. I told our visitor that if he would crawl in and get the setting goose, he could have her and the eggs. He deployed, and I could see right off that Jerry's strategy was an attack from the rear.

The city man never got his goose.

One day we heard a terrible yell from the front yard. Old Jerry had Closson, aged four, by the seat of the pants and the child was running for his life toward the house, with the goose firmly attached to him. As Jerry grew older, we had to keep him shut up in a yard behind the house, for no stranger could approach if the gander saw him first.

We enjoyed our geese, and they made perfect Christmas presents for all our city relations. But as my church work grew, and there was less time to fuss with goslings, we gave them up altogether. They were often troublesome and the city visitors who came out didn't seem to relish the nocturnal parades they staged, with Jerry marching ahead and calling the tune. We let them go with deep regret.

The family from whom we bought Jerry in the first place eventually came out and took a farm for themselves. It was a wretched place, without even a garden plot. As they knew nothing about farming, their case soon became desperate and I had to look after them. The agent who sold them their miserable piece of ground took them out to look at it in the dead of winter. All over it were large mounds covered with snow. When the innocents asked him what the hillocks were, he replied, "Why, they're haystacks. That's hay under the snow. This farm has such rich land that you just can't begin to get the hay into the barn."

It seems incredible that anyone would have accepted this interpretation of snow-covered dirt and rocks. As a matter of fact, the whole farm didn't have enough hay to keep a goat, or, as Father used to say, "enough to wipe your scythe so you can whet it." The only thing they could get off that land was firewood.

What will God do with the souls of real-estate agents?

I got the man a job on another farm, and the daughter a position with the Goodyear Rubber Company.

After that they got along all right. The whole family chippered up. One of the girls was confirmed by the Bishop and the oldest boy went back to the city and became a plumber. Later a relative died in Australia and left them considerable money. Now they often drive out to look at their "farm," riding in a better car than I ever owned or ever expect to own.

The farmer needs protection from a number of pests, and I put the high-pressure salesman at the top of the list. His technique is one of the hardest things one has to fight in a country parish, where the gullible fall hook, line and sinker for the instalment racket. To impress on my people the folly of listening to these persuasive fellows, I often tell the story of the salesman who went to a farmer who owned one cow, and before he was through with him sold him two milking machines and then took the cow for the first down payment on the machines.

One family that I was interested in sank themselves entirely by listening to these insidious fellows. The man was getting compensation for injuries he had sustained in an elevator in New York, and was using it to pay forty dollars a month on a tidy little place near Middletown. He had plenty of grass and he needed a cow and a pig, so I thought I would help him get his stock.

I was invited to speak before a Jewish club in New Haven about that time and I thought to myself, "This is no place to hit them for a pig, but I'll tackle them on a cow." So I described the family, passed around the hat and got forty-four dollars toward a cow. Soon cow and halter were installed on the farm. Things went along nicely at first. The woman worked out a little and they seemed to be making a go of it. I left greatly encouraged about this family, until I went down one day and found the birds singing, the cow out grazing, the chickens clucking in the yard, but the old Colonial clapboard house practically ruined. Roofers had come up from New Haven and talked them into covering the sides of the house with stripped green shingles. The bill for this was $172.

I never got them on their feet again. They kept running behind. The cow was sold. The chickens were sold. The woman went off and the children scattered. All their trouble began from the wretched instalment system. I wonder why the Chambers of Commerce don't take it up. Certain ethics are involved in selling things to people for which they can't pay. These fellows come to my own house, telling me that my roof leaks when it doesn't, that my mailbox needs painting, when it has just been done, that my chimney needs fixing, when I'm very well pleased with it, and what business is it of theirs, anyway? I shut them up fast and send them on their way, but the city people who have settled on the land, and who have never owned property before, are apt to fall for their wily line of talk.

At one time or another we have had all sorts of animals on the farm, even a Shetland pony and an Angora goat, but now we confine ourselves to sustenance farming. We have a horse and enough hens to supply the table with eggs and chickens. We generally raise two pigs every summer, and smoke our own ham and bacon. We have our own beef and we sometimes can thirty or forty jars of it. When we kept sheep we had sheep bakes every year, but we gave them up because with sheep the ground soon becomes infected and they need to be moved around. Our land is not extensive enough for that.

We keep this up partly as an example to our parishioners. I want them to raise things for the food they eat themselves. I urge them to have pigs and smoke their own bacon, but I can't insist on this if I don't do it myself. I have to have my alfalfa and clover looking good and no weeds in the fence rows. When the farmers come up for picnics we compare notes. I have made a point of keeping abreast of rural conditions all over the country, both because of my genuine interest in farming and because I think it helps my ministry. When the Farm Bureau was first started nearly thirty years ago, I was immediately asked to become one of the directors of the bureau in Middlesex County. This gave me a chance to offer practical advice to my parishioners. I served in this capacity for about ten years until things were so organized that some one else could carry on. After all, I was primarily a preacher and I felt I shouldn't give so much of my time to it.

In my early days in the country I gave out market prices to help my parishioners. Along the back roads people had no idea what their produce was worth and they needed guidance. When the buyers came around the small farmers often were terribly defrauded. What they got for their eggs, potatoes and particularly for their veal calves, was a shame. So I started the custom of giving market reports before, during or after the church service. I told them what their eggs were worth and I urged them to sell their veal calves by weight instead of by lumping them off. I remember one buyer expressing great surprise when he came down to get his eggs and was stalled off by a farm woman. "I can't sell my eggs today," she told him. "I don't know what they're worth. I'll tell you after Sunday." "But what difference will Sunday make?" he demanded.

"The minister will be down and he'll tell us what they're worth," she said.

This is no longer necessary because now there are state market reports, so I merely tell the farmers to get hold of them and to watch the prices for themselves. The rural scene has changed greatly in Connecticut since those days. Where once we had the native American farmer I now minister to all nationalities. I have had Bohemians, Germans, Swedes, Poles, Italians, Lithuanians, Irish, English, Scotch, French and even Indians. The young people from these families don't want to stay on the farms any longer. As soon as they finish with school, the girls go to work in factories, or as mothers' helpers. Once they get used to town life they refuse to come back to their parents' little farms. The result is that young people are getting scarce along the country back roads. And the little country schools where we used to find them are folding up at a great rate, as the children get transported in busses to the consolidated schools. I used to show my magic lantern pictures in eight or ten schoolhouses, but today these are about all closed up. While the young people from my region work in factories making cold cream, typewriters, rubber boots, brake linings, electrical supplies, toys, hammocks, webbing for Venetian blinds and so forth, their parents do small sustenance farming and engage in the rather limited economic trinity of burning charcoal, making Christmas wreaths and picking huckleberries.

Between the migration of the native American farmer and the influx of city residents who keep on making over Connecticut farmhouses and throwing cocktail parties on Sunday, the rural church is not the flourishing institution it ought to be. There will have to be some redistribution of the land before things get straightened out. I'm very much of a Socialist and I believe in public ownership of utilities. I have belonged for years to the Public Ownership League of America and I think that the old theory of rugged individualism has entirely broken down. The cry against government intervention in industry and farming is the bunk. There has to be government intervention when it comes to such things as crops. There must be some relation between what the people consume and what is raised for their consumption.

The trouble with the farmer is that if he does well one

year with a certain crop, then he and all his neighbors go in for it in a big way the following year, producing blindly, without any thought of what is to become of the surplus. People can eat only so much, and if they have no chance to export their stuff, what happens? The market is ruined.

Anyway, farmers are never content. Father was typical of the species, whether you find them in Vermont, Connecticut or Kansas. I always preach contentment to them. Why not be content? I ask them again and again from the pulpit. There are other ways of making life expansive and beautiful besides by wealth. I keep battering away at this thought. Of course, I think a terrible struggle is on to get back for the people the free use of the natural resources of the land.

When the depression was at its worst I was on the charity committee of the common council of Middletown. The town owned some land on the outskirts that was not being used, so I proposed allowing the jobless men to turn it into gardens. It was within walking distance of town. I sent to Vermont for the seed potatoes. Plots were staked out and numbered and we had about 125 of these gardens. Prizes were given for the best effects and a Negro walked off with the first prize. I got frankfurters and rolls gratis from the bakeries and shops, and we staged a hot dog roast at the gardens, with the mayor and the members of the council in attendance. Toward the close of the year I invited all the amateur gardeners out to my own farm for a picnic and supper. I butchered a sheep myself, skinned it and made a perfectly enormous lamb stew. We used huge kettles (I'm always surrounded by plenty of these) and again the bakers furnished the rolls. We had swimming, boating, pitching horseshoes and plenty of fun.

There is always something going on at the farm. We have enough kitchen equipment of one kind and another to sink a small cruiser, and we are used to handling large crowds at mealtimes just as we are in our churches. Our big lazy Susan has twirled the butter, bread and salt on our dinner table for a goodly throng in its time. I like to break bread with folks of all kinds. The farm is as lovely in summer as it is cold in winter. You never would suspect the mean dives the mercury can take when you sit by the lily pool on a June day, nor would you think that the pond was once an old hen yard, converted to beauty by the use of some secondhand boiler pipe and a lot of family elbow grease. Moms can look right out of the window as she kneads bread or works out a batch of butter and see these floating lilies, with big frogs sunning themselves on the pads and goldfish swimming all around.

I'm very proud of that lily pond. I've always liked to fish and as far back as I can remember I've been crazy about a pond, so when I got to wondering one day what I could do with that old hen yard suddenly I thought of pond lilies and how I had always longed for them. Father never would bother with flowers in Vermont. A garden to him was a place to grow good filling vegetables, and not rows of flowers. Anyway, the pond lily is a fine bloom to raise if you have water. You don't have to hoe or water it.

Closson did most of the work digging out the hen yard and laying the boiler pipe that I bought secondhand at ten cents a foot. You need soft mud for the lily roots and rather stagnant water, so it doesn't do to clean out the pond too thoroughly—they thrive on decaying matter. But my lilies no longer come out as well as they should. The first sign of trouble came when I noticed that the pool leaked. I found the leak, fussed around and stopped it, but the lilies came up poorly next season and didn't look right. Then one of my neighbors, who is a great trapper, woodsman and hunter, let drop that he was down at Conrad Moller's place trapping muskrats, because they had been eating lily roots over there. I had suspected all the time that the leak in my pond was made by muskrats, as I knew they lived on roots. To make matters worse they seemed to do the most damage to my lemon-colored lilies, which are my special pride. The yellow blooms had always been quite rugged and would blossom as late as October 20, but after the muskrats got busy the lemon ones scarcely came up at all and didn't blossom till midsummer, but the white and pink ones still continued to thrive. The yellow ones have big heavy roots and I think the muskrats favored them. The little pests come along in winter under the ice and dig right through to keep under water. I often notice the drag of their tails in the snow. They will eat out a dam as easily as not. Some people put in half-inch mesh wire when they build a dam in order to stop them. It took forty bags of cement to make a wall to check them over in our big pond. I was none too well-off at the time I spent fifty dollars on this, but I felt afterwards that I had never put money to better use, because it had a profound effect on the boys, who never have ceased to get pleasure from our swimming pool. It took us years to get it in shape, but it is a never-failing source of interest, conversation and fun at the Gilbert farm.

The big pond is about 200 feet long and 60 feet wide.

We had to dam up our brook, just as we used to do in Vermont, and with pretty much the same results at first—the rains would come, the floods would flow, the dam would be washed away. Remembering how many times this happened in my boyhood, after one washout on my own farm, I decided that we must dig the hole aside from the main channel of the brook; otherwise it would soon fill up with mud. We started digging on the flat near the brook and we worked on it off and on for ten years. The pond from the first took its place as one of the most important activities of the farm. Its enlargement, care and use were discussed as much as the crops. Just as the boys helped me with corn, potatoes and hay, so I helped them with the pond. Sometimes we used wheelbarrows, but most of it was done with horse and scraper. Help came from an unexpected source when the neighbors found that it was a fine place to cut their ice. Instead of going farther afield, they came to our place, often with two horses and a big scraper, and between one thing and another the hole steadily grew bigger and deeper until it reached its present proportions.

It has provided good swimming and skating for the whole neighborhood. We can see it from any part of the farm, and it has always had a heartening effect on us. When the boys were growing up it was good to look down at that water waiting for us at the end of a hot day's work. Sometimes we would knock off half an hour early so as to have a swim before supper. And the endless happy discussions we would have about that pond! "Well, I see the pond is very full this morning," or "The pond seems low—do you think it has sprung a little leak?" That would be in summer, and in winter the fruitful speculation would go on—"Is the pond smooth for skating today?" "How thick is the ice?"

No long cedar posts or planks around the place were too good to use for diving apparatus. We always have a row boat on the pond, and visitors think there ought to be fish in it, but fishing and a good swimming pond do not go together. Even with the brook running in, it will fill up with mud at the bottom and for good swimming, of course, it has to be cleared out. Fish require weed growth. Where my pond is concerned, I am willing to let the suckers go. I can get my fishing elsewhere, but the pond is the pride of the farm. We have a fireplace beside it and seats where we can all gather for outdoor meals in summer.

Everything about the place has been built up with the help of our boys. The amount of farming a country minister can do is often influenced by the number of children he has, and their ages. When our boys were in high school they had time to help around the farm, and it did them good. Children will do better in their studies if they get plenty of outdoor exercise. All my children seem to enjoy the farm, but I have never believed that the young should be sent out to work alone in the hot sun. I can remember only too well my own boyhood days.

We have always found it a good thing to talk over the work of the day at the breakfast table—what had best be done after school, on Saturday, or during the vacation. Sometimes the boys would say that it was pretty hot to hoe or do a cement job. Then we would plan something else for that day. Thus it has always been a partnership matter. And I never forget that a boy is always hungry, sometimes terribly so, about eleven in the forenoon. Forenoons on a farm somehow seem a great deal longer than afternoons. How hungry I used to get when I worked over at Ralph Hodges during haying time, as a boy of fifteen! I had breakfast at six, then walked more than a mile across lots, then did a regular man's work until noon—although only a lanky growing boy. The last hour or so was sheer agony. Fortunately, my children always had good dinners and plenty of food. Usually the boys and I took something up in the lot with us—sandwiches or crackers, with homemade grape or elderberry juice. Fifteen minutes in the shade and something to eat at the end of the row made a tremendous difference in the forenoon slack.

I shall never forget the look on little Clossie's face as he straightened up his back one day over the potato row and said, "After we get 'em picked up, are you going to give 'em all away?" The fact was, I gave away so many potatoes to the poor that even Clossie hated to pick up potatoes he knew he'd never eat. Moms always begins to fret a little around midwinter, lest the bin we have won't hold out, But it always does. The earth is bountiful, if one gives it a little care.

Chapter X

HUMANIZING A CHURCH

. . . .

AFTER I had been doing real open country church work for many years, the chance came in 1924 to take over Epiphany, a village church in the old settlement of Durham, six miles from home. It was on the point of closing and the Sunday school was down to four children. I thought of it only as a side line and did not expect to run it for more than a few months, but it has been stirring with activity ever since, and during one year of the depression we served as many as two thousand meals in the church on Sundays without a cent of collection.

The church, poised on a hill, was built when this region was alive with native industries that have vanished before the encroachment of the factory. In or around the hamlet one could once find a spinning wheel shop, a grist mill and a comb shop. Flax and sheep were raised on the farms and cloth was manufactured in the homes. There was a large farming community too, and the Concord coaches used to pass through the village every day. It was known originally as Coginchang, an Indian name meaning Long Swamp. The first settler was Caleb Seaward, who established a home there in 1699. Five years later the name of the village was changed to Durham. Today the population is 900 and there are three churches in the old hamlet, whose houses, churchyard and roads are reminiscent of its history, and a touch of its early nomenclature remains in such signposts as Goat Hill, Haddam Quarter, Hogpen Brook, Feeding Hill and Great Swamp.

The church, a beautiful little building with architectural features copied from English sources, was built in 1862. When I first stepped into it and looked around I realized that it had equipment not usually found in the country church—stained-glass windows, high brass candlesticks, a tall cross, a costly short cross, brass vases, silver-plated candlesticks, an engraved communion set and a fine pipe organ with an electric blower. My practical eye also observed that it had chairs that would not fold and extension tables that nearly filled the parish house and could not be packed away. This church had just about everything one could think of, with one important exception—folks. Of men, women, children, babies and grandmothers, it had practically none. How many churches are in the same predicament, with buildings and furniture guarded and galvanized against the wear and tear of the weather and rowdy children!

I went to work to see if I could humanize this church, and run it according to the God-given nature of the common folk instead of by ecclesiastical canons and regulations. Taking over this village parish, I soon found plenty of children in a neighborhood two miles away. I called around a bit, did some hair-cutting among the children, helped a man with his haying, and then gave a party at one of the houses. As it was shortly after the Fourth of July, I had some fireworks—bombs, skyrockets and sparklers. The boys made ice cream. We produced the old stereopticon lantern, slides, a curtain, and a box of hymnals with which to close the party. I announced that my car would come down the following Sunday, if anyone wanted to attend Sunday school. It did, and came back with thirteen in it besides the driver. Children sprouted all over it. One was sitting on the engine hood.

Then I went exploring other roads, and found children who never went to church. One day I ran across a real houseful—two families huddled together. I happened to have with me some frankfurters, a pot of cocoa and several loaves of bread. We had lunch first, then I produced the stereopticon and showed my pictures. We got more done in that community than in the one where I had the firecracker party. Sometimes we picked up as many as twenty passengers in our old seven-passenger Buick. Fifteen years ago, it was an unheard of thing for a minister to go out on Sunday morning and bring in children and grownups. Now many ministers are doing the good shepherd act by driving people to service and taking them home. In country parishes it is downright difficult for the very poor to get to church, when they live out of easy walking range. People won't walk two miles to church or school any more. They can't anyway—too much danger from autos. The old churchgoing ardor is a thing of the past, and the minister has to meet this as best he can, if he wishes to reach the people who most need his help.

Although church horse sheds are disappearing rapidly throughout the countryside, the church at Durham happens to have some good strong ones, so I decided to put them to practical use. I put in swings for the children—one in each horse and buggy stall—and built a strong back stop for softball playing, just outside. I had the sheds wired so that the children could see to swing when services were held in the evening. In vacation time the village children make this a playground, and for many years a tennis court on the church grounds was in constant use.

Because Epiphany was six miles from our home, and we usually went on to another church for afternoon service, we decided to have our midday meal in the church. Many of the children we had brought in stayed with us at first. Then gradually the older people adopted the custom, and began bringing in their own eatables with them. When we had Sunday school at four o'clock and an evening service at seven, forty or fifty children would stay to supper. To feed this many is not so difficult as it seems. We take two large pans of baked beans, a big kettle of cocoa, and plenty of bread. With this and the food brought in by the parishioners, we always have plenty to eat. The young people enjoy doing the dishes together, while the smaller children play outside. After the dishes are done, there is ample time for choir rehearsal. We give birthday parties with cake and candles for anyone whose birthday falls during the week.

But we had not gone far with our humanizing efforts before we ran smack into church tradition and the outraged feelings of some of the ladies of the parish. Epiphany, like many another church, had been existing on expensive church suppers. Now it is my firm belief that pay suppers, and indeed any sort of church function with a fee attached to it, create obstacles to reaching the people that the church was primarily meant to reach. True, quite a bit of money may be taken in at these ticket suppers, and it helps the church exchequer, but the poor with their big families are forced to stay out in the cold.

I always remember the night that I stopped with my own family for a church supper. We were driving along in the old open Model T Ford and we decided to stop because it was dark and we were quite far from home. We stepped into a vestibule in the basement of a church and a voice said curtly, "$2.45 please." I did some quick calculation and found that we were being charged thirty-five cents apiece, including our nursing baby, who was at the moment sound asleep. I pointed to the infant. "Thirty- five cents for that one?" I asked.

"Certainly," said the woman selling tickets. We couldn't very well back out then, so I paid thirty- five cents for a nursing baby who was asleep, and for three other children under twelve.

I have seen women going home from a church supper— not my church—with heavy baskets on their arms, while hungry little children connected with that church stood around on the steps with their mouths watering. Never so much as a bone or a crumb was offered them. Then too, I have seen a church put on a fine musical entertainment with a thirty-five cent admission charge. The building would not be half filled, and poor children belonging to the Sunday school of that same church would be standing outside trying to hear a bit of music through the cracks. Yet people wonder why the poor and the underprivileged don't crash the church doors for morning service!

"Well, I can't run a church that way," a minister's wife said to me. "You know, we have so few older boys and young men in our church. My husband has a fine boys' club with twelve or fourteen boys. The ladies are having one of their regular suppers next Tuesday night. How I should like to have those boys come to that supper and sit around a table of their own!"

"You have plenty of room for an extra table?" I asked.

"Oh, yes, plenty."

"Plenty of food?" I queried.

"Oh, yes. There's always a lot left over. But do you think I dare mention such a thing to those ladies—not in this church!"

What a pity! I feel that eating together is something of a sacrament and the fellowship it fosters is a fine Christian thing. It has been my experience that a bite to eat after a service keeps the people from going off home in a cold mood and changes the whole atmosphere from stiffness to sociability.

Well, at Durham I found a handful of women who had been running these pay suppers for a good many years. The Ladies' Aid must have had nearly $1,000 in the bank from this source, but as the proceeds from the suppers mounted, the church and Sunday-school attendance dwindled away. It makes me think of the man who stepped up to the receiving window of a bank and said, "Here is some Ladies' Aid money."

The cashier thought he said, "Here is the ladies' hen money." So he answered promptly, "Well, the old hens have done pretty well this winter, haven't they?"

There was no doubt that the ladies of Durham had done very well in this respect. They would telephone all over creation for food of various kinds, and it was up to me to chase about with a car picking it up. But I never had to carry home any that was left over. The women saw to that. I soon realized that the size of the market baskets in which they brought their contributions was out of all proportion to what came in them.

In my simplicity and ignorance I hit on what seemed like a good idea. We had choir rehearsals on Friday nights, so instead of bringing in the members of the choir and letting it go at that, I thought I would corral their younger brothers and sisters too, and have refreshments and games while the older ones were practicing. There was always so much food left over from the suppers that I felt we could afford to treat the youngsters, whose stomachs wouldn't suffer a bit from filling meals of beans and macaroni. So I put an icebox in the basement to store the ice I usually brought for their supper, and asked them to put the leftover food in this icebox but alas! there was no feast for the back country farm boys. Talk about old Mother Hubbard's cupboard! It was a Hotel Astor pantry compared to that box. But it didn't end there. One night I bought a pound of butter at the close of a supper for our own use at home. I put it so far back on a top shelf that one had to stand on a chair to reach it or even see it. When I went to get it, the butter was gone. Someone had taken it home. Butter was high. It had cost me fifty cents.

While these ladies of mine were still hanging on to the pay suppers like grim death, I decided to have some homely meals of our own for my poorer children and their parents. I saw no reason why we couldn't bring our own food, sit down in the parish house, and eat it. There should be no worry or fret ever over a free supper. Indeed, it has long been my practice to read the first part of the fourteenth chapter of St. Luke in church, announcing it as a supper-chapter, and giving directions for a church supper. I like the custom.

Pretty soon the treasured church dishes began to show signs of wear and tear. Now these dishes, I had early discovered, were regarded as sacrosanct. When I first looked into the parish house kitchen I found five dozen pieces of imported old English blue china behind the cupboard doors. The set had been packed away with extreme orderliness—each kind of dish in a place of its own. Not a piece had been nicked off nor a cup handle broken since their purchase twenty-six years earlier. But after our suppers were well under way, it soon became apparent that the dishes were to be an issue. The same hands no longer put them away in the same order. Meat plates and bread and butter plates got jumbled. Soon a couple of cups were nicked and it was even whispered through the church that a handle had been broken off. This was a serious business. Some of the sisters, thoroughly outraged, felt they could no longer worship in a church where the china suffered damage. They felt that these outrageous proceedings should be reported. So they hired a taxi and sped to the Bishop of the diocese to make formal charges against me.

Their main grievance was that I gave free suppers, thus tending to undermine their restaurant and market-basket activities. In addition to that, the cherished dishes were in danger of being damaged, and were not properly rearranged in their own niches in the cupboard. The ultimate allegation was that we had a "common rabble" around the church, sitting right in the pews and tracking up the church carpet.

The Bishop sent for me and stated the case for the prosecution, but a Bishop could hardly hang a man for feeding the poor, and we certainly had to use the china with which to feed them. They could not very well eat off the tables, even though these had been enameled white so that there would be no need for tablecloths. I had also bought ten dollars' worth of cutlery myself to replace any losses that might occur. I was genuinely glad that the Bishop called me in, for it gave me a fine opportunity to tell him about the work, and the families we were helping. One member of the vestry who had favored closing the church before we took hold, became such an enthusiastic supporter that he spent an entire Sunday afternoon interviewing the disgruntled and trying to find out, in face of the miraculous growth in attendance and offerings, just what the trouble was. He never said much about what he learned, but he summed it up in one expressive sentence, "I hope they break every damned cup in the parish house."

Well, our work went on but the pay suppers didn't. We had 95 confirmations and 108 baptisms in the succeeding fifteen years in Durham. And throughout the depression the people ate Sunday after Sunday—averaging around 2,000 meals in one year. We used to take over great pans of beans or beef stew for these really needy people. One time we had 34 men come to visit the church from Beacon Falls. I saw they would be very late for dinner if they went home, so I invited them to stay. The women were quite aghast, but I knew I was safe. We had just put a new water system in the parish house—the pump worked perfectly, and the can of beef stew I had that day went so far that I had some to take home for supper that night.

My congregations are never surprised when I vanish from the pulpit during a hymn. They know what it means. If I hustle and everything goes well, I can pump the water, get on the coffee pot, light the oil stove, put the coffee in a coffee bag and get it in the pot in six lines of a hymn.

One of the most gratifying emotions of my ministry is to see the children gathered around the board in the parish house at Durham on a Sunday night. They sit at the table waiting to sing the doxology and for me to say grace. There is no wild stabbing or spearing. Some of the older girls, who know how to wait, pass things around for these hungry youngsters. Many of them belong to families who have little or no social life. They are never invited out. So it isn't only the food they get but the warm sense of belonging that makes them enjoy these suppers. Among them nearly always is Mrs. George Keithan, who brings most of her brood of eleven to church, where they overflow a pew and tuck in afterwards at a meal that is greatly appreciated. The Keithans live close to a quarry and literally over the railroad tracks. To get to the highway they follow a path down a deep gully, then cross the railroad tracks and climb a steep hill at the other side, a feat Mrs. Keithan has accomplished innumerable times, even when the path was all ice. She has many of the qualities of the pioneer women—a vigorous creature, swinging along with free gait, doing huge washings for her endless brood, trying to keep them fed, clothed, well and comfortable on her husband's meager pay in a steel mill. He used to work in the quarry and $22.50 a week seems like wealth to them.

The Keithans were Roman Catholic and I didn't feel at first that it was my place to go to their home. They are French Canadian and the mother claims to be related to the Dionne family. Certainly some of her children bear striking resemblance to the famous quintuplets. Although I had no contact with them, one day Mrs. Keithan sent word to me that she would like to have our car stop across the tracks to take some of her children to Sunday school. After that I soon found out the misery this family endured and the efforts the mother was making to keep things going, in spite of every inconvenience. Now, no matter what assorted sizes we get in shoes or clothing, we can always send them over to the Keithans, sure that one or other of the youngsters, whose ages range up to fifteen years, will be able to wear them. There is one pair of twins in the family and George, the oldest son, is my altar boy.

When I first came to know them I found the boys trying to cut wood with axes far too big and heavy for them, so I got them smaller axes and helped to keep them sharp. As a practiced wood chopper myself, I always have a keen eye for the merits and uses of an ax. I gave the boys an old tent I had and five or six of them now sleep out in summer, which relieves the congestion in their little house. (I have another parish family whose every member grew up in a small house where they had to go outdoors and climb a wooden stairway to get to their sleeping quarters—a cheerful custom for below-freezing nights!)

In course of time I was able to give the Keithans beds, bedding, two baby carriages, a better wood stove, chairs, a large table, and solid kettles for washing and cooking. These are the things I find that the mothers of large families on the back roads need most. I always prefer to work on a whole family, instead of selecting one member for special aid. It is difficult to give real help if the rest of the family is not in sympathy with what one is doing, and the child singled out for attention is surrounded by a hostile and rather jealous group.

Epiphany, with a hundred communicants, now has a volunteer vested choir of twenty-five, directed by our boy Shelley, who has been organist and choir director of the church for a decade. In addition to the usual divisions of sopranos, altos, tenor and basses, we have a group of boys and girls whose ages range from seven to ten. We bring them to the church in carloads and we make a party of our choir rehearsal. After their work is done the social period begins, usually with a Virginia reel. Shelley plays the piano for this dance, and old and young join in a long crowded line that runs the length of the parish house. Usually I prompt for the old-fashioned dances. Then we play games, or the young people dance to swing music from our radio-record player. This is followed by refreshments, with each family contributing something to the feast. For instance, we have one boy of fourteen who makes most delicious pastry.

But we had ructions in this church choir in the beginning too. Originally there was a choir of fourteen girls, and the women of the church made vestments for them from a pattern which a leading member of the community had brought from a distant city. The cassock, instead of being one whole garment, was made with sleeves, a narrow yoke and a skirt. Over this was worn a cotta. Mrs. Gilbert remarked one day without thinking,

"It's too bad the ladies put so much work into this type of vestment. Pity they didn't make regular cassocks."

That was enough to make the fur fly. The woman who had furnished the pattern turned very nasty. Mrs. Gilbert was running the choir at the time and the outraged parishioner attacked it at every opportunity. Finally Mrs. Gilbert confronted her in open meeting with her innuendoes. The disgruntled lady left the church and never set foot in it again. While we still use some of the old vestments Mrs. Gilbert has made six or seven new sets of the conventional cassock.

Verily, the way of the country preacher is not all milk and honey. The smaller the parish, the more public his life, and venomous tongues assail his ministry. Humanizing a church means hurt feelings too, but the good of the greatest number must be served.

Chapter XI

WEDDINGS

. . . .

ONE wedding service I shall never forget was read by me while the body of the bridegroom's father lay in an adjoining room awaiting burial. It just goes to show the strange demands made on a country minister, and the lights and shadows that can cross his path at one and the same time. On a December day in 1910 I was asked to go down country eighteen miles to conduct the funeral of George Ackerman, who was burned to death when his bed caught fire. The family had only recently come to America. It was bitterly cold when I arrived at the house. I blanketed the horse and went inside. There was the usual funeral set-up always found in these old-fashioned country houses. The coffin and mourners were in one room to the right, and the men and the undertaker were in the kitchen. Opposite the mourning room, or parlor, was the "sittin'" room in which I went to put on my vestments. Just as I had all my vestments on and prayer book in hand, ready to go into the other room and begin the service, young Gerhardt Ackerman, son of the dead man, came up to me and coolly said, "Mr. Gilbert, I want to get married. I gasped. Although I have good underpinnings, my knees weakened a bit, I'll admit "When?" I asked. "In a few weeks?"

"No, I want to be married right away.

"Well then, after we get back from the grave perhaps we can arrange it." "No, no. I want to be married *right now*, before Father is taken out of the house." "Have you got a girl?" I asked, superfluously.

"I'll go and get her."

He stalked out of the parlor and came back a moment later with a husky German girl named Hetwig Erche.

I stared at her, incredulous. "Have you a license to be married in this town?" I demanded.

"Certainly," said Gerhardt, as he pulled out the wedding license from the pocket that also held his father's burial license. He had applied for both at the same time. Why not? He produced a ring and went to find someone who would stand up with him. He had all the fixins necessary, so what could I do? I knew the corpse would wait, although I wasn't so sure of the undertaker, as a good blizzard had started up. However, I turned back the prayer book leaves from the burial service and began, "Dearly beloved, we are gathered here ... to join this man and this woman in holy matrimony."

At the word "matrimony" the undertaker bolted out to see what was the matter with me. An Episcopal minister's daughter in the mourners' room said in a stage whisper, "He's got the wrong place in the prayer book." An old deacon of the Congregational church began to cry out, "What's he saying, what's he saying?"

As the service proceeded, they quieted down and put away their handkerchiefs. But their expressions were a caution when I appeared at the door with the wedding party. For once, the corpse was not the center of interest at a funeral. The bride and groom were. It was hard to get the feeling into the second service that should have been there.

Just as I was leaving, I heard a neighbor's baby cry on the floor above, and I have never forgiven myself for not going up and baptizing it, thus making it a real day's job.

I learned later that there was some purpose in the youth's strange decision to marry Hetwig before his father's body was removed from the house. It seemed that Mr. Ackerman had liked the girl and wanted Gerhardt to marry her, but he had kept putting it off. When the old man died, she came from Brooklyn for the funeral and they decided to carry out his wishes before he was taken from the house. Later they went to Brooklyn to live and I lost sight of them, but eight years later their paths crossed mine again.

I was preaching for the Rev. Frank Morehouse in Shelton, and he told me about finding two little girls sitting on the steps of his church one Sunday morning, waiting for Sunday school to begin. He took them in, talked to them and later called at their home. When he asked the father how they came to turn to his church, which was far from their home, the man said it was because he had been married by an Episcopal minister down in Killingworth. Mr. Morehouse had often heard me speak of the combined marriage and funeral service, so something impelled him to say: "Didn't your father die at the time of your marriage?"

"Yes, and we were married on the same day as the funeral."

They had turned to Episcopalianism after that, and were sending their two little girls to a church that was quite inconvenient for them to reach. I followed the history of these children. Later they were confirmed in that parish and the last I heard of them, both were teaching in the Sunday school.

Another time I drove down to Killingworth for a wedding and got there at four o'clock, the hour set for the ceremony. No one was in sight, so I waited and waited. Five o'clock came, then six, then dusk began to fall. I knew that if the wedding couple finally did show up, I would not be able to see to read the service, so I went to a farmhouse and borrowed a lamp. I can still remember it with its long base and narrow half-inch wick. The woman with her daughter and big black dog returned with me to the church.

At eight o'clock the pair turned up, unattended. By then it was quite dark. I held the lamp in one hand and the prayer book in the other, and we got along all right until the moment came to put on the ring. I had to go back and put the lamp on the altar, return and adjust the ring, then get the lamp again. At the place where the minister joins the hands of bride and groom I had to dispose of the lamp again. The light was so dim that I could scarcely see across the church. Once I caught a glimpse of the big dog, skulking among the pews. It could hardly be described as a brilliant occasion, yet this pair have lived together happily these many years. And they certainly didn't have any heavy wedding bills to give them matrimonial headaches.

One day as I was working out in the hay lot on my farm, a boy came along on his wheel and said that a man where he lived wanted to know if I would come over and marry him.

"Why, probably," I said. "When does he want the wedding—what day?"

"Oh," he said, "any day convenient for you."

"But when? This week? Next week?"

"I don't know. I think some time this week."

"But how about the girl or woman?" I asked. "Where is she?"

"Oh, she's a woman, and she lives right there."

"Did you hear him say anything about having a license?"

"No, but I guess he has one."

"Well, you tell him I'll be over tomorrow afternoon at two o'clock."

When I went over next day the man was out in the fields working. The boy went after him and he came in and stood up in his working clothes and his shirt sleeves, waiting for me to begin. I insisted he put on his coat, although I am no stickler for ceremony. He grumbled but he did it. There were two other women in the house besides the bride, so we brought them in to act as witnesses. The minute the ceremony was over the man threw off his coat and dashed back to his work. He'd lost half an hour.

Another time I was having a perfectly conventional house wedding with everything nicely arranged, when the flustered bridegroom went slightly haywire on my hands. The Episcopal wedding service falls into two parts. The first is the betrothal and is often repeated, in church weddings, at the chancel steps, when each is asked if he or she will have the other. It is quite long and a little confusing to nervous bridegrooms. This man was so rattled that I had barely started to ask "Will you have this woman ...?" when he shouted "I will," and threw both arms around her enthusiastically, hugging and kissing her to beat the band. I stood there, quite like a fool, waiting for the movie to end. At last I had to take hold of him and steer him gently back to his proper place, assuring him that he wasn't married yet.

A young deacon who came to me to get experience had more than he bargained for in the first country wedding ceremony he was called on to perform. I had a good Ford car at that time—the only brand-new car I ever owned. (It was the gift of a Congregational deacon at that.) My young assistant took it and drove over to the bride's house for the ceremony. Her father was an odd character, who had done no work for many years. He was sitting half asleep behind the old cook stove when the wedding couple stood up to say their vows. There were a lot of children around, and the house was in a state of real commotion.

As the young deacon read the words, "If any man knows any reason why this man and this woman may not be lawfully joined together, let him now speak or else hereafter forever hold his peace," the father jumped to his feet and shouted, "I object. Yes, I do. I object. I don't want this to go on."

What a disturbance! It seemed that they had had quite a time getting him to sign his consent on the license, as the girl was under twenty-one. Ever since, he had been in an ugly mood. The ceremony was suspended and great arguments ensued. There was much weeping and wailing. The minister and the entire family labored with the father. Finally he quieted down and the wedding ceremony continued. Soon the time came for the ring to be produced.

The minister held out the open book to receive it. There was an embarrassing silence, then someone spoke up: "You see, we sent to a mail-order house for the ring, and it hasn't come yet."

What was to be done? Why, nothing more than to hold things up for a while and let the bride and groom go to the five-and-ten-cent store for a ring. This took time, as it was more than a mile to the city. The minister waited patiently until they returned and lined up again for the home stretch. When the wedding was over, and the afternoon far spent, the deacon went out to get into my new Ford, but it was nowhere to be found. He soon noticed that several of the older children of the family were missing too. It seemed too bad to notify the police, so the deacon played a waiting game. By and by, sure enough, the car appeared. The young folks, not often having enjoyed the luxury of a car, had been joy riding around the place.

Speaking of deacons, another one over in the eastern part of the state, having his first wedding, cried out in a loud voice, "Who giveth this *man* to be married to this *woman?*" Who shall say, in this day and generation, that he was not speaking more wisely than he knew? In fact, it is claimed that at my first big church wedding, I asked the groom if he would "take this woman to be thy wedded husband."

One day a woman called me about her daughter, whose husband was in jail. He really didn't deserve to be there. He'd been running with a tough bunch of boys, one of whom stole a car, went for a joy ride and got caught. The son-in-law was standing on the running board when the cop caught up with them. He had been in jail two weeks when the desperate mother-in-law got in touch with me.

She was worried over what the couple were going to do when he got out. They were just married, they had no furniture, no house, no anything. There had never been a wedding party nor any shower for the bride. Hence, no presents. That was bad. I promised the mother-in-law that I would be at the jail door when the prisoner was released, and that I'd bring him into my own home, where we could talk things over and decide what to do. He had no relatives, and few friends, after serving that sentence, so it was lucky for him that I had a spare room in the house and a job for him on the farm.

This all happened in the fall, at a time when we were busy gathering vegetables. We had a lot of watermelons that year, and as we were bringing them in, it occurred to me that we might have a watermelon wedding feast for the bride and groom. The more I thought about it, the brighter grew the prospects for the feast. By the time the happy day arrived I had sacrificed several good roosters to the cause. We sent word to the mother-in-law to invite in all the friends she could seat around her dining-room table and we'd do the rest.

Next day, when the chores were done, we loaded up "Old Daredevil" (the Ford) with roast rooster, watermelon, potatoes, turnips, and a lot more, and drove down to the house with bridegroom and food. What a homecoming that was! The past was buried and forgotten in face of all that provender. We had a prayer at the table for the couple and their future, and then I carved the first rooster. After the dessert was consumed, the neighbors showered the poor weeping bride with the long-overdue presents, and the groom walked about like a man of affairs who was a total stranger to jail. It beats all, what a meal like that will do!

The wedding feast over, I asked them if they had any idea where they were going to live. The bride had seen a rental sign on a two-family house down by the brook. She said she liked it, and it was cheap. That settled the matter. Then I discovered they didn't have a stick of furniture. So I left them with mother-in-law (a few days with mother-in-law can be all right), and next day I rambled all over the countryside begging one piece of furniture here, another there. We had some pieces stored away in the barn—things people had given us at one period or another, and in no time at all we had paid the first month's rent and had the house comfortably furnished. We got the stovepipe up, and the bride tried her hand at cooking her first meal. It wasn't at all bad—a nice plain supper, or you might call it a consecration service. The parson's mind wasn't much on the car that night. He had a lot to think about during his fifteen-mile drive home.

It wasn't always easy for the brides and grooms during the depths of winter to get in to my church in the woods, and I can remember one pair arriving on a cold February day through a heavy snowfall in their trusty Model T. I doubt if any other car in Christendom would have made it. As they came into the church, the bride exclaimed: "Henry! You've come to your wedding with your everyday cap instead of your fine new wedding hat." "Gosh!" said the groom, blushing furiously.

But the shoe was on the other foot when, just as everything was set for the ceremony, the groom shouted,

"Minnie! Where's your wedding bouquet?"

Then it was the bride's turn to say, "Gosh, I forgot it.

It's under the dish pan by the window in the pantry at home, where I put it to keep cool."

But the wedding went off smoothly enough, in spite of these mishaps. Much worse was the distressing delay at another wedding, when the license could not be found. It had last been seen in a first-floor bedroom, but although the bedroom was picked to pieces, every drawer in the bureau was overturned and the bed taken apart, there was no sign of the license. Of course there wasn't a chance that I could go ahead until this vital piece of paper was unearthed. A car was sent to the city clerk's office in the hope of getting another, but it was closed for the day, and no clerk or assistant could be found. The guests waited patiently. At last one of the women remembered seeing someone pick up a heap of papers from the bed and put them in a box on the bureau. A quick search brought the license to light, mixed up with other papers in the box.

The wedding fee is rather a delicate matter to write about. In the country, the income from this source is not enough to turn anyone's head. It is a bit embarrassing when the groom pulls out his pocketbook right at the altar rail, as soon as the ceremony is over, and asks, "How much do I owe you?"

In some cases, where a fee is set by the church, and it seems rather staggering to the groom, the question is asked by the minister, "Isn't she worth that to you?" Now that puts the man in a mean and undeserved position. One might think he was buying the girl from the church. The groom is only getting a service which can be had legally, at least, from other sources, for a dollar or two. Personally, I would like to see all marriages performed by the servants of the state as a legal matter and then let the church give its blessings and its prayers.

One of my grooms put on a look of poverty and pulled out a five-dollar bill and a one-dollar bill. This had the appearance of being all the money he had in the world. I knew he wanted to take a little auto trip, so I took the one dollar bill, which did not pay for my gasoline. Sometimes a groom tells you that he is "a little short," and will see you after the wedding trip. Well, he does see you—always at a distance. When people belong to one's church, and help to support it, there is really no need for any gratuity—although the custom of giving something is, I admit, mighty pleasing to us parsons.

I think it's always a good idea to give the wedding honorariums to one's wife. They do not run large for most of us, nor do I think they should. Mrs. Gilbert and I like to give back the fee in the form of a wedding present, whenever we know the bride and groom intimately, and we usually do this by installing a telephone in the home of the newlyweds. This was done for us when we were married, and we never ceased to appreciate it. The brides always seem to feel that they must telephone us first, and one of them called me late at night some time ago to say, "I wouldn't even phone my mother until I had thanked you first."

I've seen many a young couple go on the rocks right off the bat, buying a lot of foolish stuff they didn't need. One couple I know of, who had applied for aid from the town, went in the red to the tune of $800 for overstuffed sofas and easy chairs. Another couple went to the store intending to buy not more than $150 worth of furniture, and a high-pressure salesman had them signed for $350 worth before they got out of the place—like the couple who, shopping for furniture, were led proudly to a fine antique piece. The clerk threw out his chest and said, "See that? That goes back to Louis the XIV."

"Pshaw," said the woman. "That's nothing. We've got a whole bedroom suite that goes back to Sears and Roebuck the 26th."

There is still some question about the propriety of the preacher kissing the bride. In some quarters the custom seems to have died out entirely. I'm sorry to see it go. One minister near us, who usually kissed all his brides, at last got one so mortally homely that he just couldn't do it. He got around it by saying, "The usual custom of kissing the bride will be omitted." Later, when the refreshments were being served, and the people had started to leave, the minister noticed that he still had no envelope in his pocket. The groom, noticing him lingering about, said in a loud voice, "The usual custom of feeing the minister will be omitted this time."

If there are several envelopes to be handed out at a wedding, they should be plainly marked and the recipient should take careful note of the marking. At the wedding of Gertrude Beavis, daughter of an old parishioner, one of the brothers slipped me an envelope, which I put in my inside coat pocket. I was going to a party eighteen miles away that night. Quite late in the evening, I saw Rudolph, brother of the bride, rush into the hall with a wild and worried look on his face. He was greatly relieved when he spied me. He did not know where I had gone after the ceremony. He just happened to see the light in the town hall and took a chance on my being there.

"Have you still got that envelope?" he gasped.

‹Why, yes, I guess so. I haven't looked at it," I said.

"It's the wrong envelope. It's the money for the wedding trip, and I'm afraid they've lost their train.

There's sixty dollars in that envelope."

So I exchanged with him, and he shot through the door. It was fortunate that I did not open that envelope, for I certainly would have dropped dead with surprise. I heard since that in racing to catch the train the police stopped the newlyweds for speeding and they never made the connection.

Nor was this the only occasion on which a young Beavis had the unusual occur at his wedding. When Rudolph himself was ready to get married he insisted on coming back to Killingworth from New Haven for the ceremony, and when he walked down the aisle I could not help recalling the little boy Mrs. Beavis had dragged into church years earlier on a day when I repeated part of the service so that she would not know she was late. Rudolph was marrying into a Roman Catholic family. The bride and groom were there in good time but Rudolph's sister, Gertrude, and her husband were late. The moment came for the wedding service to begin. Now I have never been a stickler for punctuality at my services. I believe that the church should be run for the convenience of the people rather than the minister. So I passed along in front of the well-filled pews and spoke about the old church. I recalled weddings we had had there and old-time conditions in the surrounding countryside. The Roman Catholic guests were greatly entertained. I had another wedding that day more than fifty miles away but I knew it would cause embarrassment if I started to fidget or look at my watch. Finally it got to be twenty minutes past the time set for the wedding and still the missing guests had not arrived. I put the matter up to Mr. Beavis: "Shall we go ahead or shall we wait longer?" He said, "Begin."

Just as the bride and her maid of honor moved down the aisle, the missing couple arrived and took their places in the line. It was the neatest timing I ever saw. Later I learned that they had had trouble starting their car. Rudolph's sister, Elsie, wrote to me later: "You know, Mr. Gilbert, you are one in a thousand. If it's God's will that I ever get married I certainly want you to marry me, and in the old church in the woods.

Now and again the country preacher has to cope with parental interference. The world is strewn with the sorrow and regret of parents who have broken up matches because of their own selfishness and their fear of what others might say. Sometimes they act as though they were going to live with the third party instead of being merely the aggrieved parents. I know of one minister in Massachusetts who was offered $1000 in cold cash to break up a match. An uncle of the groom-to-be volunteered this sum if he would talk to the young man and get him to give up the girl. The parents threatened to change the family will and strike out a $100,000 legacy to their only son, if he went ahead with the wedding. All the fuss seemed to be over the girl's social standing. They admitted she was a "nice, sweet little thing." I never heard whether or not they got married, but I imagine they did, as the man was twenty-five years old and knew his own mind. Blood is thicker than water, and I dare say he got the money, too, in the long run.

In looking back over my weddings of the last forty years, I fail to recall more than one case of divorce.

Of course, there may have been many more, but I have not happened to hear of them. I know the question arises much more often in wealthy city parishes than it does along the country back roads. The poor are much less likely to run head on into divorce than the well-to-do. They haven't got the money, and for the most part they get on well together. They are busy raising their children and making a living. When they don't agree, they usually settle matters among themselves—like the man over the hill here, who beat up his wife so that she was in bed for three days. I haven't heard of any trouble there since.

Whether the poor wish for divorce or not, it's too much of a luxury for them. I think it is wrong for the rich to be able to get divorces, often for a mere whim, while the poor can't get them even when they are badly needed to right mistakes. I cannot but believe that God wants all His people to be happy. Why shouldn't there be the opportunity to correct the mistakes of youth and inexperience? I have seen many enduring and happy marriages after a change of mates. When God looks down and sees the results, I know that He is glad. Of course, the spoiled and selfish can never be happy anywhere, nor can anyone who tries to live with them. Of all domestic problems, the most tragic is the growing number of lazy, wicked parents who rear their pampered children to fill future homes with discord and the divorce courts with business.

The Episcopal church practically prohibits its clergy by law from remarrying divorced persons. There is supposed to be one exception, which I have never had to make use of in more than forty years. An Episcopal minister once told me that because of this canon, he lost sixty-four persons from his church in a single case. He had been forced to refuse to marry the son and daughter of two prominent and beloved church families. His refusal on canonical grounds brought to light a childish escapade of many years earlier that was not known to the community at large. The families were outraged by the cruel ecclesiasticism and stubbornness of the church they had loved so long. They showed it by turning their backs on the church, and all their relations with them.

I think this is one phase of Episcopal law that needs correction, and the sooner the better. It is my belief that the canons should be changed to allow the local minister to use his discretion from his knowledge of the candidates up for matrimony. If he doesn't know, who does? Canons like this discourage churchgoing and drive people away, yet the clergy are expected to build up the church regardless of such obstacles. There is no warrant for it in Scripture, from what I read, and I don't believe in it. Nothing makes me more mad as a minister than this outdated canon.

Chapter XII

FUNERALS

. . . .

OLD Dr. Samuel Hart, of Berkeley Divinity School, used to say that the true test of a minister was how many funerals he had. If people turned to him in time of trouble then he was their pastor in the real sense of the word. Although some of my families have had their marriages and baptisms elsewhere for one reason or another, yet when it came to funerals they would usually call on me. In the last fifteen years I have had eighty funerals in the parish of Durham alone.

Country funerals do not always go off in the well-staged city manner by any means. Strange incidents crop up that the parson must cope with on the spur of the moment. Anyone who is used to a city church and city ways must be careful of what he says and does at a rural funeral, lest he give mortal offense. Some years ago I was asked to assist at a funeral where a supply minister was in charge. Apparently he knew little about country ways in the presence of death. When the ceremony was over he pitched into the undertaker because the coffin was opened after the service. "Don't ever let that happen again at any funeral I have," he growled.

Ten years later I attended the funeral of the dead man's sister and the same minister officiated again.

This time the coffin was open before, during and after the service. Obviously he had learned his lesson.

I had just finished a marriage ceremony one hot summer day when a car came to take me to the hospital so that I could baptize a dying baby. The child belonged to one of our families way down country who were working hard to get along. When it died I arranged with an undertaker to look after the body. Next day I got the little coffin and took it in my car to the family home. There I picked up the relatives and we all went together to our church cemetery, where a member of the congregation waited beside the grave he had dug. We held the service out in God's great cathedral under the sky. What better place to have a funeral? We put wild flowers on the grave.

When I left the parents at their home, I gave the father the receipted bills of the undertaker and the hospital. Before the funeral I had called on a good and generous parishioner for this aid, so that the saddened family would not have the additional financial worry. They have been loyal parishioners of ours ever since. It was William Beavis who dug and filled the grave on a terribly hot day and wouldn't think of taking a cent for it.

One of the most unusual funerals I ever had anything to do with was held in an abandoned Methodist church which was built in 1790. Bruce Edward Stannard, the deceased, was in his ninety-first year, and I asked a brother minister, Mr. Knowles, who was present, to take part in the service and to speak. He also was ninety-one by that time, and he had known the dead man for many years. The first funeral he ever conducted had been held in that church, fifty-seven years earlier—a most unusual set of circumstances. It was touching to see this man past ninety helping at the funeral of a friend the same age. "I have found old age," said he, "the finest part of my life." It was a wonderful thing to be able to say, and to mean as sincerely as he did. I have often remembered these words and have wondered how many of us, when we reach our seventies, can achieve this same feeling of contentment. It seems to me that only those who are doing something worth while can attain this happy state. I heard a wise man say long ago, "When choosing an occupation, if possible have one that you can still keep working at in your old age." What profound wisdom! I often think that this is where the possession of a bit of land fills the need in many men's lives. At almost any age one can putter around and find joy and satisfaction in seeing things grow.

To illustrate how adaptable a country preacher must be, I recall the experience of Mr. Knowles when his parish was filling up with large families of newcomers who knew nothing of the ways of our land. He was called in to a home for a funeral and on entering he asked where the body and the coffin were.

"Why," a member of the family said, looking quite bewildered, "we don't know anything about a coffin."

Just then a young girl appeared, carrying the body of a dead child in her arms. Mr. Knowles looked around and found a box. With saw, hammer and nails he shaped it. Then he tore up a discarded skirt and lined the box. He put hay in the bottom, covered it over, and gently laid the child inside.

"I suppose you are going to bury the child in Parker Hill Cemetery?" he queried.

"Parker Hill Cemetery?" The woman seemed to know nothing of any cemetery.

"You mean that no grave has been dug?"

"Why, no, no grave."

So Mr. Knowles got shovel and pick and started out in his horse and buggy. Some of the mourners went with him, and they soon had a grave legally dug. With that done, he returned and read the funeral service.

One time the body of a woman was brought in by express to the Higganum railroad station and remained there over night. That it might take up less room the coffin was placed end up. After the service, the proposal was made to open it so that friends might view the remains. At this juncture a boy rushed up and excitedly exclaimed, "Don't do it. Don't do it."

"Why not?"

"Well, you see, the old lady stood on her head all night down at the express office, and you had better let her alone."

It is easy to hurt people's feelings at a funeral. I sometimes feel that many ministers have as little tact and sense as the young curate making his first round of calls, who said to a weeping widow, standing beside her husband's coffin, "Don't cry. Don't feel so bad, my dear woman. This is only the shell—the nut has gone to heaven."

One strange experience I had concerned a parishioner named Ed Clark. He was a blacksmith and his smithy was near my church. He had never stepped inside the church to my knowledge but I often went into the smithy just to sit and talk. He would make hoops for my ice cream tubs when they rusted off and he never charged me a cent. He was a pretty tough customer but I liked him. He had a good warm heart.

I went to see him when he fell ill, and I found his wife in a sad state. "I expect to have the funeral on Thursday, and of course I want you to officiate," she said, a little prematurely. "The doctor has just gone and he says Pa can't last but a few hours at best, and there is nothing we can do. Shall we have the services at half past two?"

Since his wife was so certain he was about to die, I thought I would stay around awhile and be there when the end came. Well, I waited and waited, and the longer I stayed the brighter Ed became. We began to swap stories, and against my better judgment I told him the one about the incense pot. When I had finished it, he sat up in bed and laughed till the tears came. His wife rushed in, utterly amazed, and the upshot of it was that we didn't have the funeral that next Thursday. In fact, Ed shod horses for two years after that, and when he was taken sick again, did his wife send for me? Not much!

I've made many a parishioner, sick and well, laugh over the incense pot, which concerns a colored Episcopal minister who came up from the South to New York and attended a service at the Church of St. Mary the Virgin, which is as High Church as it can be. He decided that the ritual was just what he needed to put some life into his own church. So when he returned home he took some colored boys off the streets and organized a vested choir. For hours they practiced marching, led by a crucifer. He knew that they must have incense, and this bothered him, for a regular censer was elaborate and cost money. So he decided to have a dish of charcoal in the vestibule, where the incense boy could step out and get it, as he and the choir swung by, proceeding from the side to the main aisle. The choir was also instructed that every word uttered must be intoned.

The moment arrived for the launching of High-Church ritual, and all the surrounding preachers were invited. The church auditorium was packed. As the procession swung by, the incense boy stepped out to get the dish of charcoal. To the horror of the minister, he came back in line without it.

"What has become of the incense p-o-o-t?" he intoned.

Right on the key the little boy intoned back, "Left outside. It's too d---ed h-o-o-t."

After many years of using various hymns and poetic selections at funerals, I have found that the invariable favorites are: "Now the Labourer's Task is o'er," "Rock of Ages," and "Jesus Saviour, Pilot me," with Tennyson's "Crossing the Bar" ranking close.

One of the contingencies we sometimes encounter at a funeral is the family bitterness that may flare up over the distribution of property. Even before the service is over we see relatives at loggerheads and know that bitter feuds are in the making. When one of my parishioners died I planned a communion and memorial service. The family would soon be moving away and I thought the mother and children would like to have their dead father honored in this way. We arranged a special dinner for that day, too, so that we could all have a farewell meal together.

When the time came for the service to begin, I saw that not one member of the bereaved family had arrived. At last the mother came in, weeping sorely. I couldn't understand it, for I was very fond of the whole family. But after the service I found that there had been a terrible quarrel among the children over their father's property and they had all left the house, bitter and angry. I certainly was sorry for that woman. It recalled the incident in the New Testament where the two came to Jesus quarreling over their inheritance. "Who hath made me a divider among you?" he asked. And He gave them the parable of the rich man and his barn.

Now and again a minister gives notice that he will have no funerals unless they are held in church. The last ruling of this kind that I noticed was soon abandoned when the wealthiest man in the parish died and the family insisted that the funeral was not to be held in the church. The minister could take it or leave it.

He took it.

Another time I planned a memorial service for a city woman who had been living with her daughter in our parish. I had called on them and done what I could for the sick mother before her death. I told the daughter about my plans, but to my surprise and chagrin she failed to show up at the service, and I learned later that she and her friends had gone to a Sunday cocktail party instead.

Frequently a clergyman is asked to take a funeral, even though he has not seen the family for years. I always try to have a pleasant word with the mourners before beginning the service for I find it adds a touch of warmth and real sympathy. Occasionally, when I do this, a mother will ask me to meet sons and daughters whom I have never seen. This is one time in their lives when people don't point to their land or houses, their fine cows or stylish automobiles, but rather to the humankind they have brought into the world. On one such occasion a woman who, as a girl, had sung in our church choir, introduced me to her children and I fancied I could still see her as the little girl who led the vested choir down the main aisle of my church many years before.

I think memorial services in church are good, and we ought to mention by name in our prayers those who have gone on before, more than we do, even years afterwards. But I must say that eulogies make me uncomfortable. I think the Episcopal prayer book furnishes the best that can be had in the way of a funeral service. The burial of the dead is stately, dignified and consoling. I always feel it's much better not to "preach the funeral," as the old saying had it. It is likely that the neighbors knew the deceased a great deal better than the minister did and, while he is saying one thing, they are apt to be thinking something else. I realized this at the funeral of a woman whom I had known quite well and for whose family I had done a good deal. They were Baptists and when she died they sent to town for the Baptist preacher. Did I hang my head while he was talking, and keep my eyes on the floor! He made out that she was a great saint, but I knew her for what she was.

In the Episcopal service it is, "Judge not that ye be not judged," and rich or poor, saints or sinners, get precisely the same service. In his book *Connecticut, Past and Present*, Odell Shepard speaks of that ultimate democracy of the earth to be found in the cemetery. Perhaps we shall have to extend that ultimate democracy backward from the grave rather than forward from the cradle. In the Episcopal Church in Middletown a large shroud is thrown over every coffin as soon as it is brought in the church door, so that all, to outward appearances look alike, unless you study the family automobile and draw your own deductions. But I believe that all coffins should look alike, and that the terrible show and waste of money for floral displays should come to an end. I think cremation will be generally accepted before long. I hope so. Mrs. Gilbert and I both plan to be cremated. For Christians who believe in the resurrection, what a fuss we do make, and how our actions belie our professions! If no one can remember us except by a chink of stone, then let the memory stuff go by the board altogether. What difference does it make?

And speaking of these same chinks of stone, right in my own parish of Durham, in the old cemetery on the hill, is a rare collection of early epitaphs and carved cherubs going back as far as 1712 with a stone inscribed to Jonathan Clements. It is two feet high and has the characteristic death's head of the period, as do several of the older stones. This in time gave way to the round cherub faces of a later period, some with drooping wings, others with pinions plumed for flight. Here and there are stars in the diadems, or wedding bells on the tombstone of a wife. The urn and cypress appear on some of the later ones.

Another early one, where the poetic vein is simple and without flourishes is dedicated to:

Sarah, daughter of Daniel and of Mrs. Lydia Smith
Died June 22nd, 1761, in her 20th year
My sun is set

My glass is run
My candle's out
My work is done

The most pretentious tombstone in the cemetery,
elaborately carved with an angel with pinions, a wedding
bell and two stars in the diadem, is erected:

In memory of Sarah Johnson
who departed this life, May 19, 1790
Aetat 24
An amiable disposition, a friendly Heart
A cheerful temper, engaging manners
A virtuous behaviour, filial Piety
and conjugal Tenderness
Made all her friends lament her death
with inexpressible grief

Short and Vain are our fondest hopes
of sublunary Bliss!
This lovely Fair, joined in wedlock
With the pleasing prospect of Felicity
in the connubial state
ere one year revolved
Was called, as is humbly hoped
to happier realms,
And to mourn the loss of so
dear a Partner
Was the unhappy lot of her
bereaved husband
Thomas Johnson

But Mr. Johnson's eloquence gave out before the time came to erect a tombstone to his second wife twenty-eight years later. It stands beside the first, a small, plain stone without angel or other adornment, and the inscription seems strangely curt in juxtaposition to the earlier eulogy:

In memory of Mrs. Phebe, relict
of Mr. Thomas Johnson
who died April 28, 1818
in the 60th year of her age

A stern note of warning is struck in the stone erected to Mr. Miles Merwin, who died in 1859 at the age of 88:

Come children and grandchildren all
On you this monument doth call
Prepare to die and follow me.

A smallpox victim who died in 1771 is commemorated in another monument, and over by the fence is a plain stone rudely carved:

Ann Cornelius
A [sic] Indian Girl

Most of these brownstone monuments were carved by John Johnson, a stonecutter who lived with his five unmarried daughters in an old Colonial house which still stands intact on Maiden Lane, a street named after this extraordinary quintet. They all lived to a great age, and the story goes that they went everywhere together, moving in single file, according to their years. They must have been quite a sight, billowing into church in a row — Nabby who died at the age of seventy-nine, Almira who lived to be eighty-two, Rhoda who survived until she was eighty-five, and Eunice and Nancy who rounded their eighty-sixth birthdays before they joined the heavenly host. Each one has a plain gravestone without any of the flourishes their father gave to so many of the residents of Durham. Almira closed their earthly book, and on her tombstone is written simply "The Last One."

The story goes that Nathaniel William Chauncey, known as the squire, courted one of the sisters for thirty years, and called at the house every Wednesday and Sunday with unfailing devotion. At last the church took up the matter officially, as it had become something of a parish scandal. So the deacons asked the squire what his intentions were.

"I haven't any," said Mr. Chauncey.

"And why not?" he was asked.

"Because I couldn't bear to break the set," he replied convincingly.

History does not record which of the five sisters was the object of the thirty-year courtship, but their tombstones carry on the strange legend of their lives.

Evidence of how people had to hoard their pennies in those days is to be found on a gravestone in a cemetery in the northwest part of Connecticut:

> Here lies little Johnnie,
> He never cries or hollers

He lived for one and twenty days
And cost us forty dollars.

One of my favorite bits of churchyard history, however, is to be found in a cemetery near Deerfield, Mass.:

Here lies the body of John Smith
As snug as a bug in a rug.

When a neighbor who didn't care so much for John was buried near by, the epitaph on his stone read:

Here lies the body of Samuel Jones
A good deal snugger than that other bugger.

At Killingworth one can find a rare type of gravestone, for Mr. Knowles believed that every grave should be marked, and when a family was too poor to erect a monument of some kind, he simply took a boulder and carved it suitably himself. Or, when a family abandoned a plain stone in favor of one more ornate, he took the discarded monument, turned it back to front and carved it in memory of someone who would otherwise lie in a nameless grave. He thought better of tombstones than I do.

Mr. Knowles had the real country touch when it came to funerals. One day, as he was on his way back from a baptism, a man shouted out to him, "Oh, Mr. Knowles, will you come in and give us a funeral?" "Funeral?" echoed the startled preacher. "Why don't you get your own minister?"

"Oh, we had him," was the reply. "He's been here. But

he made it so short that it was all over before we knew what was going on. Now we want a real funeral."

So Mr. Knowles put on his vestments and gave them all the trimmings. Country folks must have their funerals right.

Chapter XIII

THE PARISH FAMILY

. . . .

ON THE old farm in Vermont we had a pump that brought up soft rain water from the cistern in the cellar to the kitchen, but we had to go down cellar for all our drinking and cooking water, and lug it up the stairs in kettles and pails. It was a great nuisance. When I began earning money, one of the first things I did for Mother was to put in another pump at the other end of the kitchen sink with a pipe running down cellar to the drinking water. This was a great help to her. It is terrible to reflect on the tons and tons of water that have been lugged up just such stairways by generations of women and children, lifting the pail up one stair at a time. An investigation made in Litchfield County showed that in one year a woman carried thirty-six tons of water from the outside well into the house—something like ten pails a day.

This makes me think of the old Yankee who decided to do something for his wife when he inherited money. "Mary," he said, "you've lugged water all these years and now I've got some money, so I'm going to do something for you."

He did. He got her another pail, so that she could carry two instead of one.

Ludwig, in his book *The Nile*, says that the water

bucket has been the enslaver of the human race. I have gone about my parish domain determined that my people, at least, should not be so enslaved by it, if I could help it.

One night at dusk, after leaving the old church in Killingworth in the rain and fog, I saw a small boy cross the road in front of my horse. I noticed that he had a tiny water pail in his hand, which reminded me that there was a spring in the bushes beside the road. Although I had twenty miles to go that night, I blanketed the horse and went into the boy's house. I found a large family of children, and terribly discouraging conditions. This little fellow was trying to get up water enough for the washing next morning, as he would have to trudge off to school early. I took a large kettle and he and I went back and forth, back and forth, quite a distance over a big ledge and across the bridge, until we filled the boiler, all the kettles, and all the wash tubs in the house. The father was away from home, working at a sawmill job.

What a strange and indescribable ecstasy seemed to come over me that night, as I started the long trek home in the fog and the rain! Few and far between are the times vouchsafed to mortal man to rise to a transfigured height and feel the unsearchable riches of the indescribable Presence. When one walks with the need of the world, and its burden seems too crushing to bear, then, and then only, can one taste of that unspeakable joy that passeth all understanding.

One might well have thought that I was in the plumbing business one Sunday when I left for church with twenty-eight feet of two-inch galvanized pipe tied to the side of the car. I also had a fine pendulum pump and a four-foot sink. These went to a family of nine children, and that pump lasted for thirteen years.

One day I saw a young girl fetching a pail of water down by the edge of the woods. I pulled up at the house near by and went inside to make a call.

"Doesn't that pump work?" I asked.

"Oh, no. It hasn't worked since we lived here."

"May I look at it?"

"Of course. Do anything you want to with it. It's no use to us."

I found that it was a pitcher-pump made in Middletown, and all it seemed to need was some leather packing. I got some wrenches from the Ford, took the pump off and carried it home with me. Next time I went down that way, I put the pump on, primed it with water, and to the great amazement of the family standing around, water came right out of its mouth. The cost was twenty cents.

This was the family of William Beavis, who were to become quite closely welded to our church after that. William was Scotch, his wife was German. They were so hostile to us at first that some of my parishioners objected strongly when I suggested leaving candy boxes at the house. But Henry Ward Beecher said, "Kill them with kindness. The language of kindness is a universal language which every man understands." And sure enough, before long the children began coming to church and eventually the father and mother too.

One Sunday we had had the regular service, having begun, as usual, fifteen or twenty minutes late. I had pronounced the benediction and the last hymn was being sung. As I was about to go through the door leading into the vestry room, one of the front doors opened and in came Mrs. Beavis with four children. She had come down through the woods for a long mile and a half with an old horse that undoubtedly walked every step of the way. That would take half an hour in itself. I could easily imagine the hurry and scurry, furor and turmoil that usually takes place in any large family on a farm getting ready for church. Probably Beavis had gone to Chester to see about buying, or, more likely, trading for another horse to do his spring work. That meant his wife would have to see to it that the cows were put in the barn after drinking in the brook, that the hens were shut up, lest they scratch the garden to pieces with no one to chase them out, and that the dog was tied up to keep him from biting a salesman, or someone trying to buy chickens. These buyers always seem to come on Sunday!

Church had no doubt begun by the time the "animal preparations" were over, with the human preparations yet to come. After a struggle, the little girl's hair would be corralled into two braids and tethered with two white grocer strings, pending the household search for two ribbons that were alike—ending in one being cut in two and made to serve. Tears would be shed over the next girl's hair, until finally two rubber bands would be snapped on the ends of the braids. Only one stocking-hole would show above the shoe top, so that would have to get a run-around knot and a quick one. One of the boys would have trouble with his shoes. The left shoe would have no string in it at all, and the other a piece of blackened twine, so out to the shed he would run, to find a matching piece of black twine.

"Someone left the cover off the blacking box and it's all dried up," would shriek a tot from the back room, so there could be no blacking of shoes that day. One of the boys would be dispatched to the shed for a stack of wood for the kitchen stove, so that the fire would keep until their return. And finally the oldest boy would arrive at the door with horse and wagon, one wheel squeaking for want of grease. How well I knew the picture from my own memories of farm life!

No wonder the poor soul was late, for it was with just such complications that she had started her four children for the day. When I saw her come in the door, holding Rudolph's small fist (the boy whom I married years afterwards), I switched sharply to the right and stood by the prayer desk again. "This last hymn seems to go so well," I said, "why not sing another one?" So I gave out another hymn which we sang through. I talked a little and then we sang some more. Finally I read a prayer or two with the "Grace of our Lord" coming at the end. The congregation noticed nothing peculiar about the service, and Mrs. Beavis never realized that she was late.

This family grew closer and closer to the church as time went on. Eventually Beavis took over the care of the church and cemetery. He built the fires and made himself generally useful, without any pay. In the Killingworth church today we have a large volume of autumn leaves and a book of wild flowers with the leaves, blossoms and roots of forty-seven varieties of wild flowers, compiled by his daughter, Elsie, while she was in school. The woods around Killingworth are particularly fine, and we have flaming autumns. We usually have what we call Foliage

Sunday about the second week in October, when we trim the church with the gorgeous reds, golds and coppers of the woods.

I used to stay with the Beavis family quite often when I went down to Killingworth with horse and buggy. No matter how late I arrived, Mrs. Beavis was always ready for me, and would get me something to eat. It was a happy place to stay and they were a fine family. I found Lily a place to work for her board so that she could go to high school. She would go down with me to Killingworth on Saturdays. The worst trip we ever had was through a heavy snowstorm, when we had to walk most of the way, Lily leading the horse, while I broke a path for us. The expedition took five hours. Eventually Lily went to New York. She comes back to the old church whenever she can and recalls the good times she had at Killingworth.

I found Elsie, the next girl, a place in a doctor's family. She has become a skilled cook and holds excellent jobs. Gertrude, the third, worked in a store in New Haven until her marriage. The older boy, Theodore, is a carpenter. He and his father fixed the partition in the old church, so that it would move back on hinges and simplify our community and cooking arrangements there. Several years ago the Beavis family moved to New Haven, but I still feel that they are my parishioners. They have come back repeatedly and I have married several of them, although they have not been baptized in the church.

There is never any telling what sort of service the country preacher may be called on to render, and I believe in keeping an open mind for all emergencies. Late one winter the telephone rang and a man's voice said, "I'm

George Shoens down in Killingworth. I have a sister in Poughkeepsie who is dying, and I want to get to her as soon as I can. I know the snow is deep around here and it's terribly cold. I have phoned all the surrounding towns for a taxi but not one of them will undertake to come up here for me—not for any amount of money. What can I do?"

I assured him that someone would go for him, and that we would make arrangements at once to get him on a bus. By telephone we learned that one went through Middletown about one o'clock in the morning, and that it might have room for an extra passenger, if it could be stopped. We got the police to watch for it. Virginia and Shelley went down for Mr. Shoens in the Ford, with chains on the wheels and a shovel inside. Several times they had to stop and put blankets over the radiator to thaw it out. There was only one track down into the woods, so if two cars met, headed in opposite directions, one would have to go in a snow drift and then be shoveled out. Fortunately they met no one, although they did have to shovel a track in which to turn around. After a thirty-six-mile trip, they got Mr. Shoens into the city, where he caught his bus. He was able to be with his sister before she passed away.

Mr. Shoens was a victim of the depression who took over an abandoned farmhouse belonging to a friend at Killingworth and brought his wife and daughter out from New York to live there. They renovated the place and took a great interest in the community. They all came to our church and were among our good friends and supporters. Mr. Shoens always used to say that he was not afraid to laugh out loud in my church. In fact, he felt I would be disappointed if he didn't. He had learned what my congregation already knew—that I am by no means a strict ritualist in my church.

Right through my ministry I have always had the most cordial feeling for other denominations. One day I got a letter from a young man, saying: "Mr. Gilbert, can you help me? I want to join the Baptist church, but I don't know how!" Now that was something of a stickler for me. I had heard of the young Episcopal minister who wired his Bishop asking if it would be all right for him to conduct a funeral service for a Baptist. Word came right back, "Bury all Baptists possible."

This request came to me during one of the worst droughts of the year. The brooks in my section were all dried up. If I waited until winter, the water would be icy cold. So I directed this fellow to the nearest Baptist church—only about three miles away. I never did hear whether he joined up or not, but I got no thanks from the admirals in the Lord's navy, if he did. I didn't report this one to my Bishop.

One of the saddest case histories of my ministry was a family down in the woods who had come out from the city and paid something down on a farm because one of their daughters had tuberculosis. It was an old tumble-down farmhouse, and when I called I found the sick girl lying in an unfinished attic that was bitterly cold. It was easy to see that she was far gone. She lay by a window which had old bran sacks tucked in half the panes. She was covered with meal sacks and blankets that did not protect her from the wind howling through the attic. I sat with her for three or four hours, praying with her and talking to her. One couldn't let her think that she was going to die. So I comforted her as best I could, then sat silently beside her when I saw how close to death she was. It's a good rule that if people are too sick to talk to you, they are too sick for you to talk to them, and the best thing to do is to sit quietly beside them, like Job's friends.

Next time I went down there the family was preparing to return to New York. Things had been too much for them on the farm and it hadn't helped their daughter. I spent some time with her the day before she left. She was quite spiritual-minded and calm about her state. It was clear that she did not have long to live. I stayed all that night with a neighbor. Next day the cold was terrible. In sheer misery the family departed, but their misfortunes didn't cease. After they had loaded their furniture on a truck, they found that the radiator was frozen and the car wouldn't move.

I helped them as well as I could and at last we got the truck moving. They proceeded as far as Madison on their way to New York. There the radiator and engine became so hot that the car took fire. It was so cold that no one could get a hose out, and the truck and everything in it was burned. Later I heard that they crowded in with relations in the city. One can picture the end of that unfortunate girl.

How often the farm women are dragged down with sickness and overwork along the country back roads! My memories of Vermont first fixed the picture in my mind, and what I have seen since of sheer human misery might startle the plush-lined churchmen of New York, whose luxurious edifices are only within motoring distance of real rural destitution. Talk about foreign missions, and the hillbillies of the South! Connecticut isn't altogether the smooth and contented state it looks to the summer resident.

A mother with a large family of children on a farm, and no conveniences to speak of, doesn't stand the strain very long. She cracks up in a hurry. I resent the fact that well-off city women with nothing to do always get long vacations, while the poor farm women with too much to do get no vacation at all. They tell of the farmer's wife who became mentally ill and was taken to an institution.

"What's the matter with her?" asked the farmer.

"Why, it's insanity," was the answer.

"Insanity?" cried he. "How could she catch that? She hasn't been out of the house for twenty years."

Years ago I got sick and tired of seeing such overworked farm mothers kiss their babies good-by, turn their faces to the wall and quietly die. That's why I've given so much thought to providing the common necessities for them. One mightn't suppose that chairs would loom so large in parish work, yet a shortage of them in rural families can seriously cramp the lives of many unfortunate children. I've often rescued chairs from church basements for just such families, feeling that they would do more good in the kitchen than in church. Any preacher with a boys' club could dig up damaged chairs for the needy. I put a church pew against the wall in the kitchen of one home thinking to myself that if I could get the family used to a church pew in their own house, they would feel more at home when they came to church. It worked!

Many of these big rural families actually do not have tables large enough for everyone to sit down together to a meal. I am sure there is not a family on my whole circuit without such a table today. Most of them come from our parish houses. These dining-room extension tables have no place in the small church parish house anyway. I believe in giving them away and putting in their place tables with screw-in iron-piping legs that can be folded against the wall when not in use. Then the young folks can dance and play their games, and the Sunday school and choir will grow bigger instead of smaller.

Perhaps nothing is harder for an overworked mother to endure than a miserable old stove, all burned out, with a crack through the oven-top to let the ashes down on the bread, and a front-door damper broken, so that the heat can't be controlled. There is no way of telling how many stoves we have distributed, to correct just such situations. Living near the city, as we do, we can go around to the hardware stores and find real bargains in stoves that have been picked up in exchange transactions. The managers are glad to get rid of them so we sometimes stumble on beauties for five or ten dollars, always getting and delivering them ourselves.

One time my son George went down country sixteen miles with a cook stove for a family with ten children. They took the old stove out and set the new one up. Then a boy was dispatched to the woods for dry bark and twigs to see if it would draw. It roared to perfection. Someone slipped out to look at the chimney. It was all afire, and the roof had caught fire too. So they doused all three fires with water, and George came home declaring the whole trip a great success.

In fixing up a number of my parishioners with pumps I discovered that it wasn't always enough to get water into a house. In many cases receptacles were needed to hold it. Kettles for a stove were often as much of a help to a harassed mother as the stove itself. For Christmas presents one year I gave each of three families a copper tea kettle. Another kettle I gave away was rescued from going to the dump. It was to be thrown out as useless, but I patched and polished it until it looked brand new, and it is now serving a family of eleven children. The mother has used that kettle for years, for everything from oatmeal to beef stew. I never see her that she doesn't mention it.

I found a stairway in one woman's house without a railing. Now I have always believed that a railing is essential for a woman going up and down stairs with a baby in her arms, a bucket of water, or any of the countless articles a mother must trundle up and down stairs in the course of a day. So I got hold of some iron railing and piping, and screwed the impromptu guard to the wall myself.

Another time I visited a woman who was worried about getting in her ice, as her husband was away. So I took horse, wagon, ice picks, ice saws and all sorts of ice tools, rounded up some young boys who lived near her home and together we got the ice out and stored away for summer. Shelley and I surprised even one of the summer residents by dynamiting her pond for her, thus clearing out the mud. She was amazed, too, to have me bring bread from my car when I called on her one day. I rarely travel without food, and I nearly always find occasion to use it. My car is like a traveling lunch wagon. Noon or supper time might find me miles and miles from home.

When I go visiting, I always try to find out in various

ways what is the immediate need of the family. It may be wood (that is always easy), or rubbers (we have a rubber factory near at hand and we get good seconds), or reading matter. I have taken out any number of subscriptions to the local paper, knowing that the children needed to keep up with current events in their school work. When possible I see that my families get radios. After all, they are normal people. They must have diversion as well as work, and they should learn how to go out to a sociable, how to eat at table, how to handle various aspects of living.

Our house is always cluttered with things we get for the needy. It may be anything from pianos to dolls.

By now I know just where to go to get what I want. I never miss a chance to give a mother a baby carriage.

Why shouldn't every mother have one? I used to have carriages at every church, but the parishioners "borrowed" them so often that finally we abandoned this custom. I often illustrate the fact that a church thinks more of its carpets and dishes than it does of its boys and girls by telling my congregation about the young couple who came out of the five-and-ten-cent store and started pushing a baby carriage along the street. Suddenly the husband looked sharply at the baby and exclaimed, "Why, Mary, this isn't our baby.

We've got the wrong outfit."

"I know it, I know it," agreed his wife hastily. "But come along. It's a better carriage than ours."

The needs in a country church all follow a pattern. They have mostly to do with stark necessity. But I maintain that when a minister sits down in a chair he has painted himself, at a table that used to be in his parish house, and drinks tea made from the water heated in a bargain kettle he bought over in town, on the stove that came down in his trailer, he feels at home, to say the least of it. And that's how it is with me.

Chapter XIV

THE PREACHER'S FAMILY

. . . .

WHEN I left the beach cottage we were occupying at Westbrook on a summer day in 1904 to conduct services at Christ Church, I didn't believe that my firstborn would be alive when I got back. How hard we all prayed—the congregation and I—for the life of my son Shelley! It was a forlorn hope for me. I didn't see how all the prayers in the world could save him, for he had looked so nearly gone when I left him on Saturday night. What a joy it was to find him alive when I returned! He opened his eyes and moved a bit, showing a flicker of life. From then on he continued to gain.

The sexton had given us the use of his cottage by the sea, thinking that the salt air would help our baby. It was a great struggle from the start for Mrs. Gilbert to keep him alive. She could not nurse him, nor could she find food that would agree with him. He weighed seven pounds when he was born and at the age of six months he weighed only six, having suffered dreadfully with cholera infantum. Mrs. Gilbert now thinks that no one but herself should have prepared his food, so much does the least variation mean to a baby's stomach.

Poor little Shelley got so thin that he looked like a skeleton. As a last resort his mother rubbed him with hot olive oil three times a day, and put hot spiced bandages on his stomach every two hours, night and day. When it seemed as if he couldn't possibly live, the doctor told us to give him a drop of French brandy from time to time, to keep his heart going. At long last the peptonized food took effect. The weather became cooler too, which helped a little. But probably the thing that really saved his life was the fact that his mother did exactly as her doctor told her, and refused to listen to the remedies suggested by her friends. Some of the saddest deaths I have had to witness have been caused by parents following a grandmother's advice, which might have been acceptable in the good old days, but no longer, with more scientific knowledge available.

I can never put into words what a loving, painstaking mother our children have. She seems to have been born to mother babies. When they were little she would never leave them except for a few hours to attend church, and then she was always sure that they were left in the best of hands. And how she could sing lullabies! A mother brings up her boys to the age of eleven or twelve, then they turn to their father, but she brings her girls up all the way. Sometimes I go into a house and find that the window curtains have been tied up out of reach, the coal hod has been put on a chair, and the cat's dish has been relegated to the freezing regions of the back porch so that the baby can't get at them. But Mrs. Gilbert never put away a thing. By spatting the babies' hands, shaking her head and saying "Noni, noni," they soon learned what they must leave alone. She ruled them by love. She could never understand mothers turning their children over to others to be cared for—either in day nurseries or boarding schools. She enjoyed them so much that she could hardly be away from them for a minute, and how sweet they all were with their "momo this" and "momo that." How old is an infant, anyway, before he knows whether he can have everything he wants just by yelling loud enough? Two weeks, say? And if by the time he is two years old he is pouty, whiney and self-centered, how can he ever be changed?

Shelley started taking music lessons when he was quite young, beginning with the mandolin. We know now that this was a mistake. He should have started first on the piano, which he took up later. He could have gone to Wesleyan University here in Middletown. Now I am sorry that he didn't, but my idea was, and still is, that one should never "send" children to college. Let them "go," if it can be arranged. At any rate he went to Yale Music School and has gone to summer schools since to keep up his music. While I was not getting a large salary, I was fortunate in having the farm, and could make enough to help send him to school. My good boys did so much on the farm that they really paid for their own tuition.

Shelley's first position brought him five dollars a week playing the organ and training the choir in our Durham church. To get paying pupils was slow work at first. We wondered how he could best get started. Fortunately he had a chance to play on Wednesday evenings for the services in an Episcopal chapel near by. This he did all one year without pay, or thought of it, although he did get a present at Christmas and Easter. Moreover, he helped to transport the congregation to and from the service. From the good will and appreciation this entailed, he began to get pupils. He bought a small secondhand car and gave lessons at their homes. Now he has all the teaching he can handle. He is married, and with what money he had saved up and we had saved up, plus the legacy of a wonderful friend who had long admired our mission work, he has a plain but comfortable house at the edge of the woods on our farm. As a boy he worked with us to build up the home place, so we feel that he is entitled to all the milk, wood and vegetables he can use, without thought of pay.

Shelley was two when George was born. When Mrs. Gilbert was preparing for him, she talked to little Shelley about the new live baby doll who was coming, and how they would love it and care for it together. Each of our children was always discussed and wanted before his arrival. Mrs. Gilbert has never believed in the "nose out of joint" babble that some women use to children, getting them to fear and hate the new baby even before its arrival.

From the start George said he was going to be a minister like "poppo," and he always liked to ride around with me, making calls and seeing the churches. When he was only four he went with me on a long cold trip to take a cook stove down to the old Killingworth church. We had a slow horse and an old toe-board wagon. The ground was frozen, and it was after dark when we got there, having had four long hours on the road. We watched for squirrels[9] nests, and counted them all, just to keep up our spirits. When we got home the next day he said "Momo, we went on that *longest* road."

When George was about twelve we had an expedition together that we shall both remember as long as we live. Although the sun was shining overhead, it was one of the dark days of my life. We went up to Vermont to pay a visit and see about buying a car. We badly needed a larger car as the *old* Model T, which was exactly George's age, just couldn't stand the work any longer. What's more to the point, even if it ran, it wasn't fit to go around in. Anyway, we had heard of a seven-passenger Chandler in very good condition that we could have. We paid $800 for it—think what that would buy in the car line today! I had never driven a gear-shift model before and was worried about driving the car home from Vermont. But I ran it around in Randolph Center and got along quite well. On our way back to Middletown we got as far as White River Junction and had dinner at my sister Rebecca's. Somehow we got on the wrong road after leaving her house and I backed into a man's yard to turn around. My seven- passenger didn't respond like the old Ford, and I was nervous about it, anyway. I must have stepped on the accelerator instead of the brake, for the car dashed across the road and struck a big maple tree, which was forced right in between the springs. (Cars had no bumpers in those days.) The radiator was wrecked and the water gushed out at once.

It was by the merest chance that we struck the tree. If we hadn't, we would have gone down a steep bank right into a flat swamp of soft mud. How our two-ton car could have been raised out of that I don't know. As it was, we scraped some of the bark off the tree—not enough to kill it, but plenty to get the owner furious with us. We telephoned for a wrecker to come, feeling quite crestfallen. We had started out rather pleased with ourselves and our new car. Now we were being towed back, our fine feathers drooping sadly.

George always was a fine lad, and we were drawn together closely that day in our trouble. It was a sad and expensive trip down on the train. We were very poor at the time and the cost of the car was enough of a burden without any added expense. We felt pretty flat coming out from town on the trolley, lugging our grips down the hill to the house, when Moms was expecting us to ride up in our new car. Later we looked up the Chandler agency in Hartford and were told we could have a new radiator for ninety dollars. This was wartime and I don't see now how I ever got the money together to pay for it. We learned later that the regular price was seventeen dollars. Some time later the son of Crocket, who fixed up Father's hair after my first bungling attempt at barbering, drove the car down from Randolph Center without further mishap.

High school was hard for George, but he was graduated and went to Dubois School and from Dubois to Seabury Divinity School in Minnesota. The day of his ordination to the ministry was an unforgettable one for us. He was consecrated in the Killingworth church to which we had taken that cook stove. I used to tell him jestingly that he'd never be a minister until he learned to cut hair, and just by way of emphasis I gave him for an ordination present a fine new barber's outfit. He has as many mission stations as his father now, out in Minnesota, and a much larger circuit.

Henry Closson came along four years after George, so there has always been a little boy to ride around with me. Mrs. Gilbert started him with the violin, and he has enjoyed it all his life. He has been a great help to us in our church work, playing the violin at our services. He still plays for Grange dances and for every other entertainment he has time for. While he was still in high school he attended trade school in the afternoons, to study weaving.

We added a room to the house in which he has his loom. He is now an instructor of weaving for the government.

I mention building on an extra room because one great trouble with large families in crowded quarters is that the children have no place in which to keep their own things, and thus develop a property sense. If anyone uses a necktie or a hair ribbon that he is lucky enough to grab first, he has little incentive to take care of it. If brothers and sisters use one another's things all the time, it is natural that eventually they should fail to see why they can't take things outside that don't belong to the family. If it is only a box under the bed, every child should have some place of his own to keep his things neat and clean.

I have never put my work-bench tools out of reach, or locked them up. To be sure, I have had some dreadful times trying to find a hammer or a saw and have made some horrid fusses, only to discover that it was just where I had left it. It doesn't do to be too sure that we fathers are invariably right. Always acknowledge a fault if you expect your sons to do likewise. Father used to go to extremes and raise a perfect blizzard of a storm if he couldn't find a tool in a minute. But he learned his lesson one day, and was never so bad again. His best pitchfork had been missing for some time, and, of course, as always, the loss was laid to us boys. It just wouldn't occur to Father that he might have left it somewhere himself. After haying, someone would go down and mow out the old rail fence along the pasture, then throw the green feed over to the cows. Father had always done this job while we boys were busy with the milking. Well, one night I went down along that old rail fence and, sure enough, there was the fork stuck right in the ground just where he had put it. I left the fork where it was. I suppose this was mean, but I simply couldn't help it—he was always so ready to blame us. I let him storm around over that fork for a week or two, and then I took courage to suggest that he might have left it somewhere himself. This audacity threw him into a tantrum, but when he cooled off, I said, "Didn't you have that fork down by the rail fence cutting grass for the cows?"

"Well, yes, I did. But what of it?"

"Nothing," said I, "only I saw it down there right where you left it. It's there now, in line with the big elm you pass going from the barn."

He stood speechless. I hope he thought of all the things he had said in connection with that fork, but I don't think he did. I do know that he was never so quick to blame us for lost tools after that. I was more than once tempted to remind him of that little pitchfork matter, but I never did, for his death before my eyes from a ruptured blood vessel would have been an unhappy experience.

These memories of Father made me a little cagey about storming at my own boys. Shelley, George and Closson were all getting along when a sister came to join the family circle. "It's a girl," said the doctor, after having said, "It's a boy," three consecutive times. The Bible speaks about a mother who forgetteth anguish for joy that a man is born into the world, but I think Mrs. Gilbert forgot just about everything for a while, out of sheer joy that a woman had at last been born into her world. But there was a bushel of anxiety to temper this joy, for the poor little mite tipped the scales at four pounds and indeed was weighed in a silver bread-boat for three months. Mrs. Gilbert had had a bad fall and Mary Virginia came into the world far too soon. I have always thought that no one, except perhaps Dr. Dafoe of quintuplet fame, could have raised her. "Man is born unto trouble, as the sparks fly upward," said the old prophet, and so was little Virginia seemingly born unto afflictions of every sort.

When she was about two weeks old, an abscess developed on her right shoulder. By the time this was cured, she couldn't move her right arm at all. The doctor thought that even with patient care and persistent rubbing and massaging, she would never be able to bend it again. But her mother remembered an accident she had had which resulted in her knee being in a cast for fourteen weeks, and how her doctor, too, thought that she could never bend it again. On the advice of an aunt, however, she kept bending the knee and rubbing it until it was cured. And so Mrs. Gilbert kept working at Virginia's little arm, rubbing it and trying to make it bend. The baby would scream and cry, and her mother would cry too, to think it hurt her so much. Time proved her right. Although this arm is not all that it ought to be, Virginia with characteristic spirit drives a car and pounds a typewriter with no sense of handicap.

When two and a half years old she fell the length of the stairs and broke her wrist. At the age of three, she sat in a pail of potato skins that had just been taken off the hot stove onto the back porch floor to cool.

The doctor said the shock of such a terrible burn was

worse than the burn itself, and her mother hardly left her side night or day for three weeks. The little one had to learn to walk all over again. Still her ill-luck did not desert her. At the age of four she went sliding with her brother. The sled went off a bridge and she suffered a great gash in her face that took five stitches to close up. Soon after this, the barn door blew shut and banged her head against a wagon wheel, cutting it open and breaking her nose.

Her troubles seemed to be over then until she was fourteen, when she had to be operated on for a ruptured appendix, with peritonitis having already set in. The doctor told the neighbors that her life would ebb away in a few hours. Again her mother gave her the courage she needed. She was so weak that she couldn't even turn her head. For six months she wore drainage tubes. It seemed as if she had had enough when she finally recovered from this siege, but at the end of six months another abscess formed, broke, and she had to have another operation for peritonitis. With her mother at the hospital, the boys and I would gather around the table at mealtime and, all of us crying, pray hard that God would spare her life. In the end He and the doctors and her mother did save her.

People were good to us during these anxious days. They gave us not only sympathy but financial help. The money seemed to pour in—sometimes even gifts of one hundred dollars at a time. Bishop Acheson's wife was one of those who sent us this substantial sum, also Berkeley Divinity School. Some gifts were most touching. One never realizes how many friends one has until there is sickness.

Virginia pulled staunchly through everything and in time went to the College of William and Mary in Virginia, and liked it. We learned something about eyes the first year she was there. She had always worn extra strong glasses. By the middle of her first year her eyes ached so much that she had to come home. She was much discouraged, thinking she could never go back. But, upon going to a specialist, we found that all she needed was new lenses for her college work. She returned and finished the course successfully.

She earned considerable money at college, sitting up with children in the evenings while their parents were out, managing the house during the prolonged absence of the grownups, and sometimes staying for weeks at a time. She waited on table in a dining hall to pay for her board, and she earned a lot more by acting as circulation manager on the campus for *The New York Times*. There was no delivery service on the campus when she arrived, but when she left more than two hundred customers were having the paper delivered every morning. The Woman's Auxiliary also helped her a good deal by giving her a scholarship. She is an inspiration, I think, to the young who despair of a college education because they haven't any money. Today she is on the local high school faculty.

Charles was born six years after his sister. I had begun to feel like the chap who had twelve daughters and one day was told he had a son. "Good," he shouted. "Now the boys have begun to come!" Well, we thought the girls had begun to come with Virginia, but no, it was another boy, who is now the life of the household and greatly missed whenever he's away. He is the only one left to help on the farm, and he hasn't much time for that, either. Like Closson, he is six feet two inches tall, and musical. He takes clarinet and voice lessons twice a week. With their music to keep them occupied, the children of this rectory, at least, seem quite content to spend most of their time at home. I recommend music for every child.

Children are great helpers, but they should never be sent off alone on a particularly hard job. Those farmers who order their small sons to hoe corn or pull weeds, while they go off into town with the milk and hang around talking all forenoon, are storing up trouble with their children. You can't fool all the children all the time. I have no use for those who are forever talking about the good old days, and how saintly the boys and girls all were when they were young. In speaking to young people I tell them about the father who got after his boy for not being more saving. "Why, son, when I was your age I worked in a grocery store for five dollars a week, and in five years I owned the store," he said.

"Well, that may be, Dad," retorted the boy, "but you couldn't do it now. They have cash registers."

Money matters in our house have always been an open book for the whole family. Just how much I make is known to all, and if I go off speaking some evening everyone knows all about it next morning at the breakfast table. Things are different from what they used to be in the country parson's house. Our grandfathers didn't have to contend with potato bugs or our grandmothers with jitterbugs, but boy-nature and girl-nature is the same as it was then, and it is just as necessary as ever to keep the confidence of the children in the home.

Mother and I often remark on what good and thoughtful children we have. The boys are forever saying,

"You mustn't do this, Dad," or, "You just can't do that. Let us do it." They insist that I never go off alone at night with the car, which is probably just as well, considering the speed hogs we have along the Connecticut roads. One night when Virginia and I were on the way home from Norwich, going along at about fifty miles an hour, a car passed us like a bullet. It must have been doing eighty or ninety miles. Within five minutes we came upon the worst accident I have ever seen—one boy died while we were there, and the other soon afterwards in the hospital.

When it comes to family life, we can all have screaming discord and distrust in our homes if we want it, or we can have merry laughter, co-operation and mutual confidence just for the asking. It's up to the family, and that's the way I like it. We could ill have spared a single one of our children. We have found every stage of their lives most interesting, and I have no patience with those who talk of children as "brats," or who refuse to give something out of their own selfish lives in order to bring up youngsters. They may be a lot of trouble, but aren't they worth it? Frequently I speak at father-and-son banquets and I always point out on these occasions that there isn't much difference between children and grownups. Boys know far more than we give them credit for knowing. I had one who informed me that, "The Bible begins with Generation and ends with Revolution." Not a bad description at that.

People have been wonderfully good to us over the years too. When we have needed aid, it has come to us unsought, and sometimes it seemed to be heaven-sent, in times of illness particularly. One year, just before Christmas, I received a check in the mail for twenty-five dollars with the specification that it was to be used for Mrs. Gilbert and me but not for anyone else. The letter began, "Dear Saint George." We had no idea from whom it came until a friend finally told us that the donor had shaken hands with me somewhere and had noticed how hard and calloused my hand was. "I found a minister who actually works with his hands," she commented.

Among our other personal benefactors were two ladies from Westport who lavished kindness on us for years after attending a service at Killingworth one day and seeing what we did for the poor. Their nephew had been reading my pieces in the *Rural New-Yorker* and felt I was on the right track. He liked my brand of practical Christianity. Every Christmas he sent me something—first five dollars, then ten, then fifteen. Finally he brought his wife to church one Sunday and she interested her two aunts, who gave a great deal to missions. One Sunday soon after that, all four filed into church. The two aunts didn't seem to mix very well with our parishioners, but went straight to their pews, bowed their heads in prayer, and looked so stiff that we thought they must be disapproving our informality. When the time came to bless the offering, I was startled to see four ten-dollar bills on the plate. Nothing like this had ever happened at Killingworth before. They shared in our usual repast at the church and after it was over, one of the aunts said, "We didn't bring anything for the dinner," and she insisted on leaving another ten-dollar bill to pay for this. From that time on, their interest in us and our work continued. They would come to our house and look quietly around to see what might add to our comfort. They sent us $600 on one occasion so that Mrs. Gilbert and I could have conveniences upstairs in our bedroom. They provided us with new hardwood floors and helped us in many thoughtful ways. I could never begin to tell how much these ladies did for us.

Day in day out I have learned to love this part of the country where my work lies. I don't believe I'll ever leave it or ever want to. Sometimes I am asked why I have stayed so long in country work—didn't I ever have the chance to get out of it? Yes, I have had opportunities to go elsewhere, but I have done so many new things that automatically vestries and bishops have steered clear of me as being radical and not very "safe." Most city parishes—in fact, most church parishes anywhere—are pretty conservative. If a parson breaks new ground, or does the traditional thing in a different way, look out for trouble!

I think that interest in our people and their families has kept me hitched more than anything else. After I had assisted for a while in the work near our present home, I was asked to become assistant minister in a large city parish under Doctor Edwin S. Lines, who later became Bishop Lines of New Jersey. I was so concerned about the large families, and my new parishioners whom I had managed to interest in the church, that I did not want to leave. I knew I would miss them terribly, and they seemed to depend on me.

Then, later, when dear old Doctor Bradin of Hartford was getting along in years, he wrote to me twice, asking me to assist him and ultimately to take his place. It was an attractive offer, as I had worked with him for three years while at Trinity College, and I knew him well and loved him. But we talked it over, and decided not to go. It would be this boy or that girl, this family or that one, that we found it impossible to leave, for we couldn't quite see what would become of them if we went. No doubt we were foolish. Certainly we were from a material point of view.

At another time I had a letter from a Bishop in Pennsylvania asking me to go there and take a parish. He said he would furnish me with a new Ford car. As we had our terrible old rattletrap Model T. then, I declare this offer was a real tug. Then Bishop George W. Davenport, whom I knew very well and admired greatly, sent for me to go down to Maryland. He wanted me to take charge of his social service work, have several country stations, and be a canon of his cathedral church. A second time the Bishop insisted on my joining him and he offered additional inducements. Things were going rather hard with us at this time. There are always those around one who will fight any new way of doing things, and we were having trouble in our work. Indeed we were almost down and out, and so great was our struggle to make ends meet that Moms had become soloist in the Baptist Church to help the family exchequer. At that time she was ready to go South, but something held me back. God seldom speaks straight to a man—He speaks to him through people.

I made up my mind to stick to my guns the day we went to a Berkeley Divinity School commencement. Dr. Miel, my old Hartford friend, was there, and as he had always backed me up so well through trying times, I decided to talk the matter over with him. Mrs. Gilbert, he and I were in Dean William P. Ladd's study when I stated our case. Mrs. Gilbert says she remembers his exact words; "George," he said, "you are too valuable a man to this diocese to leave it. I and my work, when I'm gone, will be forgotten, but you stick to it and you and your work will never be forgotten." He said so much more besides that on the way home we decided to stay.

I also had a call to a parish with a much larger salary, near New York City. It seemed a better place to bring up the children, with more opportunities for schooling, but again we said no. When one has worked as hard as I have with a large number of poor families, and begins to see his efforts bearing fruit, he can't help wondering what will become of his families if he leaves. I was just plain afraid they'd lose their faith and their church connections, so I stuck. And I've never really regretted it.

Chapter XV

"I WAS A STRANGER—"

. . . .

I THINK it must have been Father who gave me the idea of taking in strangers. I remember one night he stayed up till morning with a tough-looking customer, for fear he might burn down the buildings. They sat in chairs by the old wood box until dawn. Father claimed that never once in his life had he turned a stranger from his door, and I believe it. He took them in, even if he had to bed them down in the haymow.

His prize package was a fellow with a long white beard who claimed he was with Napoleon in Russia, and had suffered with "Bony" in that terrible retreat. Father gave him a broom and put him through an army drill. He knew it perfectly and also every last detail of the Russian campaign. "If it hadn't been so cold," he'd say, "Old Bony, he kill them, every one."

Once, in the dead of winter, three college students came pounding on our door. Two of them were white and the third was a Negro. Father took them in just for one meal and they stayed a week. This prolonged visit was the result of three things—there was a blizzard, so they couldn't travel; they had such a good time with Father that they didn't want to leave anyway; and last but not least, Father kidded them so much about their business that they just stayed on to get even with him. They were selling books, but not getting far with it.

The day they arrived one of them approached him with his nice little sales speech: "Sir, I have here a wonderful book—a book you must have, a book you need." "What's it about?" asked Father.

"Etiquette," replied the brash young man.

"You've insulted me," said Father.

"Insulted you, sir? What do you mean?"

"Do you mean to say, sir," shouted Father, "that my manners are so abominably bad that I need a book on *etiquette?*"

The boys hadn't thought of that. It seemed to take from them what little enthusiasm they had left for book-peddling. They never canvassed another soul. But how those three fellows could sing! The old sitting room was opened up (a thing unheard of in winter), a fire was built in the big stove and the old square piano was wheeled out and put to work. We boys would rush through the chores. Never did the cows get fed in such haste; never was there so little stripping done. It was a wonder they didn't dry up. We'd rush back into the house, so as not to miss a word or a song. Father entertained us by reciting Shakespeare—Hamlet's soliloquy, Polonius' advice to his son, and powerful moments from Macbeth. Always Macbeth, for in his wanderings with Levins, this had been the leading opus. But it was the singing I remember best: *I'm off to Louisiana, For to see my Susianna, Singing Polly Wolly Doodle all the day!* I loved it.

The funniest man Father ever harbored bore the name of Jones—no one knew his first name. He was a peddler, and he went around with two tin cases containing pins, needles, trinkets and extracts. He always walked, and invariably stopped at the Gilberts. It was his custom to leave one case with us and then walk to the same three houses down the street—the Eddys, the Carpenters and the Haydens. Then he would return past our house and go to Luther Blodgett's, where, after selling what he could, he would take out his Bible and proceed to read for several minutes, standing in the middle of the floor. Our place was too noisy and we were too numerous for him to try anything like this. With us he would open his cases, to the great joy of all of us, and proceed to show his wares. Curiously enough, he seemed afraid that any one might want to buy something. He cherished all his possessions. Laying out his goods carefully, he took one extract after the other, unscrewed the cork, lapped it with his tongue and commented on its excellent quality. He then shook each bottle again and passed the cork around for the adult members to lick, hoping the taste would please them. He made quite a rite of this. It was good salesmanship although questionable hygiene.

At the table it was most difficult for us boys to keep from laughing when Jones was around. One morning Mother brought in oatmeal. It seemed to be very mystifying to our guest. Mother asked him if he would have some. He looked at it doubtfully as if he had never seen oatmeal before. "Guess I will, guess I won't," he chanted. "Guess I'll eat my apple-sass first."

In view of Father's open door, it came naturally to me to hang my latchstring outside. We have taken in something like twenty boys and girls in the last forty years, and are still at it. While in college I was more or less put in charge of a Hartford youth named John Kellogg, who had had a nervous breakdown. Ever since then he has divided his time between our home and the family place at Randolph Center. Next on the list came a young girl whose mother was widowed and out working. She had no idea what to do with her daughter, and was much relieved when my sister Martha and I took her in. She is now an assistant superintendent of nurses at a large New York state institution.

For the last six years we have had as members of our family two young Bohemian girls, Lillian and Frances Platenka, one of whom is due to enter high school and the other, having graduated, is studying beauty culture. They were in a sad plight when my path first crossed theirs, for their mother had just drunk poison and killed herself. They lived near Maromas and she had been trying to make a living by taking in boarders. In winter there was no income from this source and she was nearly frantic with worry. She had seventeen different kinds of part-time payments and instalments falling due constantly, and a mortgage on her hands too. After her suicide, the father went to town and returned with a housekeeper. Before long he followed the same course as his wife and shot himself. I conducted the funeral service and afterwards a selectman of the town asked me if I wouldn't become guardian of the children and settle up their very muddled estate. At the time they were seven and twelve years old. I found it a complicated job to handle. The father had some insurance, but all sorts of bills and part-time payments were outstanding. I closed these out as fast as possible. The children stayed with the housekeeper while I was trying to get their affairs straightened out, but soon it became apparent that the only thing to do was to take them into our home until we could sell their house. They have been with us ever since, living exactly like the members of our own family.

One morning soon after we were married and just before we moved out to the farm, our front doorbell rang at six A.M. Mrs. Gilbert's morning greeting, "What are you getting up so early for?" hadn't yet been spoken but I dressed hurriedly and went downstairs. On the porch stood the town's bad boy with his mother. She shoved him in, saying, "Here he is, Mr. Gilbert. I've tried for thirteen years to do something with him, but I give up." She ran down off the porch and left us there, looking at each other. The boy's father was dead.

Well, we took him in, and soon he began to live up to his reputation. We never knew where he was, what he was up to, or when he might come home. There was no telling whether he would condescend to sleep in our house at night or not. I talked the matter over with him and explained that we couldn't go on that way. He agreed and promptly became worse than ever. I might as well have been talking to my horse. It took less than a week for things to come to a head. He had wandered off again with some of his old ne'er-do-well chums, not bothering to tell us where he was going. I drove into town to see if he had any record in the town court. He had. His papers were all made out for reform school. So I decided then and there that a real impression had to be made on the young man. It turned out to be quite an impression, not only on him but on the kitchen floor. The dents in the floor, where his heels came down, are there to this day.

It may seem harsh to give any boy such a licking, yet I think that he was more scared than hurt. Sooner or later we have to learn that we can't do as we please in this life—and the sooner we learn it, the better. I kept him in bed all the next day to think things over and ponder on his future. We took food up to him, but not enough to distract his thoughts from the main business in hand. Meanwhile Moms did her best to sew up the coat collar of his jacket. There seemed to be a real improvement after that. We had no more trouble with him while he stayed with us. We got him a place on another farm, where he could work for his board and go to school. He went to church with that family every Sunday and they found no fault with him. Later he went to the city and joined a Baptist Bible class. For years he was president of it.

A minister in a near-by town called me late one night to plead for a fellow who was due to be called into court the next morning. It meant four and a half years in the state reformatory, the offense being stealing. The judge didn't want to send him there—it would "complete his ruin." So he said that if someone would find a home for him, he would put off the case. Naturally, inasmuch as I seemed to be running an open house for all those imperiled by the threat of reform school, my help was commandeered. I got busy on the phone and found a home for him, without having to take him in myself. Later I found him a second home. His case was never called, he never went to reform school, and today he is a respected citizen. Several times I've "cheated the law" of men like this, and I wish I could do it oftener.

I was preaching one morning to about six hundred inmates at the state prison in Wethersfield. During my talk I said that if any man there had no place to go to when he got out, he could come to my home. It wasn't two weeks before Moms glanced up from her ironing board and saw a big fellow shuffling up the walk. The minute she saw him she knew where he came from. She invited him in, just the same. He sat there intently watching her iron and suddenly he asked her if he couldn't do a shirt for her. She hesitated a bit, then decided he couldn't hurt my shirts very much anyway, so she handed him the iron. He did one of the best jobs on that shirt that Moms had ever seen, for he had worked in the prison laundry, and he knew his business. That laundry experience was all in his favor when we debated whether or not to keep him. He came in August and stayed until the following January. This man had been sent to prison several times and had done a total of eleven years behind the bars for stealing. Yet we never locked up anything, or put anything away, while he was with us. He had a bed on the back porch with our boys and he worked with them on the farm during the day, having the time of his life. He helped me mightily at the church.

One night I had a stiff job to do there. The stove smoked so badly that it was driving me nearly crazy. It isn't easy to talk of heaven in a room full of smoke. One inclines more to talk of the other place. Once before I had found a squirrel's nest in the pipe, so I took my ex-convict and a heavy eighteen-foot piece of tractor chain, drove twenty miles to the church and got to work. One or other of us had to go down a rope from the belfry to the ridgepole, then walk nearly the whole length of the building to the chimney, carrying the chain with him. My helper picked up the chain without waiting for me to ask him to do it, and started out along the ridgepole in the howling wind and bitter cold. I was worried about him, but he made it. He got as far as the chimney and found that the chain would go down only a few feet. Sure enough, there was a squirrels nest about four feet down. So he crawled back along the roof again, got the stove poker, went out a second time and cleaned the pipe thoroughly. He was blue with cold when he got through, but even on the long drive back home, he never once uttered a word of complaint. He was real, that one.

One night he said he thought he'd go to town by bus. He wanted to take in a movie. Moms was nervous about it. "We'll all be in bed when you get back," she said. "You'd better take the key to the back door, and come in quietly, so that you won't wake us all up."

"Not me," said he. "I don't need any key, and I won't wake anybody up, either." He got in all right and we heard nothing. Second-story work was his business. I often tell my listeners that I learned a lot from that man.

He had taken up cooking as well as ironing in jail, and at the end of his stay with us he got a job in a bakery in Hartford. There he has been ever since. He's married now, and he often drives out with his family to see us. They send us a Christmas card every year. He never forgets that he might easily have been sent back to jail.

I had several interesting talks with this man, as we worked the fields together. He told me that ninety per cent of the prisoners in the pen should be outside. Only about one-tenth of them really made trouble, and should never be let out, he declared. There was another thing he said that made me think hard. "You know," he told me, "we talked over what you said that day you preached at the prison, about our coming to your house, but not one of us would have come if it hadn't been for an inmate who knew you. He said, 'That minister's a regular guy. It's O.K. to go to his house. I know him.'"

"But why," I asked him, "should you be afraid to go to any minister's house?"

"Well, it's hard to express it," he replied, "but a good many of the fellows felt they would be out of place and uncomfortable in a minister's house."

That gave me food for thought. When a minister's home is looked upon as an uncomfortable place for the lost sheep, there must be something wrong. We piously read to our congregations, "I was a stranger, and ye took Me in..." but we have little or no idea of taking strangers under our own rooftrees. We'd better be sincere about it, or keep quiet.

A doctor called me one morning to tell me about a fourteen-year-old girl he was treating for a leg badly crushed in a motor-cycle accident. He said that her cries could be heard a great distance from her house. Of course we took her in. We found the leg bone badly infected. The city doctors, unable to do anything for her, had told her to get out into the country where "the sunshine and fresh air might make her leg heal." That was nonsense. No sunshine could cure that kind of infection. Many times, I think, the city doctor tells his patient to "get out into the country" because he doesn't know what else to tell him. Fifteen or twenty years ago the rural areas were overrun with patients suffering from digestive troubles or nervous breakdowns.

I talked over her plight with our doctor, and we decided to put the girl in a hospital. A bone specialist near by took the case without charge, and so did the hospital. The girl improved rapidly and in a month she was walking around our house on crutches. She stayed with us until she was graduated from grammar school—about eight or ten months in all. We bought a complete graduation outfit for her, and she insisted upon paying me back when she finally got a job. I looked at her on that commencement platform and almost cried. Kindness worked a miracle here that mere medicine never could have done. She is happily married now and has a son and a daughter. She comes back often to visit her folks and comes to church if she can.

When we first moved to the farm, the mail carrier drove a horse, and would go by as we were eating dinner. The boys were not big enough to do the milking then, and I had a lot of work to do. You can imagine how pleased I was to receive a letter from a man offering his services on the farm. It ran something like this, "I will be no burden to you in any way, as my work will be entirely free, and I will pay my own board somewhere." One could hardly refuse such an offer!

The writer of this letter arrived in due time, but would not stay with us for fear of giving Mrs. Gilbert extra work. He was perfect on the farm. He knew how to do the work and he did it well. It was planting time in the spring—the ideal season to have a helper like this drop in. He was a great Granger and shortly before coming to us had been to a national Grange meeting in Portland, Maine. He seemed to be a free lance with money enough to live on. He was unencumbered with domestic ties and went where he pleased, staying as long as he pleased.

I was putting in my first patch of alfalfa that spring, seeding it in oats as a nurse crop. We had two horses. This man was so thorough that it was a treat to see him prepare that piece of three acres. It was harrowed as mellow as an ash heap—the stones pushed off, and then properly fertilized. The results justified the care. We mowed that piece of land for seven years without replowing. Of course we top dressed it with something every spring. One of the strange things about our able helper was that he never wanted to be thanked for anything, or have a word said about his good offices. He left as mysteriously as he came. The only time we heard from him afterwards was when he wrote to tell us he had left a whip in an apple tree, after he had finished harrowing. We had wondered where it was. Sure enough, we found it just where he said we would. But we never knew what brought this man so opportunely to our door.

I had been off on a missionary trip one Saturday and was getting home quite late when I noticed, about two miles from home, a boy sitting under a tree by the side of the road. As I came nearer to him, I recognized him as Red, an orphan whom I had known but had not seen for some time.

"Hello," I shouted, as I pulled up the old car. "What are you doing here?"

" Not much of anything," came the answer.

"Any place to go tonight?"

"Nope."

"Had any supper?"

"Nope."

"Had any dinner?"

"Nope."

It developed that Red's half-brother, burdened with a large family of his own, had turned him out to fend for himself and he had been knocking around the countryside, sleeping anywhere and eating anything he could lay hands on.

"Well, get in," said I. "We'll go down to the house to see if we can find anything there."

On the way home I asked him where he had been that day, and he answered, "To Hartford."

Hartford was twenty miles away. He had gone to the home of another half-brother there and had again been turned away.

"How did you get there?" I asked.

"Bummed a ride."

"How did you get back?"

"Walked."

I saw that Red was in a terribly upset state, and that his hair was a perfect sight. I gave him a good supper but in the yard, and then took him into the woodshed to clean him up. It was the worst hair-cutting case I have ever run up against—the only one I have had where a comb was of no use whatever. You couldn't have run an iron rake through that thatch. But I got some of it off at last, just as one would shear a sheep.

We fixed a place for him to sleep in the shed, but before

he went to bed the boys took him over to the pond and made him scrub from head to foot. They burned every stitch of clothing he had on, even his shoes. We had enough clothing to fit him out anew—thanks to the people who give donations. It was three weeks before we got this boy in such condition that he could sleep in the house. Now, it's quite a task to make anything of a fellow like Red, who has grown up wild and never learned how to do anything, or to mind anybody on earth or in heaven. He would come out of the barn and slam the door behind him, never even looking around to see if the latch caught. He would fling the screen door back and let in all the flies for miles around. He would never think of cleaning his shoes or taking off his cap before entering the house. Instead, he would come in from the stable and plant himself right in a parlor chair. When the mood struck him he would wander off at will, saying nothing about where he was going or when he was returning.

Things came to a climax with him in a very short time. He seemed to think that he could get up any old time in the forenoon that suited him. I called him one morning, and he answered, but that was all. It wasn't long before he was helped out of bed and he was all over the floor in less than a minute. He soon saw that it would be much more comfortable to rise and dress without my assistance. He too, learned for the first time that in this life one isn't altogether one's own boss. He stayed with us for a year and a half. I was appointed his legal guardian by the court, and by the time he was twenty-one I had one hundred dollars to turn over to him. But it didn't do him much good. In his harum-scarum days Red had spent so much of his time swimming that his ears had become infected, and although Moms and I took him to one doctor after another, he never got well. He died of that ear infection, several years ago. That was one we lost.

We took in one girl whom Moms couldn't stand for more than two weeks. She never saw a thing to do, and she wouldn't have done it if she'd seen it. But she was honest, and never pouty or sullen. We found her a home after carefully explaining her peculiarities to her employer. She stayed at this house for a month, and with her next employer nearly all summer. Finally she settled for several years with a family that happened to live near her sister, who worked in Hartford.

We still do a great deal of placement work with these girls, sending them out to good homes. We usually arrange for them to stay at least two weeks. By that time both the girl and her employer know whether or not they want to go on. In this way no girl is ever "fired," and no one quits a job. The girl's mother can say, "Susie has been helping Mrs. Smith out for two weeks." But they seldom leave at the end of that time. Usually the employer wants to keep them. We insist that these girls eat with the family, especially when there is no company, and when they are not required to wait on table. While there is no need for them to be under foot all the time, neither is it necessary for them to spend all their spare time alone upstairs. When the employer agrees to this, they usually get along in great style. I've known many a mother and many a child to cry when the "visiting girl" went back home.

When speaking to city congregations or groups of women, I tell them that I cannot see how any Christian woman can say to herself, "Here's a good stout healthy girl. I can get a pile of work out of her."

Instead may she think, "Here's a girl that Mr. Gilbert has carried back and forth to church, has baptized, has seen confirmed, and has cared for over the years. Now he is turning her over to me, to carry on the work of character building."

A case in point is the Nedobity family, on whom I called several times, becoming well acquainted with them as we drank coffee together. The father was quite ill, and I soon learned that they were greatly worried over their taxes; indeed they were in danger of losing their home. About that time I was asked to preach at a union service in Shelton. The collection amounted to twelve dollars, which I promptly sent to the tax collector on behalf of the Nedobitys, and told him he would get the rest in due time. The family had raised a number of turkeys that year but had no way to get them to market, and no telephone to solicit buyers. It wasn't long before I took a buyer to their home who gave them an excellent price for the entire flock. Maybe the Bishop wouldn't approve of my taking that collection to pay a tax collector, but it seemed to me to be the Christian thing to do.

When the daughter of that household was sixteen, I got her a position as helper in a splendid home for five dollars a week. The woman who took her in became interested in her family, and supplied them with many an article of clothing and other helpful things. Every two weeks that girl took home ten dollars. They paid up their debts, bought a horse to cart wood and eventually a Model T. The girl's employer, meanwhile, taught the girl how to sew and encouraged her to take painting lessons, with the result that she won a prize at the county fair. Now she's happily married and has a fine home of her own. Her father seems quite well. He was suffering merely from tax sickness.

The people we have helped have without exception been appreciative. Nedobity didn't have much of this world's goods, but he insisted on giving me a fine old pestle and mortar made in his native country, Bohemia. It was such a beautiful piece of work that we hesitated to take it, and only accepted it when we saw that he would be hurt if we didn't. I also have two brass pieces that an Italian woman gave me. One is a kettle, the other a covered dish. She said, when I demurred, that I could have them and gladly, for her husband didn't like them and they would be given away somewhere else if I refused them!

The story of another boy we took into the family for a short time is a rare one. It all started with a call I paid on a wealthy, generous and public-spirited citizen of Connecticut—Edward Hazen of Haddam. Mr. Hazen and I were on the first board of directors of the County Farm Bureau. We worked together for a number of years, and even after I gave up this activity, we remained firm friends. I stopped in to see him one day, when he was not feeling well. As I was leaving he said, "Gilbert, you've never asked me for money."

As he was a deacon in the Congregational church and I an Episcopalian missionary, his remark took my breath away. "Why no, I haven't. Why should I?"

"Well," he said, "I've been watching your work, and I'd like to have a hand in it."

Just then I was wondering where I could get hold of

some money to shingle an old Methodist church that the Episcopal church had bought for me to use as a mission house. When I left Mr. Hazen I had a check for $100 from a Congregational deacon to an Episcopal missionary to pay for shingles on a Methodist church. Furthermore, Mr. Hazen remarked that if I happened to run across a good deserving boy who needed help, he would like to know about it.

Soon after this I was showing some of my pictures at a rural schoolhouse, and I noticed in the congregation several children from the same family who looked as if things were none too good at home. (I usually find out where such children live by giving them a ride home, and then I stay around outside for awhile to give the mother a chance to slick up her hair and change her apron before coming out to see me. I've learned never to rush that process. A woman will come down to see the preacher when she's ready, and not till then.) I found seven boys in that family, and a father who was the most savage-looking individual I've ever met, with jet-black whiskers and a tough manner. He was a carpenter by trade and a fighter by nature, and he was forever fighting and brow-beating his wife, thrashing his children and going to law with his neighbors. He sold the lumber on his farm, and, though desperately poor, immediately got into a fight with the sawmill owner who bought it, and as far as I could find out, never saved a cent from the sale.

The mother was taken sick shortly after my first visit to the home, and the neighbors phoned us about her. Moms and I went down to see what we could do for her. That day we took her to a hospital and we brought home the baby, keeping it for three weeks. A few days later we took in the oldest boy, a clever youngster who had just been graduated from grammar school and who wanted to learn to read plans and blueprints so that he could become a builder. I laid his case before Mr. Hazen, who promised to help. We put the boy in trade school. His mother was highly pleased, but the father was mad. That was the way they agreed—on everything.

One night while we were eating supper there was a rap at the door. My daughter went to open it and found the boy's mother there. She asked to speak to the boy and as he stepped toward her a hand flashed in from the dark and grabbed him, trying to pull him through the door. My sons and I seized him from behind and held on. In came the father, and was there a rumpus! He pulled, fought, kicked and bit everybody. He tried to draw a knife from his pocket, and we got him down just in time. The room was a sight when the fracas was over, with chairs and rug in a heap, the table turned upside down and dishes and food all over the place. We had to call the police before we could get the man and his wife out of the house. We learned afterwards that he had planned to bring his shotgun and shoot me through the window, but one of his boys, learning of it, had hidden the gun in the barn.

That's the price we sometimes pay for trying to help. Occasionally it may be dangerous, but more often it's funny. There was a funny side even to this fight. During the heat of the battle my daughter phoned the neighbors to say "There's a fight over here!" Men came rushing in from all sides, with pails, buckets and ladders. They thought my daughter had said "fire" instead of "fight"!

After this episode, we moved the wife and her eight children into the city. We let the boy return home, but he finished his course at trade school. They were quite destitute, so it was up to me to furnish the rooms for them with a gas stove, beds, mattresses, bedding, dining-room table and chairs, silverware and kitchen utensils. We even dug up a rocking chair in which the mother could rock her baby to sleep. This was one of the biggest outfitting jobs I ever attempted. They were Italians and, of course, never came to our church, but what of that? People are people, whatever their church, and it is up to all of us to help them. I have had many a Roman Catholic family on my hands in the country. Shockingly as this man treated his wife and children, the woman was reluctant to give him up, and time and again, she went back to him, to suffer more punishment at his hands. He was unrelenting towards me and did a carving of me and the first selectman as devils with horns, which he mounted on his front gateposts.

Once, believe it or not, I played the Good Samaritan to a crateful of chickens. A widow who lived on the banks of the Connecticut River wrote saying she had heard that I was kind to strangers, and she wondered if I would look up a shipment of pullets coming to her through Middletown by express, and give them water to drink. I did, thinking to myself meanwhile, "You can't say I didn't obey the Lord's injunction to give a cup of cold water..."

They seemed quite appreciative.

Chapter XVI

POLITICS

. . . .

As MOTHER fed us religion so Father fed us politics. I was no stranger to either. Politics was Father's meat and drink. If he had spent more time studying poultry bulletins than the political editorials of the New York *Sun,* we'd all have been better off. He was a great admirer of Grover Cleveland and when Cleveland ran the second time Father had a sign at least five by ten feet painted to hang over a limb on a large maple tree in front of the house. It gave the prices of butter and eggs during Republican and Democratic administrations. One night it disappeared and we found it later down in a swamp near Dana's woods. No wonder! Father was an ardent Democrat, and that was something in those days, for it was even harder to find a Democrat in Vermont then than it is now. Indeed, when an invitation was sent on one occasion to the Governor of Massachusetts to come up to Vermont and speak to its Democrats, he sent back word that he was a very busy man, but if they would come down to his office, he'd address them there.

By some odd chance we were Democrats on both sides of the house. Grandfather Blodgett came from New Hampshire and was always a staunch Democrat. He and all his family were keenly interested in the underprivileged and, as Aunt Kitty used to say, "were naturally Democrats." The Gilberts were very independent thinkers and were never inclined to go with the crowd, which probably explains why they held out for their own political convictions in the Republican state of Vermont. Father was always at white heat during elections, challenging all comers to debate as they sat around the stove in Will Fargo's store. For several years we boys sold sandwiches at the polls, so we knew our way around politically. Under Grover Cleveland, Father was appointed postmaster at Randolph Center. Immediately, the Republicans got busy and saw to it that he could not find a building in which to establish his post office. Father had to erect a new building on a piece of rented land. He put Martha and me in the office as clerks, and what a time we had! (Eventually, in the time of Woodrow Wilson, Martha was appointed postmistress at Randolph Center, and for the last twenty years, as Mrs. Edward F. Kibby, she has held this post.)

We would keep the unclaimed letters that came in for several days, and then mark them "Try East or South or West or North Randolph." It always seemed that five minutes after they went out, someone would rush in and ask for them. We would search the place high and low, even taking mail out of the boxes. Then we'd say that the letters would probably arrive in a day or so. We'd send a tracer out after them, and sure enough, in a day or so we'd have them. We had a number of lockboxes in that office that nobody ever rented. There was one poor half-witted fellow who used to come in for his mail but he never got even a postcard. One day we fixed up one of the lock-boxes for him and gave him a key. He was overjoyed. But there remained the problem of getting something into that box. Now, even in the smallest post offices a lot of almanacs and mail-order catalogues come in, addressed to people who have long since died or moved away. So between mails we fixed these up, readdressing them to our half-wit with the big empty lockbox. We loosened the glass in the box, so that it would rattle when anything struck it. Then we sorted the mail, with half the town waiting outside, and let down one of those heavy catalogues into the box. You could have heard the clatter out on the street. The poor fellow would step up, proud as punch, take out his key and open the box. He would hardly have it locked when "bang!" in would go another Sears Roebuck. He had all the mail he could carry home, and it saved us the bother of burning it up.

Father lost the post office when Cleveland went out, and the building had to be moved off the rented ground and down the road a mile and a quarter to our farm. It was a job we never would have tackled had we known what was coming, but we had a lot of fun out of it too—thanks to Charlie Blodgett, comical, dirty, fat and disreputable, but a soul I hope to meet in heaven. I learned one of the most valuable lessons of my life from Charlie, and that was to maintain perfect cheerfulness under the most trying circumstances. There is no man living you can't learn something from, and although Charlie was regarded locally as a rough and brutal character, he made a lasting impression on me. Indeed, everyone liked him and there was a great turnout for his funeral when he died. He was a big, tough, cursing fellow, who beat his horses and cared for the Opinion of no man. He didn't look at a church when he rode by, and we were supposed to keep away from him, lest he contaminate us. But when it came to moving the post office, Charlie had to be called in. He did odd jobs with horses and he moved buildings. When some one asked him one day if he hadn't a horse for hire, Charlie said that he had six, and there wasn't one in the lot that would draw your hat off. That was correct. He had the finest collection of old plugs in the country—the Blodgett touch again, although he was not related to my mother's branch of the family.

But even Charlie was stumped by that plagued post office. Day after day we struggled with it, Charlie cursing like mad—hot, red and filthy, but always cheerful, and usually singing the old Civil war ditty, *Stick to her, Jack. Stick to your mother till your Dad gets back.* About the middle of the week he went to the brook to take a bath. On his return he proudly announced, with a string of oaths, "Well, I roiled up the brook for over two miles."

We worked with planks and rollers, moving the post office on a capstan, with a horse going round and round. When we got it down to the edge of the hill we decided to have a bee and get people to bring their oxen and horses to help in our mighty task. I was dispatched to ask the people to come, and the bait was the dinner we would give them. The people grumbled. They didn't see why they should use Republican horses to pull a Democratic post office. Well, we finally hitched on seven pairs of horses and seven of cattle and did we have a time! We had to feed this army of men and animals. The road was narrow. The skids were narrow. The post office wouldn't go straight. It kept going off the road. We had to jack it up. The ropes would break.

It was terribly hot as we lugged these heavy planks around. Charlie had boasted that he would stand right in the window and drive these Republican sons of guns, but it didn't work out just like that, even though he did turn a heart-breaking job into a holiday. Father in the same circumstances would have had a thousand fits, but Father was steering clear of this undertaking. Our weak calves usually became Father's cows. He had given me the building in order to get me interested in moving it. Well, in the end Charlie's horses triumphed and the building found a resting place after a week's labor.

From Charlie and my Uncle George, a humorist of the first rank, I came to understand what an important place humor has in a minister's life. I think Mrs. Gilbert is right when she says, "The two main essentials for a country minister are a good sense of humor and a leather stomach." I found that both were badly needed when I went into politics. The boys and I were husking corn in the barn one morning in the fall of 1924 when we saw a group coming down the walk. They came right in on us, for you don't rap when you enter a barn. They turned out to be a delegation from the town Democratic committee. They tried to husk a bit, but they were pretty bad at it, so they just sat awhile and then they sprang the news. They wanted me to run for State Senator. It was hard for me to arrive at a quick decision, sitting there with my lap full of corn husks. But when it occurred to me that I might help my country folks get electricity into their homes, I said, "Sure. I'll run." And that was that.

As national elections come in the fall, corn husking and politics have always gone arm in arm in the country. The kinship was strong that night on my barn floor with the committee doing their best to be good farmers. There wasn't a chance in the world of a Democratic senator being elected that year, but I had a great time campaigning. Since high tariff doctrine always threw Father into a fever of excitement, if not of rage, I had always laid most of the country's ills at its door, and still do. So that fall I took a much worn woolen sweater with me, and tramped up and down the aisles of a hall showing people the garment at first hand and telling them what it had cost and what it should have cost. I pulled such a good vote that I was considered by the opposition to be a man who would bear watching.

After that experience I turned more and more to local politics and began writing "Open Councils" for the local paper. The parishioners didn't seem to mind my getting into this, as they knew that my fight was for the poor folks and the farmers. I announced that I wanted open and aboveboard government, for I was convinced that public affairs were being run, not by the men for whom the people voted, but by the boys in the back room. I considered that the mayor of Middletown was a mere figurehead and I said so in blunt language, which was quoted in the local press.

About this time I had a run-in with the Chamber of Commerce. I don't say that this organization does not have its uses, but, if it has, it should keep in its place and not try to supplant the voters. The organization became quite excited over my accusations, but they were never shown to be untrue. As far as I know, the Chamber of Commerce has never undertaken to run the city since. A man came to my farm, trying to get me to join up, saying that one of the members had offered to pay the ten-dollar membership fee. But the town at that time would certainly have thought I had fallen from grace if I had joined. And I would have been sure of it.

The question of taxes and the expenditure of public money seemed to grow worse and worse in the town and, after protesting plenty in the local paper during the summer, I set forth on the greatest venture of faith I have ever attempted—a poor country missionary on a little old farm on the outskirts of town, scandalously invading the strongholds of the mighty, facing the sneering derision of the schooled politicians of the party who had had absolute sway over the city for years, and hiring the big town hall for a public meeting of indignation and protest.

If I ever did any hard praying in my life, it was over that meeting. I honestly felt it was the Lord's work and a straight moral issue. Such a bold stroke had never been attempted in this section, and no one seemed to think there would be anybody in the hall. I certainly would have been the laughing stock of the town, and goodness knows how I could have shown my head upstreet again, if only a few had turned out. One of my friends told me later that as he sat in his home that night, he felt more and more sorry for me as he pictured me sitting there alone in that great hall, so he decided to look in on the meeting just as a gesture of friendly comfort. He was blocked before he could reach the door. The place was packed. I gave a long talk to this crowd of voters and answered questions, then they voted their opinions on various matters. They all wanted more meetings. I suggested that we take up a collection to pay for the rental of the hall. So much more was received than was needed that we had to elect a treasurer. After the meeting, two men came up front and said they were with me heart and soul and would do anything they could to help. This took courage on their part, for I was far from being in the good graces of the upper crust of the city, and I had expressed rather liberal— some thought even radical—views from time to time. (Friends phoned out next morning to see if our house had been bombed during the night.)

One of these two men was Frederick J. Bielefield, a grocer who had a store on Main Street, and who was known for his straightforward honesty and fair dealing. Thanks to his knowledge of grocery-store chat, he had helped me a great deal in gathering data on how the city was being run. My other ally was a young Jewish lawyer named William M. Citron, just out of Harvard Law School and ablaze with liberal ideas. He had come from a poor family in the city and had worked his way through college and law school washing dishes in a restaurant. He needed a start, and it certainly wouldn't help him on the road to a lucrative practice to join with the honest grocer and the so-called militant parson, but he had the courage of his convictions. Together we continued our League, with Citron as secretary, Bielefield as treasurer, and myself as president. Before long we realized that a local election was upon us. We boldly put forth our grocer for mayor. He was elected by an astonishing and overwhelming majority, and three times after that was reelected, holding the office for eight years, which shows what the people thought of a real mayor. Right after this came the state election, and young Bill Citron and I decided we would run for the House of

Representatives in Hartford. No Democrat had been elected there since Woodrow Wilson's time. The city was overwhelmingly Republican. Well, we put on a hot election. We stumped the city from one end to the other. We had the people all stirred up. We spoke in front of every factory, big and little, at the noon hour, and continued to hold our meetings in the town hall. I remember once when I was speaking, the crowd blocked the sidewalk right in front of the police station, so that even the trolleys were stalled, and the guardians of the law had to come out and clear the way. Fine sight! Episcopal minister snarling up traffic in front of the police station. We filled school-houses and halls all over town, and I got my audiences going with stories. Mix anecdotes with politics and a talk is bound to go over.

Mrs. Gilbert said Citron's voice was so bad that it would kill the cows, and that neither of us would get anywhere, but he improved, and in time became a good speaker. Later I stumped the state for him when he became congressman at large. Citron is a socially minded fellow and he and I instinctively linked right up together, although we were considered a strange combination— elderly Episcopal minister sponsoring young Jewish lawyer. Our ideas were quite revolutionary in some ways. We stood out for government control of public utilities, and extension of electricity to the people, with lower rates. We condemned the boss rule under which the state had suffered for years, taking the same tack as we had in civic politics. The wealthy were against us, hook, line and sinker, but the common people heard us gladly. When I spoke at a factory owned by the family which dominated

Christ Church, I noticed a stenographer down front taking shorthand notes on every word I said. I drew attention to her and jested along, telling some stories, until finally she was so embarrassed that she put her notebook away. The factory heads who assigned her to this task never got the detailed report of my speech that they sought.

Another time, speaking at a typewriter factory where we were under suspicion, we thought it best to keep off the premises, lest legal action be started against us, but our voices were so strong that we could easily make ourselves heard, even though the building stood well back on the property. We talked from the street and the employees stood outside the factory and listened with interest.

When election time approached we obtained sample ballots. We took them with us wherever we spoke. Holding them up we showed our audiences first how they could vote for our opponents; then, as an especial kindness, we demonstrated how they could vote for us. But we always urged them to vote anyway, whether for us or against us, and to study the issues well. In this instance they were clear-cut enough. Did they want to be governed by a man who was governor himself, or by a man who was governed by someone else, not on the ballot at all, yet the real power behind the throne? We called their attention to the way in which the power franchise of the state had been turned over to J. Henry Roraback, boss of the Republican party. We asked them if they knew how he got it and when he got it. We asked them if they wanted their candidates to represent them, or the private interests of franchise seekers. We asked them if our opponents had told them how they stood on the questions that would come up, or were they voting in the dark? We told them we wanted them to feel that if we were elected they would be taking an active part in making their own laws and their own government, for we would bring down the bills while they were still "in the works" and all of us openly discuss them in the town hall.

Soon our opponents for the legislature were calling for "facts" as to boss rule. To prove to them that we were not talking of something we knew nothing about, just because one of us was a minister and the other a young man who had not been in public life before, we quoted from the New Haven *Courier Journal*, one of the strongest Republican papers in the state. It had admitted editorially that King Roraback had named all the principal officials of the state for years, and added that if anyone outside the sacred circle was "rash enough to invite support at the polls, the immense Roraback machinery, with political wheels, municipal, county, state, even in Washington, begins to revolve and he is crushed."

I kept hammering away at the electricity issue, using the arguments that are as potent today as they were in 1926. What has New England got left? Her building lumber is practically all gone. She has few if any natural resources for her immense manufacturing interests. What does she do when it comes to textiles? She sends 990 miles to Alabama for a bale of cotton, and 1266 miles to Iowa for a piece of beef for breakfast. She sends 1763 miles to Dakota to get a bag of flour to make a loaf of bread for a workman's lunch, and 460 miles to Western Pennsylvania for a ton of coal. The workingman goes to the factory and he makes a shirt, which is sent 965 miles to Sears Roebuck in Chicago. By the time it gets there, the workingman's wife makes out a money order which she sends to Sears Roebuck for the shirt, and it is sent 965 miles back to the workman's wife. The man puts the shirt on his back and he wears it to the factory where it was made in the first place. None of it makes sense. What then has New England got left but the pure gold of her water power? The Connecticut River has a fall of 500 feet, and the Merrimack a fall of 1,159 feet, and it is well said that two-thirds of their flood waters would furnish light and power for the whole southern part of New England.

We demanded cheap electricity in every campaign speech and in so doing we were hitting directly at King Roraback, who was head of the Connecticut light and power interests, and at the same time chairman of the Republican State committee. We argued that adequate electricity was the only thing that would keep the boys and girls content on Connecticut farms.

Excitement ran high the night before the election. Some admitted the possibility of my being elected, but as for the staid old town sending a representative to Hartford who not only was a Democrat but a young Jew as well, that was beyond even the shadow of a doubt. However, we made it, Citron and I, to the confusion of the prophets. When we started for Hartford on the first day of the session in my trusty Model T Ford, a crowd gathered in front of the post office and gave us a great send-off.

We found the old boss rule stone-crusher tactics in full swing, and I was quickly shelved to the committee on unfinished business—a committee that was not supposed to meet and never did meet. After this appointment I wrote an open letter to the press, saying, "I accept, O King, with the understanding that the unfinished business is your dethronement." How much I had to do with it is not for me to say, but in any event Roraback was utterly unseated several years before his death, and Dean Wilbur L. Cross, of Yale, was elected Democratic Governor, and then re-elected and re-elected.

A surprising and interesting feature of Dean Cross' campaign was that he began at once to invade the smalltown Republican strongholds. He told Yankee stories to the farmers, and everyone wondered where he got such a fund of them. It is my guess that he picked up a number from Father. One summer, some years before his campaign, Dean Cross went to Randolph Center for his vacation. He had rooms at my sister's house, and took his meals at what was then the Maplewood Hotel. Father had retired from the farm and had all the time in the world to go around visiting. He had a very fine driving horse— Desdemona, called Dess for short, who was a joy to ride after and could go like the wind. So what was more natural than for Dean Cross and Father to go riding around the country day after day? If anyone ever was full of old Yankee stories, it was Father, and he must have peddled them out to the future governor over many a mile.

Dean Cross told a good one about helping our old church. The building needed painting and Father persuaded him to give a literary lecture to help raise the money for it. The event was well noised abroad. The city boarder crowd turned out, and a neat sum was cleared. The church people, however, promptly got into a terrible fight over the color of the paint to be used, with Father leading his battalions on one side, and the minister leading his on the other. The minister's side seemed to have come out ahead, although how he could have won over Father I cannot understand. Anyway, a painting bee was staged. The job was practically completed in one day. But feeling as to the color still ran high. Just as the paint gang was going home, the Lord Himself took a hand in the affair. A terrific shower came up, with the wind and rain whipping the building from all directions. Such paint as was not washed off was all streaked up. The church looked considerably worse than it had before, and Father, telling Dean Cross about it afterwards while visiting at his home in New Haven, announced that he "was damned glad of it."

Well, before the good days of Dean Cross, there were the bad days of Roraback, and we made things as hot as we could for him. Citron was made minority leader in the House but that didn't get him very far. The few Democrats who were there were seated in a corner where it was convenient for the Speaker to ignore them, when they wanted to be heard. Such satisfaction does one little good, but I can't help mentioning the fact that soon after the session ended, this boss-picked Speaker was arrested, tried, convicted and sentenced to prison. This was the sort of gang we had to work among.

I spoke and worked with all my might for better roads in the country districts, and a movement was started that resulted at a later session in a bill appropriating $3,000,000 a year from automobile license returns for dirt roads. This has been a great boon to my country flock. I can't think of anything that has a greater effect on the comfort of the rural population than good roads and cheap, abundant electricity. One spring morning while I was still in the legislature a member of the House left his home and soon got stuck in the mud. He had to leave his car and walk two miles to a state road. When he reached it and tried to get a ride, what was his fury to find two trucks and a big gang of state men setting out shrubbery and flowers—a sort of posy garden! But the Grange got back of the dirt-road movement, too, and now in many towns in this state there are virtually no unimproved roads left.

It is no less gratifying to see the changes that have come about in electrical facilities. I can scarcely believe my eyes as I look around me now and recall how we had to fight for the smallest concessions. In one locality we had meetings in the church with agents of the electrical company. The lowest minimum rate we could get them to set was twelve dollars a month. The absurdity of this is apparent when one considers that this actually was more than any house in that section would rent for at the time. But we kept plugging at it. We brought in a public utilities man and an engineer from Connecticut University, and things got warmer and warmer for the electric company. Now we have electricity all through that section and also in our own church for a minimum of $3.75 a month.

In another region, the company offered to install a line for a minimum of eight dollars, giving a lot of electricity with it. But of what use is electricity that you have to pay for and don't use? It merely gives the company a chance to say in effect, "Why, look here, you're paying for a lot of juice you aren't using. Your bill wouldn't be a cent bigger if you had an electric cleaner, or an electric stove." And at this point the agent steps in to sell you these appliances.

The backing offered to farm folk by the Roosevelt Administration seems to me to have been of the very greatest help to the country sections. A government offer of aid is always in the background. The reason I am such an ardent advocate of public ownership of public utilities is that these necessities must be run for the benefit of all, and not for private profit.. The T.V.A., to my mind, is one of the greatest boons the country could have.

After my legislative experience, I consented to run for the city common council for a four-year term. I was elected but refused to run again, for someone else could do that work just as well as I—quite likely better—and after all, I was a minister first and foremost. As councilman I headed the charity committee and established the custom of having stated hours in the municipal building for people to come and see me when they were in trouble, financial or otherwise. Most of those who came were in distress over the small-loan finance companies. One mother came in weeping bitterly because all her furniture, even the cook stove, was about to be moved out. I immediately telephoned to this company, telling them who I was and my position in the city. I told them that if they pressed their intention I would have a photographer at the house to take a picture of them removing the furniture. It is needless to say that they made no move against the unfortunate woman after that.

I was able to help another family who were afraid of losing their home, by telephoning to officials of the insistent company and telling them that I would take the matter to court and engage a lawyer to fight it. They had threatened to send in the sheriff on the following Monday with eviction orders. The family still live there and the children come to our Sunday school. It means a great deal to poor people to have some one they can go to when they are in need—some one who will stand up for their rights. In this connection I like the old joke about a man's choice of a church. What church do you go to?" he was asked.

"Why, I go to the Episcopal church."

"You do? You like that one best?"

"I certainly do. You see it never meddles with politics or religion."

Aside from the question of whether the church meddles with religion or not, one might well consider whether a minister should not strictly "stick to the Gospel." One thing I will say is that in all my political efforts, stumping over the city and state, broadcasting and writing for the press, I heard hardly a word of criticism from the bishops, fellow ministers or my parishioners— many, if not most of whom, belonged to a different party from mine. I say "did," because now I no longer know in advance which ticket I shall vote. In this respect I am less consistent than Father.

Chapter XVII

BY WORD OF MOUTH

. . . .

SAY, Gilbert," said the chairman of a country church meeting in Clinton at about the time I was getting started in the ministry, "if we run short of program a little later in the afternoon, can't you come out front and say something?"

I tried to get my wits together in a hurry, for I knew it wouldn't be long before I was called upon. While sitting in the back pew of the church thinking what I might say, I unconsciously began swaying back and forth, an echo of my Divinity School days when I had fallen into the habit of rocking my sermons into shape. Soon one of the women of the church came to me and whispered, "You seem to be ill and in great distress. Can't we do something for you, and get you something to take?"

At any rate, I got along quite well with my talk that day, telling my audience something of my church work, which, from the first, was inclined to be different. I don't think that at that time I even bordered on telling a story, but soon in my talks I found that stories were a tremendous help. If you have a growing list of anecdotes that you keep in readiness all the time, you can generally find one that is appropriate. One never can tell how a new story will take until it has been tried out on a crowd. A story that one group finds excruciating, another may receive in stony silence. It is my theory that a good story is much more than a means of amusement. It is relaxation, for it diverts the mind of the listener for a moment and sharpens his appetite for the more serious discourse that may follow.

I make a business of "warming up" a crowd at the start. I generally start off with a few stories to get my listeners with me, and into a good humor. Sometimes a group is chilled by too much introduction. One can always recognize the symptoms. They sit back and coolly eye the speaker when he gets up, as much as to say, "I doubt if this guy is as big a shot as the chairman thinks he is, and as for his being such a wonderful humorist, he won't get me to guffawing in a minute. I've heard good speakers before." The old slogan for toastmasters is still good, "Get up, speak up, and shut up."

In one place where I was speaking, a toastmaster got off a lot of ministerial stories, and such good ones that I bagged two of them right off the reel, but it made it rather hard for me to begin, since stories are my own long suit. However, I took my usual tack of telling stories on myself. If you are a minister, tell stories about long sermons, and notice how they capsize. If you are a lawyer, it's a safe bet to dish up some stories about lawyers. And if you are bald-headed—well, my bare pate has saved the day for me more than once.

People fight shy of anything that looks like profound learning in a speaker. They think that the scholar must needs be tiresome. One night Mrs. Gilbert was sitting in an audience in which no one knew her.

When I got up to speak, my Phi Beta Kappa key

happened to show.

"There!" exclaimed a woman in front of her. "See that key? He's a Phi Beta Kappa. We're in for a dry time tonight."

People may have the best ideas in the world, but if they can't put them across, of what use are they? I just can't read anything when speaking. It seems to put up a screen between me and the people. A speaker may have some headings on the table in front of him, and glance down to get a few reminders of what he wants to say next, but beyond that the written speech seems to me to be a great handicap.

It is a good thing to go to church conferences and get all the ideas one can, jot them down, and then use them. One can generally pick up some stories on these occasions. The clergy know how to tell good stories but just won't use them in their sermons. Many of them go to meetings and hear excellent stuff—new and fresh, but never take a bit of it home to their people. They seem to have the old-fashioned idea that nothing will do but a long set sermon every Sunday. I go to most of the annual meetings of the New England council held in Boston each year and get a lot of dope about the economic and vocational conditions in New England. Hence I can give many talks on the "New, New England."

I find that everyone likes homey talks. When I enlarge on the problems and pleasures of bringing up seven children (five of our own), I usually get a warm response. If they like what is said, they are liberal toward my mission work. I have raised many thousands of dollars during these forty years with homely sermons and talks packed with jokes and anecdotes. Once, before the depression, when I was speaking at a luncheon club in the Hotel Taft in New Haven, I insisted that the underprivileged children of the back roads should have the same advantages as other children, even in the matter of skates and hand sleds. "A child in New England who can't have a hand sled to take to school with him is deprived of his natural rights," I argued. I got enough money there and then to buy hand sleds for every family that didn't have one within a radius of a hundred square miles. And we were able to throw in lengths of clothesline rope for good measure.

And again the money flowed at a big Old Home Day event in Sherman, attended by a number of summer people from the city. Several came up to me after the evening meeting, at which I had spoken. As I was about to leave, in rushed a well-dressed man with his overcoat on, and apparently in a great hurry. He thrust a ten-dollar bill toward me and said, "Here, take this. I got started for New York when I thought to myself, 'What good did all those smooth words I said to that man do him? Words will get him nowhere so I turned around and came back."

When I spoke before the woman's auxiliary of St. Bartholomew's Church in New York on one occasion, a woman rushed up and shook hands after I had spoken, leaving a ten-dollar bill in the palm of my hand. I like to tell my audiences now that after that I tried to shake hands with every woman I met in New York!

One night I was asked to go over to the western part of Connecticut to speak and run a party in a little Methodist church. I knew it would spoil two days, but I have always enjoyed going to small country churches, and it turned into a fine evening. By chance Robert Erskine Ely, at that time director of Town Hall in New York, was on vacation in the vicinity and was present at the meeting. He booked me right away to speak in Town Hall and put on an old-time country social and dance in the evening. Did I have a time trying to teach that city bunch how to do the Virginia Reel! We had sent the music down in advance and I called off the dances, but our country high steppers could show the city folks a thing or two. It was an odd experience for me, the country parson, ordering around all these smooth city people, dressed up to the nines, and not the type I was used to. At that time I had seen very little of city life. I hadn't got around as much as I have since. I have never had a more trying time putting on square dances than I did that night. If any of them had ever tried them before, you wouldn't know it from their performance. As prompter I was boss of the floor. I had to tell them where to stand, what to do, to stop in their own stalls and to keep the figure straight. I called "Pop Goes the Weasel" and "The Girl I Left Behind Me." I had three or four sets and went from one to another, trying to straighten them out. Every minute or so we would have to stop "to make repairs," then off they would go again. I wasn't so vociferous as I am in the country barn—maybe that was the trouble, but we didn't get far, although they all had a good time. They did pay attention to the music and they didn't treat it as a roughhouse affair, the way city people are apt to do with the barn dances. I had a good Vermont partner in Dorothy Canfield Fisher, whom I steered around the floor. When I was handed a check for $150 for my labors after the dance, I was in need of being steered around myself by somebody.

In addition, I had raked in the shekels from the platform for our work. After I spoke, people crowded up to the stage to talk to me, and as I greeted them with one hand, I stuffed the greenbacks into my pocket with the other.

Another time I took part in a debate at a club in Hartford that gave me quite a kick. I was assigned to the negative side of the argument, which was in effect that in spite of all the current controversy about it, New England was continuing its steady advance and was not slipping in any way. It was not exactly the side that I would have picked for myself. I found that my opponent was a lawyer from Boston, smarter than blazes. He had the cool manner and the cool facts. I saw that I was up against it, but he was pretty long-winded and that helped. I remember I cited the increase in mental cases in New England, but although I was short on data I did have a raft of New England stories. I tried out the audience with a few to start. I saw at once that that crowd of intelligentsia, mostly professional men, were avid for this light stuff. I fed it to them for fully three quarters of an hour, and how they roared! Before I finished, I saw the Boston lawyer leave the stage and the room. They said he boarded a fast express for Boston. I was showered with congratulations, and was unanimously declared the winner. I was handed a check for $50 and laughed to myself all the way home. So true it is about "a little humor now and then ----"

One winter I was scheduled to speak at a religious education meeting in a Congregational church at Comstock's Bridge. It was set for a Sunday afternoon, and the roads were all ice and snow. It was a hard trip, but Mrs. Gilbert and I arrived on time, having hurried our heads off.

The local minister came to the door. "We're here," I cried, "right on the dot."

But he didn't seem to reciprocate my rejoicing. "Why—er," he stammered, "we are having a series of meetings. You are to speak at the next one. You are two weeks early."

They had to put us up overnight, as we couldn't repeat our trip that day. We attended the meeting anyway, and had a sort of preview of what would come at our next appearance. It worked out perfectly, for the next time we had a full house.

Now the laymen in a city church would holler if the service began anywhere from half to an hour-and-a-half late. Yet I don't think one banquet in fifty begins promptly. The last one I attended started just an hour after the time set by letter for me to be there. But on one occasion I had time to spare. I was told to arrive for a meeting at six o'clock. After making many train, trolley, and bus changes, I finally covered a distance of 50 miles and arrived on time. It was a Grange Pomona, and every Past Grand, Present Grand, and Future Grand had to make a grand speech. I, as speaker of the evening, was put on at twenty-three minutes past eleven. There were more than 600 present, and I should say, off hand, that I had to wake up about 400 of those farm folk from a sound sleep.

I don't speak before as many men's clubs connected with the churches as I used to, for literally hundreds of them have gone to the wall. One reason is that the ministers view these clubs as bait to get men to go to church. But the church service must stand on its own merits. It can't rely on a pillar of Rotarian breeziness for its attendance. The fellowship of these clubs was all right, although the doughnuts were heavy and the coffee strong, as my stomach will bear witness, but every club must have something more—downright, worth-while service which should smack of hard work and not a little sacrifice. All the luncheon clubs that lasted found that out. Now they are sponsoring or supporting all sorts of good works—Boy Scouts, children's summer camps, *Herald-Tribune* Fresh Air Fund, child placements, keeping old couples together, looking up and acclimating newcomers to town, introducing their wives in congenial circles, and guarding their children against the hardships of new surroundings. Clubs thus engaged do not lack membership, any more than a church doing a good job lacks the support of the community. When the church does nothing beyond supporting itself, and working for itself, money comes hard.

A city girl, visiting in the country, went to the barn to see the men milk the cows. When she came back to the house, they asked her how much the cows gave.

"Why," came the answer, "they didn't give any."

"Didn't give any? Nonsense, of course they gave some. Why should they be milking them?"

"Well," she said, "they didn't give any. I was right there, and every drop they got they had to squeeze out of them."

It has come to be a byword in some of the parishes, "Be careful about Gilbert getting in, or he'll carry all your cash away." True enough, a number of years ago I cleaned up in a Congregational church in Stafford Springs. The minister invited me over, saying "I have tried to get the deacons to promise you five dollars but they refused to do it. They said the collection would never amount to that much and they had no intention of making it up. I hope you get something out of it, but they refused to promise a cent.

That got me rather nettled. "All right," I said, "you advertise it well and leave the collection to me."

The trip over was forty or fifty miles. I knew the Episcopal parson there, so I asked him to come and bring his flock. The result was that the church was packed, and the adjoining Sunday-school room that had not been opened since the dedication, also was filled. I told some pitiful tales of my mission work as well as plenty of stories. The collection was taken up. It was twenty-three dollars. The deacons were upset. They were thoroughly mad that I was getting so much. They felt that they ought to have some of it. They had "furnished the place, the lights and the janitor." "Glory be," said I, remembering the five dollars, "give them two dollars for lights." I bagged the rest.

Something similar happened to me on another occasion at a Lenten service, when the minister forewarned me to expect little or nothing from his congregation for my mission work. He said I could have what was on the plate, but if he knew his people, it would be mighty little. They didn't believe in missions. That worked like a challenge with me, so I preached hard that night. When I got through I knew that I had the congregation with me. When the time came for the collection to be taken up, I could see the men putting their hands inside their coats instead of in their trouser pockets. That meant the wallet instead of loose change—a significant sign always to the preacher. When it was counted, it turned out to be the largest collection they had ever taken up in that church, not barring Easter or the Pension Fund offering.

Maybe the city parson has little need of a joke book, but if you're going to preach in the country you'd better have a stock of stories on hand, and funny ones at that. There's nothing like a good story to illustrate a point or to wake up a tired farmer in the pew. Henry Ward Beecher used to say that the sermon period was "twenty minutes in which to wake the dead." I've found that good stories waken them up quicker than anything else, so I've made a study of the art of storytelling in the pulpit as well as on the platform.

I've discovered that the first rule is that the story must be relevant and should always have some connection with the thing you're talking about. Often I've been asked to return to the same place two or three times, and I've always been afraid I'd repeat some of the yarns I told on a previous visit. So I protect myself by telling the story of the man who spoke in the same town three times. He made a good speech the first time. The second time he came, he gave the same speech. The people wondered if he'd try the same line a third time, so they decided to try him out. After quite a spell they invited him back. Sure enough, they got the same speech, word for word.

When he had finished the toastmaster got up and said, "Now, brother, you have been here three times. And three times you've given us exactly the same speech. We appreciate that, and we're going to give you a little token of our appreciation. I have in my hand a watchcase—a good one, but only the case. If you ever make that speech in this town again, we'll give you the works." I must have used that one a dozen times.

There are occasions when a speaker, going back to a place for the second or third time, wants to take up where he left off. I've often used the following story to prepare my listeners for that: In a farmer's family were two boys, both of whom he wanted to send to college. They were twins, so the none-too-rich parents hit on a happy scheme to get that college education for both their sons. George went to college first. He would go for one term, then send the work and the exams back to brother John. Then John would go for a year and send the work and exams back home to George.

So John went up the second term, and his father said to him, "Now, John, don't let them rattle you. You just take up where George left off." John kept thinking of that, when he arrived on the campus. It worked perfectly. He went into George's class, into George's fraternity, into all George's outside activities. He even decided to pay a call on George's girl, who lived down on Faculty Row. Dressed in his Sunday best, he mounted the professorial porch and rang the bell. The door burst open and out rushed a beautiful girl. She flew into his arms with "Oh, George, George, I thought you were never coming to see me again."

John made the most of that moment. "I know, I know," he cried, taking her in his arms. "I'm not George, but I'll begin right where George left off."

Many times, when I am introduced, the host will speak of my numerous occupations—farmer, minister, barber and so forth. That always gives me a chance to tell of the barber who cut his customer all over the face, and then tried to patch up the cuts with pieces of brown paper. The man looked at himself in the glass when the torture was over, and he was so mad that the barber feared for his life.

I'm sorry," said the barber. "I had bad luck with you."
The customer pulled out a dollar bill and passed it over.
The barber started to give him back his change, but the
customer roared, "Keep the change, man, keep the change.
It's the first time I've ever met a man who was a barber, a
paperhanger and a butcher at the same time."

Stories on the various denominations always go over
well at any sort of gathering, but especially at a church one.
The minister who can crack a joke on his own
denomination gets off to a good start. I've done it many a
time by telling about the Episcopal clergyman who was
fatally ill. It seemed fitting for him to leave a message to
his vestrymen. They brought him a pad and pencil and
with trembling fingers he wrote:

> Go tell the vestry that I'm dead,
> But they need shed no tears;
> For tho' I'm dead I'm no more dead
> Then they have been for years.

Whenever I speak to Methodists I tell them about the
fellow who dropped in, a total stranger, on a Methodist
meeting, and heard the preacher announce that after the
sermon there would be a special meeting of the official
board in the room downstairs. The sermon was a dry one,
and about an hour long. At the close the preacher shouted,
"Don't forget the meeting of the board." After the last
amen the stranger appeared in the room downstairs. The
preacher was embarrassed.

"Er—this is just a little business meeting of the board,

my friend," he stammered.

"I know," replied the stranger, "but I heard you say it was a meeting of the board, and if there is anyone in this place more bored with that sermon than I was, I'd like to meet him."

I used one that got over quite well at a meeting of Southern Baptists. It seems that a colored preacher was walking home from church when he met a parishioner who had been fishing all day. As he was upbraiding the backslider, his eyes fell on the fine string of fish at the rascal's side. Immediately he wilted.

"Nice string of fish you've got there, Rastus."

"Yas, suh!"

"What kind of fish is they?"

"I allus calls them Baptist fish."

"Baptist fish? Why?"

"Cause they spoils so quick after coming up out of the water."

City people coming out to the country always know a lot more about farming than the natives, and they often provide good illustrative material for the country preacher. I know of one city woman who came out our way and sent for a native to help her make a flower garden. He dug out a bed, rounding it up nicely and smoothing it down with a rake. Then he asked, "What are you planning to plant here, ma'am?"

"I plan to put salivas in here," she replied, proudly.

"Salivas? Salivas?" repeated the old farmer. "You don't mean salvias, do you?"

"I mean what I say. Do as you're told."

He did as he was told. Then the city farmerette said,

"Samuel, what would you suggest as a border around this bed?"

"Well, I'll tell you, ma'am," came the quick answer.

"If you're going to have this great big bed of salivas here, I would suggest that you have a mighty wide border of spitoonias around the outside."

I wonder if farmers in general aren't inclined to be critical of the clergy. Perhaps because they have to work so hard at manual labor, they get the feeling that the minister has too soft a time. The Rev. Charles Allison, now passed away, who was a rural missionary in New York State, used to tell how his car got stuck in the mud one evening and seeing a light on top of a hill, he went up to see if he could find a farmer who would pull him out. Yes, the farmer would help him. He got on his coat and his boots, and, with lantern in hand, he started for the barn to hitch up. Suddenly he noticed the clerical vest and collar on Mr. Allison. "Are you a minister?" he queried.

"Yes," said Mr. Allison, "I am."

"Then there's nothing doing," he snapped, as he put down his lantern and ripped off his overcoat. "I wouldn't ask a pair of horses of mine to pull a clergyman out of hell."

Whenever you are called on to talk about some local job a church or other organization is doing, something for which money is needed, you can hit the funny bone with the story of the little girl who asked *the* old man for a dime.

"Will you give me a dime for the Lord?" she asked

"How old are you, my child?" asked the old man.

"I'm nine," was the answer.

"Well, I'm sixty-nine, and the chances are that I'll see the Lord long before you will, so I'll give it to Him myself."

Speaking at clubs is a job that calls for a lot of good humor, deftly mixed with a little flag-waving and Fourth-of-July stuff. Whenever you find an up-and-coming club, congratulate the members, and perhaps start in with the story of the girl who suddenly began to call her boy friend Pilgrim this and Pilgrim that, until he cried,

"What's the idea, calling me Pilgrim?"

"Well," replied the young lady, "I don't know why I shouldn't. You sure do make progress every time you come to see me."

Stories about sermons or misdirected prayer delight an audience beyond measure. I often tell the one about the little boy who came out of church and met the hack driver waiting outside.

"Isn't he through yet?" asked the hackman.

"Sure he's through," replied the youngster. "He's been through for a long time, but he can't stop.

"That may be a good place for you to stop, too.

Then there is the one about the little girl who prayed for a baby sister. No sister came, so she stopped praying. But one wild night, twins arrived. Nonplussed, she took to prayer again that very night, saying on her knees, "Oh, Lord, I thank Thee that I stopped praying when I did."

Bishop Brewster used to tell one which was hooked up to the story of the Good Samaritan.

"Why do you suppose these two priests passed by on the other side?" a minister asked a boys' class.

Up went a little boy's hand. "Why was it, my little man?"

"Why, sir, you see, he'd been robbed already."

A minister mustn't always crack the first joke that comes into his head, however. He must think fast on his feet. His audience won't stand for the wrong joke in the wrong place. The tale must fit the occasion. But the Lord loveth a cheerful giver, and the audience loveth a cheerful talk. I'd rather be accused of impiety than of dullness.

Chapter XVIII

DOGS

· ·

WHEN I found the Keithan boys with a new dog one day I wondered where in the world they had got him. I knew that their old dog had been killed and that they had all been disconsolate.

"Well," one of them explained, "we saw a car stop beside the railroad tracks and some people putting out a dog. We heard them say, Good-by, Brownie,' and then they rode right off and left him. So we tore down the gully and over the railroad tracks to get him. Now we call him Brownie. He follows us everywhere and tries to go to school with us."

Good for the boys! I was so glad to hear what they had done that I bought the license for Brownie. Indeed I've bought many a dog license in my day for many a poor boy, because I feel that boys and dogs belong together in the country. Sometimes I let the boys work out the fee on the farm, if they are big enough; otherwise, I just pay it and forget it. But no little boy has lost his dog in my parish for want of that license fee. Sometimes I take along a bag of bones in my car for some poor pup on the other side of the tracks, in homes where food is scarce. I've often pitied the city boy who can't have a dog, for dog-affection in a boy is like doll-affection in a girl. I feel it's like a benediction to see a dog running out to meet a crowd of farm children coming home from school. I think God planned things that way.

On the old farm in Vermont, I had a brown spaniel named Curley. As Closson was nearly always away, it made a great difference to me going down to the woods for the cows every night if Curley was along too, and he usually was. A boy and a dog have a great deal in common. They both love to run and play, and make a great deal of noise—the boy trying out his new voice as he would a willow bark whistle, and the dog barking furiously as he tries to entice a woodchuck out of its hole. Curley would sit on the big snow drift near the barn and wait for me to come home from school. Sometimes, when I was late, he'd go into the house and get warmed up and then come out and take up his watch again. When I whistled by boxing my hands near the old watertub half a mile away, he would come dashing across the flat and up the hill.

I went to normal school one morning during the blizzard of '88—there *was* a blizzard!—and I got snowbound in a house in the village. I stayed in that house from Monday to Saturday and on the Saturday afternoon I heard a mad scratching on the door. I opened it, and there was Curley! The men had shoveled a path to within a quarter of a mile of the house, and Curley had floundered and fought his way from there on. It was a lesson in love that I never forgot.

When I started my mission work we had a little dog named Maida. How that dog loved me! She went with me when I rode my circuit on a bicycle, often on trips of forty miles or more. Only once was the trip too long for her.

Then she just turned around and left me, to trot home, disgusted. When we used the horse and buggy she liked to run by the horse. In some of the unheated bedrooms down country Maida would sleep under the bedclothes at my feet all night, keeping me warm as toast. She always went with me to church and no one thought anything of it. They took it for granted that where I was, Maida also had to be. Mrs. Gilbert was busy at home with the babies just then, and she never got over appreciating the fact that I could have Maida with me when I couldn't have her. Maida didn't altogether like the babies at first. For a week after each of them was born she would shun the nursery and show great jealousy. Then she'd give in. She would steal into the room and put her little paws up on the edge of Moms' bed. Moms would pat her and explain that we still loved her, babies or no babies, and after that things seemed to be all right. She was a most intelligent dog.

One Sunday I took Maida to a strange church, where I had to fill the pulpit for a sick minister. I left her in the Ford outside, but she wasn't one to take such treatment as that, and just as I was reading the prayers she crept in, and quietly walked right up the chancel steps to sit down behind me. The senior warden spied her, and he was speechless. This was horrible! A dog, in the chancel!

I saw him steal out the front door and come back with a rope big enough to tie up a herd of elephants. He made a noose at the end of it and crept up the main aisle to face the poor little dog at my feet. I thought it best to hold my peace and watch the performance, for I had the sneaking feeling that he was never going to get that lariat around Maida's neck. He reached for her quickly with one hand,

and at that instant she curled back her upper lip, showed her glistening teeth and gave a growl that would have put a she-bear to flight. But no she-bear could possibly have gone through that door as fast as the warden did, dragging the rope behind him.

I have sometimes wondered if that man could get so perturbed over this little dog, what he would have done had he been with me the morning I saw the snake. We were celebrating Holy Communion, and I was standing in the chancel with the elements in my hand when I turned around as a signal for the people to come forward. I spied a good-sized snake curled up in a corner right in front of the rail, running his tongue out at me. I had to think fast. Fortunately, there was a kneeling hassock near me, and I stepped back, encircled that hassock with my foot and worked it up in front of the snake, so close that a communicant could not see the reptile, yet not near enough to frighten him into action. I managed to complete my strategic maneuver just as the first person arrived at the communion rail.

After the service we looked for the snake, but he had disappeared. All we could find was a small hole in the corner of the church wall. I mentioned the episode after service, and the children promptly scampered home and told their folks that there were snakes all over the church. Did we have a time then!

Oddly enough, a woman named Butter lived near the Killingworth church. The family living in the house before her was named Grease. Thus was I cheered to think the country was improving. Mrs. Butter had a German dachshund named Yudie, and Yudie always came to church with her. He would follow her to the communion rail and sit quietly behind her until she was ready to return to her pew. One Sunday there was a special service, and Mrs. Butter decided that Yudie had better stay at home. She closed the windows, locked the door and left, leaving Yudie inside. As she crossed the bridge near the church, he dashed past her. He had gone right through the dining-room window, glass, sash and all. When the church bell rang, if Mrs. Butter did not appear to be getting ready, Yudie would tear around the house, bark, and pull at her dress until she *got* ready.

For many years we had a little white French poodle with a black nose named Bijou. He was my shadow. I call him poodle, for he was part poodle, at least; for the rest he was just dog. Someone asked Virginia, when she was very young, what kind of dog he was, and she said she thought he was part mongrel. But how smart these mongrels are! They eat anything, sleep anywhere, and never know what it is to be sick. Our little mongrel was allowed to sleep in the house, and he was a real companion. I never went upstairs without having him at my heels. Every time I go up into the pasture lot, even yet, I think of him. We always played a game in that lot, when Bijou and I went for the cows. Our fences were mostly sheep and hogproof, and I would shut the gate ahead of him and shout "You can't get over!" He'd run furiously down the line of the fence to a little hole he'd dug for just such an occasion. Then he'd slide under the fence and race past me with his ears flat, barking his head off. We never got tired of repeating the game.

We had a good many more dogs around the church in

the early days than we have now. A good dogfight outside offered stiff competition to my preaching on more than one occasion. It was worse than a woodmouse running along the chancel, and that was bad enough. But I think the funniest dog story was born one Sunday when Bishop Brewster came for confirmation. The boys and I had been mowing down near the swamp that week, and we caught a big snapping turtle. "Just the thing," I said. "We'll have snapping-turtle soup for the Bishop's Sunday dinner." We cut off the big brute's head and took the rest of him up to the house. The womenfolk had one good look at him and washed their hands of the whole affair. The boys and I had to do the rest of it.

You scald a turtle as you would a chicken, and the outer skin peels off. Then you disjoint the shell and dress him off, and the meat that's left is meat worth eating. We looked in a cookbook and found we should brown some flour in an oven to use for thickening, so we put in a dish of flour and gave it a great baking. It came out black as ink on top and white all the rest of the way. The womenfolk laughed and said we should have stirred the flour. We used an old cook stove of our own back of the barn.

We finally got the soup made, flavored well with potato and onion. We poured it into a six-quart milk can to carry down to the church for the Bishop. We left the can in the kitchen outside the door leading to the church auditorium, and got under way with the service. It went well enough. The Bishop was directing some earnest and touching words to the confirmation class when we heard a sudden knocking and rapping just outside the door. I looked around to see if the boys were all in their places, and they were. The knocking became louder and seemed to be coming nearer and nearer. The Bishop, standing directly opposite the door and at the head of the aisle, saw it first— a little white-haired dog had thrust his head into the milk can, trying to get at the soup, and his head had stuck. The dog came down the aisle with the can bumping at every step.

In the Episcopal church there is a slogan, "When in trouble, go to your Bishop." The dog had apparently been to church enough to understand this perfectly, for he headed straight for the amazed diocesan. The Bishop's voice began to quaver and then the words stopped altogether. Whether or not "his heart beat in two directions" I do not know, but his eyes certainly went in two directions—one on the dog and the other on the class. As the dog came nearer, Bishop Brewster looked down at Mrs. Gilbert, and she says she never saw a man who wanted so much to laugh right out in church.

A woman headed off the dog, and out he went. And it may as well be added that the sermon was out, the service was out and the people went out forthwith.

Chapter XIX

PARTIES

. . . .

WHAT'S the use of singing "Seeing Nellie Home" when there's nothing to see Nellie home from? With the influx of races and the change in conditions generally, I saw the old social life breaking up gradually through our section. The quilting party, husking bee and kitchen dance passed into the discard forty years ago, as new stock came along and were eyed suspiciously by the natives, while the newcomers themselves regarded one another with some hostility. They dressed differently, ate differently, talked differently, and for the most part had different church backgrounds. The minister's task, then as now, it seems to me, was to build a new civilization out of all these conglomerate parts.

The newcomers were reluctant to attend church, partly because they knew so few people, and partly because they didn't have a common meeting ground with those they did know. While many city people have too much social life— gadding about all day and staying up all night—the country dwellers are apt to have the other extreme and need a healthy social life in the worst way. I have always felt that newcomers to the rural regions should eat together, play together, dance together and say their prayers together.

This way antagonisms are broken down and in their

place grow warmth and understanding.

Instead of having regular country dances just for the young people of dancing age, we launched parties to which the whole family could come, from babies to grandmothers. We had games for the young and dancing for the mature. It might be said it was a fifty-fifty proposition—like that wonderful sausage meat that was fifty-fifty rabbit and horse, one rabbit to one horse, with the dance end being the horse. I have often thought that we boys, when we were young in Vermont, should have gone out to dances and parties more than we did. I can see all that now. When Cousin Caroline and my oldest sister, Rebecca, got up a birthday party for Closson, and had some girls and boys of the neighborhood in, Closson wouldn't even go into the room where they were. I can see him now, sitting back of the kitchen stove and refusing to change his clothes or have anything whatever to do with his own party. Poor Cousin Caroline mixed bitter tears with her pleading and, by the time the first game of Needle's Eye was over (minus the kissing), the old kitchen stove was a veritable breastwork, with Closson in a broken chair on the one side and the enraged family on the other. It is wonderful how quickly rage can dry up tears. I say "family," but Father wasn't on the attacking front. Sensing what was on that night, he hung around Will Fargo's store and post office, fighting with the Republicans over their high tariff notions—his favorite sport. I rather think they did get Closson in for the refreshments finally, but I can't recall that he ever entered the parlor. It was certainly the social event of the season—in fact the only one for us.

I remember once getting up a birthday party for

myself. Carl Tracy lived down the road a ways, and we went to school together. Our birthdays came on the same day, though he was a year younger than I. "If only we could have a roast chicken!" I thought. I talked with Mother about it, and she got up courage to speak to Father. It was January, and, of course, for a hen to have laid an egg in January on our place, or, in fact, to have laid one anytime between September and April, would have been a miracle. If there was anything Father hated worse than a cow, it was a hen. They were wintered in a cold, damp, dark cellar on the north side of the barn under a bay of hay. They were all sizes and colors. No one knew anything about their ages, except that they were so old that their occasional deaths, I always supposed, were due to their antiquity.

At last Father agreed that I could have a hen, but *not* "one of those brown leghorns." With great anticipation I killed, dressed and picked a mongrel bird, and Mother stuffed and baked it. We young fry were to eat by ourselves after the others were through, and I was to carve. What a thrill! We were to devour the luscious feast as we pleased. It came to the table a perfect brown. I can see it now. Proudly I attempted to apportion a large cut to my birthday chum. I thrust a carving fork into its breast— honestly, I believe it squeaked when it went in. Its joints seemed wired together. I tried to pull out a sliver with the fork, and it stretched out and snapped back just like rubber. Neither the teeth of youth nor the appetite of a stone crusher could separate a strand of that flesh from the bone—-they had been wedded for too many years.

A little later Father decided to give up the aged and infirm poultry home for the winter, and I took two bags full of chickens to a family by the name of Sargent in East Bethel. The local news item had a note of praise for the generous donor, but I knew better than to be seen in that village for years afterwards.

It can readily be seen from this that our social life was not a hilarious one. Indeed, I had never danced until I entered the ministry, but I made up for lost time then. I can't carry a tune, and it was quite a job for me to learn the old fashioned square sets, but I was determined to master them, and I did. In kitchens and schoolhouses we would sing hymns and read psalms, have a talk and then go into the Virginia Reel and Pop Goes the Weasel. We had good times.

I have a theory that boys living on poor farms should get out and go places, dressed up in fancy neckties and polished shoes. They should learn to make themselves really presentable and to handle themselves in society. They should learn not to hang around the outside looking in, or stand staring through the door. A gang outside always means trouble. When talking up a party, I emphasize the fact that it is to be held inside and not outside. Of course, in small-church parties, everything depends on the minister. Indeed, most social effort is ruined if there is any lack of discipline on his part. There is usually a fresh youngster who must show off by getting tough, perhaps by putting his foot out to trip somebody. A good strong right arm is generally needed to put such a boy where he belongs. The minister should get to a party early, and be there right in the middle of the floor, running the show with a high hand, from beginning to end, or the children will get away from him.

Years ago, we used the graphophone, which is really not quite loud enough for a party in a large hall. Then the children came along with their musical instruments— Shelley with the piano, George the trumpet, Closson the violin, Sister the saxophone and Charles the drums. Sometimes Mrs. Gilbert played the piano, and Shelley the banjo. With an orchestra like this, and a big freezer of ice cream, it didn't take all summer to get up a party. But now that my children are all grown up, it is different. As they have other interests, I have fallen back on the radio-graphophone combination, a tremendous improvement over the old model. We get records from the mail-order houses, and the boys have had some made from their own playing. When we went to a party in those days we were laden down with graphophone, records and needles, dishes and cones, gas tank, stereopticon slides," and six gallons of ice cream. We would never have a party in summer without taking our own ice cream, which for years we made ourselves. Ice cream seems to me to be one of the essential features of any sort of party.

Running these combination gatherings is not always easy. One night a burly, half-witted fellow who had evidently had a drink or two of cider blew in on us. The girls wouldn't dance with him. This made him ugly. Suddenly, as I was passing out hymnbooks to have a song before going home, he sprang from his seat, rushed out on the floor and landed me a terrific blow right between the lamps. I was completely floored and that parting hymn never was sung. The men present rushed up and threw him out. I was helped to my feet, the blood was wiped from my face and fragments of my glasses were cleaned up.

(For several years now that fellow has been a patient in a mental hospital.)

Later I got even, quite unwittingly, with this man's father for bringing up such a boy. The old fellow himself had been to a party, although over eighty. He lived across the street from the church and on his return he bethought himself to sit on the doorstep a little while and have a good smoke. I was the last person out of the building. Just before leaving, I had rinsed off the cups and kettles, cleaned up the old coffee pot a bit, and tidied up generally. I took up the dish pan hurriedly, to throw out some dirty cold water. It was dark outside. I gave the water a fling and it caught the old man right in the back of the neck. As he was not a confessor of religion, his remarks didn't seriously damage the reputation of my church. I believe he came around next day looking for his pipe.

In the old days "confessor" was the regular word for a Christian. When my sister went to teach her first school in West Brookfield, the huge woman with whom she was to board (her first name was Lodosky and she was called Dosky) placed both her beefy arms on her hips and loudly asked my sister two questions, even before she had taken off her hat and coat. The first was, "Have you a spark?"

My poor young sister was as nonplussed as she was frightened. It seems that by "spark" Dosky meant "steady," and the answer to this question might make a difference to the wood pile, on account of the parlor fires.

"Be you a confessor?" she asked next. This was merely a bit of curiosity on Dosky's part.

I find that young people like active games. They don't want to sit around seeing how many words they can get out of the letters on a penny. Those of high school age like what might be called "preference" games, in which they can show a bit of preference—this boy for this girl, that girl for that boy. In forty years we have never had kissing games. There is no need of it.

Old-fashioned dancing is an active preference game set to music. One can have wonderful parties that will hold and satisfy young people without any dancing, but the games must be different. Pinning the tail on a donkey all evening long isn't enough. In "Wink" the boy can lure the evening's apple of his eye to the chair in front of him and by vigilance strive to keep her there. In "Jacob and Rachel" he can call his Rachel into the ring, and have the thrill of trying to catch her. Of course "Tap on the Knee" also gives preference, as does "The Virginia Reel," in which he may ask her to dance with him, and perhaps she will. Or perhaps she won't. "Three Deep" is a good game for alertness and activity, especially in a large group. For smaller ones, "Toss the Handkerchief" works well.

There is no need to buy game books. It is enough to have four or five standard games. They will be enjoyed at any party if they involve activity. A party is a good place to study character, and, if need be, to try to improve it. Some children are so self-centered that they can hardly play a game at all. Others are the "pouty" kind who if they can't have their own way don't want to play at all. The type that causes the worst trouble is the lad who is always on his toes looking for mischief. He'll sneak out doors when you are not looking; he'll holler "Jacob and Rachel" when he shouldn't, just to spoil the game. He needs to be sat on like a ton of bricks. Probably more than one good shaking up is needed. Even then it's hard to do much, considering the short periods we have him, and the amount of time he spends in what is often an undesirable home. But such boys must be made to behave, even if they don't come back to the next party.

It seems strange, but after forty years of observing the young (with sixteen of them spent on the school board), I am convinced that the more book learning parents have, the worse they bring up their children. Of all the parents who make trouble in schools, none can touch the professors and ex-school teachers who have the tomfool self- expression bug in their heads, which they won't give up even when they see they may have carried the idea too far. Heaven preserve their offspring from these misguided parents!

Chapter XX

SPECIAL DAYS

. . . .

CAN you come down and give us a quiet day in my parish?" asked a young preacher of his bishop.

"Quiet day!" exploded the Bishop. "What you need down in your parish is not a quiet day, but an earthquake."

We have found special days to be miniature earthquakes that shake up those who may have become lax, and get new people interested in the church. It seems to me that any church that has plenty going on has both the people and the means to maintain its vitality. All the survey results I have ever seen have shown that the country church with a special life for its young people is by far the most likely to do well.

Putting into practice our idea of creating a family spirit in every small church—a spirit of co-operation and mutual helpfulness—we started at Killingworth the custom of observing the church family Thanksgiving. At first we held this on Thanksgiving Day, but soon we saw that this interfered with the home celebration, so we changed the date to the Sunday before Thanksgiving Day. We have kept this up for a quarter of a century, and each year it seems to be as happy an occasion as ever.

Eating is not overemphasized. We have a Thanksgiving service in church first, with a celebration of

Holy Communion. None of the women has to stay away from the service to prepare the meal that is to follow. One of them may take a minute to step out and put on the coffee or shove wood into the stove, but she soon returns to enjoy the service.

We have made it a point to eat the good things we raise ourselves. We discuss the bill of fare on the Sunday before the event, so that each one knows what he or she is to bring. On one occasion we had a forty-pound pig right on the middle of the table, with a red ribbon on his tail and a red apple in his mouth. He looked nice. (One cuts the pig in halves to bake him, and then sets the two halves close together on the platter. The dividing line is easily camouflaged with a few celery leaves.)

The attendance at these Thanksgiving Sundays gradually increased until one time we had eighty-nine participants. All the tables were set up that we could squeeze into the parish rooms, and we put some table tops on the pews. One time, when the weather was hot, we ate outside in our shirt sleeves. In 1938, however, the snow was so deep that nobody got through to the church. Such is New England! In the old days, I have known the bread to be frozen so hard that you couldn't cut it with a knife. When this happened we put it under the stove to thaw it out. After our Thanksgiving dinner we generally gather in the church and launch into discussion of all sorts of controversial topics, but in quite good spirit. Democracy, as someone has said, is respect for someone else's opinions.

Christmas, of course, is the big day of the year for us. I remember trying to get to Killingworth on one occasion for our church Christmas tree, and running into plenty of obstacles on the way. "Here, we're stuck," I said to the girl whom I was taking down to her home in Killingworth. "And it's quite a job we're up against."

We were then more than two miles from the church and, while the streets of Middletown were as clear of snow as in June, when we hit the hill that went up into the dense woods, we found that the roads were all glare ice. Chains were unknown in those days, and we could not even get the car off the road. In it were all the gifts and trimmings for the tree. It was already dark and cold. The outlook was gloomy. So there was nothing we could do but leave the car, after letting out the water, and walk nearly two miles to a farm, where we got a horse and old bobsled. The horse was an enormous beast with a stiff knuckle ankle-joint, causing it to walk on its toes. It couldn't or wouldn't trot a step. At last we got back to the old car and hitched the rear of the sled to the Ford to pull it back off the highway far enough to get it through a gate.

The old horse gave a long, hard pull, and creakity crack! the sled came all to pieces. What a scrape! I kept thinking of the people who would be waiting for me at the party. Fortunately, I had some stovepipe wire in the car that I had brought to cut into short pieces which, by bending into a double hook, I planned to use in hanging the oranges on the Christmas tree. Well, I took this wire, got on my knees, and managed somehow to wire that sled together so that we could get the car off the road and through the gate. Then we put all the stuff into the little old sled and poked along, step by step, through the two miles of woodland. We borrowed a cedar tree from the banking of a house we passed, and picked up many children on the way. At last we landed at the church. Then we got the tree set up and hung the gifts. We lighted the kerosene lamps and built a roaring hot fire in the big box stove. We kept the graphophone going full tilt, and everyone seemed to have a very good time.

About midnight I drove the old horse back to the farmhouse, where I stayed all night. What a job it was to start the Ford next morning, with the engine white with frost! But it wasn't quite so bad as the time we had to leave it right in the middle of the road all night, stuck fast in the mud. That next morning it was frozen in solid; but, luckily, this time it was not. On the earlier occasion we put lanterns on each end of the car and just left it there until it thawed out. This time we warmed up the car with hot water and kept it going.

It was foolish to have our Christmas way down there in the woods at night, so after a few years we planned our celebration for the Sunday after Christmas. We're no sticklers for the calendar. The large Episcopal Church in Stamford makes a practice of sending me boxes of presents the children bring in and some left over from their parties. But they always came in two or three weeks after Christmas. One year we received none at all, and when I asked the Stamford preacher what had happened, he replied, "What good are they to you a week after the holidays? We're keeping them this year—holding them over for you. You'll get them next Thanksgiving." A man after my own heart!

We have found it best to have the children recite pieces instead of giving Christmas plays. I've always considered a

Christmas play a terrible headache. Sure as guns, little Jimmie or Susie will develop a cold the night before, and then where are you? In small parishes, it's good to work closely with the public schools. A program given in the school can usually be put on again in the church. Children get enough cheap candy, oranges and apples at home or at the school party, so there's really no need to give them more at church. Why not substitute something Christmasy or really religious—pictures to hang on their walls, for instance? They cost little and they last a long time.

Before so many rural schools were closed, I used to get in as many as nine or ten Christmas parties. The old stereopticon lantern with about twenty Christmas slides, and the story of the Nativity, led to a fine program. I never fail to recite a Christmas piece which I have not been able to trace to its source, but which appeals to me greatly. I first heard a little girl recite it in a country schoolhouse:

Used to think that Christmas was nothing but a day
To get a lot of presents and to give a lot away.
Shouted, "Merry Christmas," and helped to trim the tree—
Just a day of Christmas was all that I could see.
Since I found that Christmas is more than any day,
Since Christmas came to our house and never went away.

Struck of a sudden that friendliness and cheer
Was meant to be on duty more than one day in a year,
If you're happy Christmas, why not the day before?
And the day that follows, and so on, evermore?
Got to thinkin' of it, an' that is why I say
Christmas came to our house an' never went away.

Lots of us go plodding along the road of life
An' think one day of gladness will make up for all the strife,
But the Christmas spirit can show you how you need
To make each day a Christmas in thought and word and deed.
Used to pack the kindness in camphor balls next day,
Till Christmas came to our house and never went away.
We just keep on givin' to strangers and to kin
An' find that what is going out is always comin' in;
Makes the sunshine brighter, where we've got to live
To learn that givin's keepin'; what you have you give.
Holly in December, violets in May,
And Christmas came to our house, and never went away.

We are particularly attached to Old Home Day. What good times we have then! In a way, it is quite a lot of work, but when one looks forward to an event with great anticipation and the memory is filled with fine echoes of the past, the work becomes not a labor but a joy. The people bring their own dinners on these Old Home Days and the church furnishes the coffee. They like to sit around a table to eat, instead of balancing coffee cups on their knees. I usually go up and down the tables, picking up a sandwich here, a chicken leg there, and a piece of peach or apple pie somewhere else. With paper plates and paper coffee cups, there are few dishes to be washed.

At Killingworth, we begin the Old Home Day service a little differently from the way we do it elsewhere. Before the processional hymn, I step out in front of the congregation and have a get-acquainted, warming-up time. I welcome the congregation and tell them an appropriate story or two. I talk about the old church building and how the people used to make a living in that district. After describing how we sawed in two the ledge that was in front of the gallery choir, I entertain them with the story of what happened behind that ledge one time long before my day.

A couple came to Mr. Knowles to see about getting married. They wanted the ceremony to be utterly quiet and secret, with no one present but the minister. (But does not the Good Book say that the wedding shall be furnished with guests?) Mr. Knowles, however, promised he wouldn't tell a soul. So, when the time came for the wedding, he took special pains to go out the back door of his home, walk across the lot, and trudge a long distance through the woods until he came to the back door of the church, where he found the bride and groom waiting. Proud of their unnoticed arrival, they slipped into the church for the ceremony.

The wedding service started with the couple facing the altar, of course, and the minister facing the choir gallery. Mr. Knowles had just finished saying, "Wilt thou take—" to the young and bashful groom and he, as though not very sure of the bargain, had said, "I will," when the minister noticed something moving up on the ledge. It distracted his attention a bit. Was it a mouse? No, it was too big. It didn't act just like a rat. In a moment several moving objects could be seen. Doesn't St. Paul talk about being encircled with a great cloud of witnesses? Well, that very secret wedding was soon encompassed by a regular cloudburst of witnesses.

Some of the women—the more talkative ones—had planned to sweep up the church that day. They happened to be wielding brooms in the gallery when they heard someone open the back door. Childlike, their first impulse was to hide, so they dropped down to the floor, back of the ledge. Before the wedding was half over, a whole row of gossips were nudging and whispering. It was fortunate that the couple did not know they were there until the ceremony was over.

After a few such anecdotes, we continue our service with the usual morning ritual and a celebration of the Lord's Supper, making it a memorial service for those who have gone on before. We always sing the hymn, "For All Thy Saints," and now we have our own special hymn written in 1937 by Arthur Everard Laing, a member of the congregation, and dedicated to our beloved church in the woods:

O little church Emmanuel,
Men built and have preserved thee well,
Through winter storm and summer heat,
To grace the spot where three roads meet.

Though all about the wilderness
Within are peace and friendliness;
Though long the way and rough the road
Where'er we meet is God's abode.

O little man with troubled soul,
God made and will preserve thee whole;
He set thee, too, where three roads meet;
Within thee, too, life can be sweet.

In thee no less than in His Son
Faith, Hope, and Love are met as one,

And thou art all men's friend as well
As little church Emmanuel.

After the morning service we have our dinner. We put the tables end to end, lapping them over a bit so that we need use only half as many legs, or "horses." I find it makes it more sociable to have a great many eating at the same table. For many years now, one of our former members has brought two huge watermelons each Old Home Day, and a large knife with which to carve them. I stand at the head of the long table and give these melons what is considered by all a very fancy cut. First I square off both ends of the melon so that the two parts, after cutting, stand upright by themselves. I give the melon a regular saw-tooth cut and then pull the two halves apart. By doing it this way, I can readily cut off pieces of equal size for each person.

The afternoon service is quite informal with talks by visiting clergymen or laymen who have returned for the day. We sing many good old gospel songs: *I Will Sing the Wondrous Story, Jesus Savior, Pilot Me, I Love to Tell the Story, Blessed Assurance*, and *Sweet Hour of Prayer*. We always close with *God Be With You Till We Meet Again*.

One day I received a letter from a woman in another part of the state saying, "I don't go to church any more. There are so many calls for beans and salads, and for seven of us to go to the supper it costs $2.45. So my family just had to quit." But in my churches no one is ever held up for money. No one is ever stopped at the door and asked for anything. When I mentioned that we planned an Old Home Day with a dinner afterwards, a woman who works very hard, without getting anywhere, said to me, "You don't know how much it means to me to go back to the parish house and have a nice talk over a cup of coffee. You know, I've never been able to give much to these little lunches and dinners we have together. Now I have a lot of ducks, and for this Old Home Day I want to give six of them."

I thought how fine it was of this woman to offer them. We got four more and the feature of the dinner was ten roasted ducks, and succulent too. Eighty-four men, women and children from the congregation stayed to enjoy them, including a family of eleven children garnered in by Virginia. When she arrived to pick them up she found that only one out of the eleven was ready. Everything had gone wrong in the family that week—a little girl had had her finger nearly cut off, and a boy had hurt his head that morning.

"How long will it take you to get yourself and the children ready?" asked Virginia of the mother.

"The best I can do is an hour," she said.

"Well, hustle all you can and I'll come back again and get you all. Even if you can't get there in time for church, we can enjoy the dinner together."

So Virginia left before the service was quite over, and returned with the whole family, arriving during the recessional hymn. But, even though the service was over, Old Home Day was just beginning. There was the doxology to sing and grace to be said, followed by a happy leisurely dinner together. This woman sat at the head of one of the tables with her eleven children around her, and what a feast they had! At a table like this, you can usually tell how many children there are in the community for they'll all be there.

Every year I expect these church home-coming days to peter out, yet when the time comes, the church is full again and the people go home declaring it the best of all the reunions. We send notices to eleven newspapers in the towns round about. Without fail some former church boy and his family will read about it and come. As we all linger over coffee after the second service, I feel like saying, as an apostle said of old, "Master, it is good for us to be here."

Old Home Day is held on the third Sunday in August at Killingworth, and in twenty-seven years it has rained only once, so we have always been able to eat out of doors. It is quite a sight to see us gathered in that sheltered woodland spot, away from the haunts of men, with the trees whispering around us and the peace of the Sabbath in our hearts. Looking into the faces of our congregation, one can see the sturdy peasant features of half a dozen European races, as well as the native American characteristics.

We have had some good Old Home Days also in the Rockland Methodist Church in Madison that I persuaded my own church to buy twenty years ago. Most of the people who returned there were Methodists and they had interesting stories to tell of early days in the church. It was considered nothing then to walk a mile and a half to and from church. Catch people doing this nowadays!

One of my funniest experiences with this church was the time we decided to fix up and paint the building. It was quite large, but we laid a new floor in a day. More than a dozen men worked at it, and boys from the neighborhood kept the stove going, and big pots of hot coffee bubbling on it. Then we staged a bee and painted the place. I had

Roman Catholics painting the north side, Jews the south side, Presbyterians the east side and ourselves the back of the church. George painted the belfry. I always use my big four-wheel trailer for Old Home Day, and I need it too, for I carry with me the following carload:

Painted planks for seats
Nail kegs to support the planks
Tables
Big milk cans to hold water
Copper kettles for coffee and to heat water
Dippers to dip coffee
Can of milk
Box of assorted cutlery
Hymnals
Irons to lay across fireplace for kettles
 Sheet iron to protect kettles from getting black
Big iron poker
Sharp ax
Newspapers to start fire
10 lbs. of frankfurters
10 loaves of bread
Enamel cups
Water can with faucet for drinking water for the children

I can seat and feed seventy-five people and think nothing of it. Truly, Old Home Day is the most human of our celebrations, although I like them all. It may not be down on the Christian calendar but it lends warmth and life to a church. We make a great deal of the seasons in the Episcopal church, but I have always been considered a little weak on proper observances. A parishioner asked me on one occasion in grave and serious tones, if I believed in the seasons. I told her I most certainly did. I believed there was a season for everything, but that a chicken supper in December was quite out of season. When they tried it at a near-by church they had a dreadful time getting enough chickens to go round. The farmers wouldn't loosen up, for if a hen had been wintered that far, they thought it better to keep her, as she would soon begin laying.

Once, when the ladies of my church decided on a chicken supper, I said, "Certainly, in the proper season." They thought I meant the proper church season, but at the moment it was the farmer speaking, not the churchman. I knew that we should have our supper in the "settin' hen season," to avoid falling into the same pitfall as our neighbors. So around the first of May I announced that there would be a chicken dinner right after the service the following Sunday, provided, of course, that we could get the chickens. Did we get any? Need I ask of anyone who knows how a farmer hates a persistent setter? Why, we had so many hens that I had to go up and down the street giving them away. Yes, I believe in the seasons.

But, joking aside, the Christian year is a fine thing. It helps to keep a man out of a rut in his preaching and aids him in covering the main lessons on the life of our Lord—the Advent season leading up to Christmas, the Epiphany season with the story of the Wise Men and its missionary teaching, the Easter season, Whitsuntide with the coming of the Holy Spirit, and Trinity with its emphasis on the Three in One, giving a long summer period to dwell on Christ's teaching.

An Episcopalian loves the Collects of the Christian year with their superb balance and rhythmic English. They come along as old friends. I believe everyone should learn by heart the First-Sunday-in-Advent Collect and the Ash-Wednesday Collect. The second Sunday in Advent is Bible Sunday, with its beautiful Collect, *Blessed Lord, who has caused all holy Scriptures to be written for our learning; Grant that we may in such wise hear them, read, mark, learn, and inwardly digest them, that by patience and comfort of thy holy Word, we may embrace, and ever hold fast, the blessed hope of everlasting life, which thou hast given us in our Saviour Jesus Christ.*

"Stir Up Sunday" is the Sunday before Advent. Old Dr. Hart used to say that in the minds of faithful women worshipers, at least, the "stir up" not only referred to "the wills of thy faithful people" but also to the stirring up of the pumpkin pies for Thanksgiving. *Stir up, we beseech thee, O Lord, the wills of thy faithful people; that they, plenteously bringing forth the fruit of good works, may by thee be plenteously rewarded; through Jesus Christ our Lord.*

The pranks and parties of Hallowe'en have rather overshadowed the deep and sacred feeling of All Saints' Day, which falls on November first. Throughout the calendar year, the nation bears in mind on certain days the great men of her history. So, throughout the church year, the church has in mind her saints who have gone before— the apostles, blessed martyrs and others. But at the blessed All Saints' time, each one of us has in mind the souls of his kindred, and with penciled finger and memory sacred, makes up the number of the scroll. I love All Saints'. I think we should make more of it.

Chapter XXI

THE CHURCH WITHIN

. . . .

PREACHING is by no means the heart and soul of the country church. And I sometimes doubt if it should be so in the city churches where voices and theology seem to dominate. Of course, a good sermon is a fine thing, but the minister should remember that Jesus was not a preacher. In fact, none of His followers seems to have been impressed by His oratory at all. A brief report of one sermon is all that we have at best. He told stories, He made parables, He used homely outdoor illustrations familiar to everyone. His power lay in what He was, and that is the greatest power for good that anyone can have.

Christliness is one thing and ecclesiasticism and church organization quite another. The church must get back to the simple practice of its own precepts and the humility and unselfishness of its founder. Somehow or other the so- called mature churches must adjust their programs so that they will attract all sorts and conditions of men. They may have what they call the "best people" of the community. Too many of them, I fear, delight in this fact, and close their eyes to the others.

But these churches are heading toward disaster. This is not the class of society that reproduces itself on a lavish scale. In fact, it is declining. The lower cultural level supplies the cities with its youth, and the churches must look in this direction for the men and women who will replace a passing generation. It is because this great group of the underprivileged do not feel at home in our church denominations that more than a score of eccentric sects exert so much pull over them. These are the churches that are growing in strength and volume as we decline. Why? Because they are full of fire and zeal. They push their cause in factory and in field. They go after people and take them home after the service. They have rousing meetings with a lot of singing. They are not sunk in the inertia that has overtaken the traditional church. These are not boom days for Christianity. The church at large is said to have lost about half of its following since the World War. Had the church been with the lowly and exploited in Mexico, in Germany, in Russia, would she have been cast out?

I object to pretension in the church, whether practiced by bishop or deacon. When the plain and the homely feel uncomfortable in church, it's time to call a halt on glistening floors, rich carpets and high ritual. They should never be conscious in the House of God that their hands are calloused, their clothes are shabby or their manners rough. Ministers and church officers of all sorts should be careful not to let their cars or material possessions savor of opulence, remembering that the Christian religion has always been sacrificial, and is not a religion of ease and extravagance. Frequently it is the sacrifices the clergy make and the difficult things they do that influence people. In the country particularly, people still take careful stock of what the parson says and does. I feel that in my own work it has always been an advantage to live quite simply.

In the early days, if my horse was well groomed and my wagon clean, I let it go at that. I left the floss to others who cared about such things. When cars came along I was right in the band wagon for them, but what jokes some of them were—old style models always one step behind anything a parishioner might own! I have had only one new car during my long ministry—the gift of my friend, the Congregational deacon.

If the country preacher fails to put on a service that is interesting to all sorts and conditions of men, and to all ages, then he must take himself in hand, instead of blaming the automobile, or the radio, or cocktail parties, or any of the other distracting features of the era. I believe it lies entirely in the personality of the man himself—not in what he says, nor in how high-flown his sermons are, but in what he is himself.

Years ago a parishioner gave me Fiske's *Beginnings of New England.* I think the church in New England is still suffering from the same blue-law stiffness that he mentions. The long dry sermons, and the hard, uncomfortable pews in our churches are apt to make us feel still that we're Pilgrims. The Pilgrim Fathers were pious all right, but I'll wager the Episcopalians and the Roman Catholics were a lot more pleasant to live with. I believe we are improving as we drop that Puritan hardness for sympathy, that sternness for kindliness. It must be so, if religion is to amount to anything.

"I just want to ask you a straight question, may I? You won't be offended?" a Rotarian asked a minister, as he was coming out of a meeting.

"Of course not," said the minister.

"Well, what I should like to know is this: Why can't you preach on Sunday the way you talked in Rotary today?"

It was a pertinent question. Why can't a minister do that? He may need a set lecture style in a big city church, but it seems to me that the day for that in the small church is past. It isn't hard to get the range and feel of a congregation, or to see if they are responding or not. And if they aren't, why waste time and breath? Why not just quit, or take a different line with them?

I haven't one written sermon today. I don't believe in that way of doing it at all. I just talk to the people—the more informally the better—trying to fit the subject to my congregation. In the country church there has to be the intimate touch from the pulpit. Why should a minister be a different man as soon as he enters a church door? And a worse one when he enters a pulpit? Why should he sterilize his voice, frost his face and lock his arm joints when he starts in? Most ministers persist in having about as much expression in their faces as an Indian image in front of a cigar store. And how labored is pulpit recitation from a manuscript!

Of course, there must be a point of contact at the beginning of a sermon. Interest must first be aroused, before it can be sustained. But a good way to kill all interest is to launch in with an exegetical discourse on the text. The old-fashioned theologian cannot resist the temptation to point out that somewhere else in the Bible it says so-and-so, and the Greek word (to show off his learning) is a shade different in meaning. By also quoting the revised version and probably Goodspeed's, he can kill a fair part of the sermon period and have the congregation stupefied with boredom. The church needs a fresh and living message— one that the average congregation can relate to its daily way of living. And it should be delivered in a good strong voice, for it is tiresome straining to hear, and a monotone is terrible.

How long should a sermon be? Wasn't it Henry Ward Beecher who said that a sermon should be as long as one had something to say, and knew how to say it? Certainly when you finished reading one of his sermons, you sat back and said to yourself, "There's simply nothing more that could be said on that subject." They are chock full of living illustrations. Many times I have quoted the one he used when people complained that he talked about things that were not in his line: "You don't have to take a cock to bed with you to have him wake you up in the morning. It is because he is aloft and sees the rising of the sun that he can arouse you to your early labor."

When a man found Beecher looking over a book on medicine in a store, he commented that he seemed to read books on all subjects. "Yes," the great divine agreed, "on all subjects except theology."

"The difference between your sermons and mine," said a young preacher to me one day, "is that you get your sermons from humanity, and I get mine out of books." One doesn't have to be a thousand years old to have had plenty of human experiences from which to draw illustrations. I have found that nothing impresses my hearers as much as stories about my own country experiences. It's always a good idea to intersperse whatever one has to say with humor and anecdotes. This gives the congregation a chance to change position and relax. And I never frown on laughter from the pews. If we continue to have so many stiff, long-faced frigid services, it simply means churches with fewer people in them than now—and that's saying something. I knew one minister who put up "silence" signs. He didn't need these signs. His church was silent as the grave, day in and day out.

Of course, there is a balance in a sermon between ideas from living persons and ideas gathered from books. I like to do my reading in bed at night. The rest of the time I'm on the go. When I was starting out in the ministry I used Dean George Hodges' sermons for lay reading, and I loved them. They were always practical and never dull. I still like to read Edersheim's *Life of Christ,* especially at Christmas time, during Holy Week and on Palm Sunday. To no book in recent years do I owe more than to Denny's *Career and Significance of Jesus.* This book expresses my ideas of the theology of the four gospels. I read it over and over and just can't help preaching it, for it's so reasonable and sensible. Ainslie's *Scandal of Christianity* impressed me a great deal. I am a believer in church unity and many a time have I taken my Episcopal congregation to worship in a Congregational or Methodist church. I also like Rufus Jones' books, although I may not be a mystic. I find it helpful in my ministry to go to church conferences of all kinds. I like to meet the various men and get their ideas, but I'd just as soon have a conference without any big shot speakers. Who ever saw a ministers' conference in which the speakers weren't from big city parishes, and usually telling the little parish man how to do his work?

The country preacher could tell the city man a thing or

two about human beings, more often than not. He gets them in the raw. And it isn't high-sounding theology they're looking for when they file into his church. I'm a great believer in following up a certain line of thought and ramming it home with practical lessons that my people understand. An isolated sermon one Sunday and then a different line of thought the next make little impression, but keep on mentioning something Sunday after Sunday, and the idea may take root. I harp considerably on plain, native honesty, and when I hear of falsehoods among my flock during the week, or notice the infiltration of fake propaganda, I speak of it on Sunday. For instance, one of my parishioners called up one Sunday and said he couldn't come to church because he had a cold. Well, I was suspicious of this, and discreet inquiry disclosed that the real trouble was he couldn't get his car to go. Now why in the name of blazes couldn't he have told me that instead of making up a foolish lie? When I pin them down on things like this—episodes that are close to their own lives—they understand me better than they would if I let loose some of the high-sounding theology I picked up at Berkeley.

A minister should have several sermons in his head besides the one he intends to preach on a given day, for sometimes he walks into his church and notices a new group of people, or he is faced with a situation that seems to call for different treatment. I sometimes switch on the spur of the moment, for I carry around a number of sermons in my head. I think it is no insult to give a congregation the same theme over and over again. In fact, repetition seems to carry weight. I love to use the same text and even the same sermon time and again—my sermon on trees, for instance. "Come and rest yourselves under the trees," said Abraham to the three strangers. I make it a simple talk, understandable to the listening farmers, their wives and children, like this:

It is good to sit under a tree and learn the lessons the tree teaches. Tolerance. God might have made a sort of general purpose tree—wood not too hard or soft, not too dark or too light, and used it for everything. How monotonous that would have been! As it is, I don't believe mortal man will ever know how many different kinds of trees there are. Trees of every conceivable shape and size and color of wood and of bark. And yet the lordly oak need not make light of the humble hazel nut tree. So, too, there are many different kinds of men of all shades and sizes, but not any one race to look down on any other race.

Trees not only furnish shade but they are refrigerators in themselves. They become cool at night, and the bark is a perfect insulation, making them stay cooler than the surrounding air during the day time.

All good lumber comes from forest trees. They grow together and depend on each other. They push up and up looking for the sunlight. When, as boys, we cleared up a piece of old first-growth wood lot, we left here and there a tree standing. "Father will need some hemlock planking for the cow stable," we said.

But when Father saw these great high trees standing out alone, he looked queer and said nothing. Of course just an ordinary wind blew them flat. They had never withstood the winds alone. Like children whose parents have always shielded them, they know nothing of the world. When the storms of life come, they utterly give way.

Then too, there is the healing of the scars that come from the trimmer's ax and the woodsman's saw, or the ruthless wrenching of the branches by the storm. How quietly, how silently, yet instantly these wounds begin to heal. Of these deep black scars where once there were limbs there is now not even a discoloring.

So God is ever healing the scars and bruises of life. The great bereavements, the great disappointments—quickly the healing process begins and the balm of making right again never ceases till the work is done.

I go on in the same vein but never at great length, for I think long sermons are one of the abominations of church life. If I keep my congregation listening intently and see them laugh a bit now and again, I am satisfied, for I feel that my words are sinking in. It is much the same with prayer, although the prayers of the Episcopal church, of course, are pretty well standardized. I have always gone on the theory that instead of having certain set times for devotions, one should try to keep in touch with God all the time. "He walks with me, and He talks with me," says the good old hymn. How much the forest and the brooks and the meadows and the flowers are always telling me about God! Or is God talking to me through them?

Perhaps I never made as much of Bible readings and praying in my parish homes as I should, but I have found that these can be overstressed. When a family asks me to say a blessing I give a short earnest prayer. Too often people are strong on creeds but short on deeds. Prayers and creeds have their place in the Christian life, but I notice that in speaking of the last great day, Jesus made no mention of either. He asked whether we had clothed those who were ragged and shivering, whether we had given something to eat to those who were hungry (say, at church suppers), whether we had been persistent in helping those who were sick. I often think that if people read and studied more of what Jesus Himself said, instead of so much of what others say about what He said, they might move a little closer to perfection. Too often we forget that He told us to pray for His Kingdom to come "on earth." The doctrine of "you'll eat pie in the sky by and by," has no charm for me whatever. I'll have mine now, thank you, and I prefer to see hungry children get theirs here below. It's just as silly as the sanctimonious twaddle about God wanting little children up in heaven. It's my philosophy that God wants people to live to a ripe old age, having their share of the good things of the earth which He has given them, and being mighty happy about it. There's no use having so much religion that no one can live with you.

From my childhood I have been steeped in prayer book liturgy, and of course know many of the collects by heart. I have always been impressed by the fact that these prayers begin by recognizing power in the Almighty to grant the petition. So when I became Chaplain of the Senate in Connecticut, I could not see why the prayers should not cover the work in hand—the bills to be considered that very day, especially if they were important to the people. I tried to carry out this idea. One senator half humorously remarked that he planned to be in his seat at the time of the prayer, not only for the inspiration, but to learn what the calendar was for the day.

The whole proceeding when I was a member of the

House of Representatives seemed to me to border on futility and I was determined to make it more worth while, for I felt that a great opportunity was being lost by the casual way the Chaplain was accepted. "The doorkeepers will close the doors," the Speaker would say at the beginning of the session. Then he'd add, "You will give your attention to the Chaplain." The Chaplain would say the prayer before a mere handful of members. Then the doors would be opened and everyone would pile in. They stayed outside purposely until the prayer was over. Well, I didn't let it rest at that.

I was much disgusted with the lobbying that was going on all the time in the Senate. Men high in party circles, who had patronage to hand out, stood right behind the Senators' chairs influencing them as to how to vote. In one prayer, having in mind the passage, "Get thee behind me, Satan," I asked that they guard against the wiles of the devil "whether he be behind or before." The leader of the opposition immediately moved that the prayer be printed in the journal, and it was.

On a day when I was sure some legislation in regard to children and child welfare was coming up, "starred on the calendar" for action, I offered the following:

O Lord, our great example in human life and living, who didst take a little child and place it in the midst, and didst say "whosoever among you shall receive a little child receiveth me, and whosoever receiving me, receiveth Him that sent me," grant that we may be guided by such an intense desire to guard the lives and promote the welfare of children as shall lead us to promote legislation that will best protect and prosper the children and youth of our whole country. As He held the little child upon His knee, so may we in spirit hold the children of our fair country upon our hearts.

One of my favorite prayers, perhaps because of my love for the soil, celebrated the coming of spring:

O, Almighty God, Who hast given us the grass of the lawns and of the fields as the great benediction of man, Who has given us the succulence of the mountainsides to feed the cattle upon a thousand hills, Who hast given us the verdure of the rough places to be the great forgiveness of nature for the marring and the scarring of the face of the earth by the hands of men, grant that we, like this God-woven coverlet of the land, may be as a covering benediction to the mars and scars, the cares and worries and the sorrows of our fellow men. And, as Thy bringing of the spring- time grass foretells the bounty of our fall-time harvest, so may our bursting love of all life foretell in us the continuing harvest of human happiness throughout the coming years. Through Him Who said "as a man soweth, so shall he reap, as a man scattereth, so shall he gather," Amen!

St. Patrick's Day, Ash Wednesday, and Maundy Thursday were all occasions for special prayers. I had been told that long prayers were not acceptable, so I deliberately kept them brief, and after I had been functioning for a time, James A. Harrington, special legislative writer for *The Hartford Times,* commented on them as follows:

In their brevity the prayers in the Senate have lost nothing of their force, their beauty or appeal. They have been quoted more generally by the press of the state and beyond than have those of his predecessors in either branch of the assembly. They have been timely, they have been sensible.

Who is this minister who, within three months has won the love and esteem of the Senate, and the attention of spectators who so attentively have listened to him? It most certainly was not because of his affiliation with any particular church, but rather because of the man himself. He inspires confidence; he radiates good nature.

He has been described as one of the most unusual and interest-compelling personalities that Connecticut has developed in years. He is just that. He is known throughout the state and beyond as a minister who does not subscribe to the theory that the way to Heaven is paved with personal discomforts. He believes that religion has a much deeper meaning than the generally accepted version.

I offered a prayer I am not likely to forget on the day the Senate was due for a banquet that had many repercussions. It was the most expensive and elaborate affair I ever attended in my life, costing ten dollars a plate. I might add that we all thought the Speaker of the Senate was our host, paying for the spread, and we thanked him profusely. He happened to be the mayor of a Connecticut town and later he was arrested, tried, convicted and sentenced to prison for conspiracy in irregular use of the city funds. I noted then that one of the questionable expenditures was an item of more than $400 for this same banquet.

As I look back on my chaplaincy, I feel that I should have had greed and covetousness more in mind, for selfish interests rather than the public good did seem to predominate over the place most shamefully. If I were to do the job over again, I think I should be more explicit in my speech as to what I thought were the sins about me, and whether they liked it or not, let those whom the coat might fit, put it on.

On one occasion I opened the Senate proceedings in Washington after my friend Citro became a Representative at large. I found this an interesting experience.

Years ago I heard Anson Phelps Stokes, then secretary of Yale, speak to a junior clericus. He said that in predicting that His disciples might do greater things than He, Jesus meant that they would prevent ills that He was only curing. Mr. Stokes illustrated his idea with the story of the doctor whose job it was to find out whether certain patients should be admitted to a hospital for the mentally ill. He would get them all in one room, and then he'd say to one of them, "I hear the water running in the other room. I'm afraid the basin will run over. Will you please step in and see to it?" One patient would go in and begin to dip water furiously and pour it into another sink. He was admitted as a patient, on the spot. Another would go in and turn off the faucet. He would not be admitted, but would be sent back home instead, for he knew enough to stop the trouble at its source.

It is a fine thing, of course, for a doctor to set a broken leg, but what about the man who goes out in the morning and sprinkles ashes on the ice on his sidewalk so that no such accident will occur? An ounce of prevention is worth a ton of cure. That goes for the work of the ministry, as well as anywhere else.

I am a cynic on the subject of straight conversion. I have seen too much to expect the miraculous just because the Holy Ghost seems to have taken hold. "Turn thou us, O Good Lord, and so shall we be turned," run the words of a petition in the Ash Wednesday service. My experience shows that it is one thing to turn them, and another to keep them turned. Pearl Buck's father, as she tells in *Fighting Angel*, turned a good many of the heathen Chinese, but keeping them turned seemed to break his heart. It's a case of a little here and a little there, with a long process of guidance and of growth. You can't take a wild, harum-scarum, long-haired, dirty-shoed boy, constantly looking for mischief, and make a Christian gentleman of him in a minute.

Some years ago, we dragged a boy out from behind the furnace in the parish house, where he had been hiding. What a family he came from! What clothes, what everything! Later on, I saw him grown to manhood, baptized, confirmed, marching down the aisle in choir vestments, kneeling for communion and well married. Of course, they don't all turn out to be saints, but on the whole our church children throughout these forty years have come on wonderfully well. This is one of the reflections on my ministry that I cherish most. In my churches I have always built up large Sunday schools and this has resulted in big confirmation classes. I look back with great pleasure to these occasions, some of them held in schoolhouses, and even in abandoned farmhouses, with the Bishop placing his hands on the heads of my young people and uttering the prayer that begins: "Receive, O Lord, this Thy child—."
I have never needed the sanctity of a building to perform

the offices of the church, but it seems to me that it is of the utmost importance for a minister to establish cordial relations with his flock. For instance, what reaction does a mother have to the coming of the parson? This has great significance. Does she accept him as a nuisance and hatch up some excuse for her failure to send her children to Sunday school, or does she welcome him as a friend who will find work for her idle daughter, have the family pump fixed, or pick up her children in his car and take them to Sunday school?

To me it is wonderful to sit around a table with children and just visit, talk and suggest. And it's good for the young people to work around a church. With us the girls clean up, sweep and work around the altar. The boys chop wood, clean the parish house, organize games. It's the only way to get anywhere with them. One can develop great influence over the young with all these close contacts. On the drives to and from church I draw them out, get to know their problems, build up their self-esteem, harp on the importance of truth, but without the nagging note. And, somehow, they respond better to the idea of fixing themselves up for parties than they do for Sunday school. Fundamentally, of course, the Sunday school is a school of character, but in a group meeting held once a week for thirty minutes, how much real character building is done or can be done? Careful investigations show that the influence of the Sunday school on character ranks lower than one per cent, or practically the same as the public school. The home, the group, or the gang of adolescent age, are the big factors.

City people don't realize that their slum areas can be

matched and sometimes outdone in the country. One doesn't associate such sordid misery with the green fields and the forest, but as the more enterprising move to the city, the leftovers intermarry and produce a troublesome, dangerous slum area. By their fruits ye shall know them, and the first fruits of such conditions are the theft of chickens. Then, pretty soon, automobiles disappear. Drunks land in the lockup. Family feuds grow, and the community is startled by having a murder on its hands, with a trial costing thousands of dollars. All this goes back to fundamental conditions. As soon as settlers in the country get a little saved, they move to town, taking their money with them. Usually they drain the soil of its fertility and the woods of their lumber before they leave. The youth that go with them represent the same drainage. The dregs are apt to be left behind.

When the money is taken to town, the support of the church goes with it. When the district school closes, a bus gathers up the children and takes them to a consolidated school, but when the crossroads church closes, no car or bus goes out for the children. This is the situation that the country minister faces, and it has to be met by a practical and immediate form of Christianity. Can one denomination, one church, put on so diversified a program that it will reach widely different cultural levels of society?

It can't be done from the pulpit, essential as preaching is in the minister's daily calendar. Sometimes we put too much emphasis on the wrong thing, such as the necessity for holding services every Sunday at such an hour, such a minute, come heat or cold, rain, snow or shine. While a parson should be conscientious about the forms of the church, yet an overworked conscience may be worse than an overworked body. I am always willing to relax a few of the rules of the church in the interests of common sense—the greatest canon of all.

God loves people more than he loves the calendar. During a blizzard in 1937, my old roommate Holcomb started out to preach in his three rural churches. He made the first one, and pushed his way through snow and cold wind to the next. There could hardly have been anybody in the congregation. Then, after the worst struggle of all, he reached the third place, put on his vestments, sat down in a vestry-room chair and died of heart failure and exhaustion.

Will it do for me to tell what I did that same Sunday morning? I, too, was booked to preach in three different places. I got up, took one good look out of my window and said, "Wife, if the Lord is going to send a blizzard like this on Sunday, he'll have to look after these sinners himself." I went back to bed and stayed there.

That reminds me of the time I went to the old Killingworth church and found the walls covered with mosquitoes. The church was situated on the edge of a swamp. I never saw such a sight in all my life. And I could just see myself in that room with my poor bald head! So, as the people gathered outside, I said to them, "The Lord seems to have supplied this church already with a congregation. I propose we go down to the shore (ten miles away) for the day." Which we did, most enjoyably. The next Sunday all the mosquitoes were gone and we took possession in due order.

It is not church form that makes good Christians. The

essence of the Christian ministry lies deeper than that and is rooted in human relationships. Too often the theologian doesn't know how to get along with people. The church cannot fail to be ineffective unless its clergy reach the poor, and that can only be done by long and friendly acquaintance in their homes, ripening gradually into mutual affection—a link which brings them finally into the fold. When preachers begin to visit with their congregations in the true and intimate sense of the word, and not with the stuffy formality I remember from the days of my youth in Vermont, then will the children want to sit around in church and listen. But not before.

THE END

What Reviewers Have Said About FORTY YEARS A
COUNTRY PREACHER by George B. Gilbert:

"What a relief it is to turn up a life-story without a shade of
self-questioning, uncertainty or disappointment. This
story, simple as it is, deserves the strongest
recommendation. Its spirit cannot possibly be
counterfeited." — Albert Jay Nockin, Atlantic Monthly

"His reminiscences are filled with so much humor and
homely philosophy that the reading of his biography
becomes a rarely delightful experience." — Baptist Leader

"The record of a fine adventure in ap-plied Christianity
under rural conditions." — Christian Century

"A high-spirited and absorbingly interesting book." — New
York Times Book Review

"No author more original or American has been discovered since Mark Twain." — Christian Herald

"He has been described as one of the most unusual and
interest-compelling personalities that Connecticut has
developed in years." — Hartford Times

"There is not a nickel's worth of theology in this book but
there is a quality of rural philosophy and of human interest
that should appeal to everyone." — Advance

Made in the USA
Middletown, DE
27 November 2019

79524583R00199